The Introspective Art of Mark Twain

The Introspective Art of Mark Twain

Douglas Anderson

Bloomsbury Academic
An imprint of Bloomsbury Publishing Inc

B L O O M S B U R Y
NEW YORK • LONDON • OXFORD • NEW DELHI • SYDNEY

Bloomsbury Academic
An imprint of Bloomsbury Publishing Inc

1385 Broadway	50 Bedford Square
New York	London
NY 10018	WC1B 3DP
USA	UK

www.bloomsbury.com

BLOOMSBURY and the Diana logo are trademarks of Bloomsbury Publishing Plc

First published 2017

© Douglas Anderson, 2017

All rights reserved. No part of this publication may be reproduced or transmitted in any form or by any means, electronic or mechanical, including photocopying, recording, or any information storage or retrieval system, without prior permission in writing from the publishers.

No responsibility for loss caused to any individual or organization acting on or refraining from action as a result of the material in this publication can be accepted by Bloomsbury or the author.

Library of Congress Cataloging-in-Publication Data
Names: Anderson, Douglas, 1950– author.
Title: The Introspective art of Mark Twain / Douglas Anderson.
Description: New York: Bloomsbury Academic, 2017. | Includes bibliographical references and index.
Identifiers: LCCN 2016040892 (print) | LCCN 2016040991 (ebook) | ISBN 9781501329555 (hardback) | ISBN 9781501329548 (paperback) | ISBN 9781501329562 (ePDF) | ISBN 9781501329579 (ePUB)
Subjects: LCSH: Twain, Mark, 1835–1910–Criticism and interpretation. | BISAC: LITERARY CRITICISM / American / General. | LITERARY CRITICISM / Short Stories. | PHILOSOPHY / General.
Classification: LCC PS1338.A47 2017 (print) | LCC PS1338 (ebook) | DDC 818/.409–dc23
LC record available at https://lccn.loc.gov/2016040892

ISBN: HB: 978-1-5013-2955-5
PB: 978-1-5013-2954-8
ePDF: 978-1-5013-2956-2
ePub: 978-1-5013-2957-9

Cover design: Eleanor Rose
Cover image © Tate, London 2016

Typeset by Newgen Knowledge Works Pvt Ltd, Chennai, India

Touchstone's question, "Hast any philosophy in thee, shepherd?" will never cease to be one of the tests of a well-born nature. It says, Is there space and air in your mind, or must your companions gasp for breath whenever they talk with you?
—William James, "The Teaching of Philosophy in our Colleges," 1876

CONTENTS

Illustrations viii
Preface ix
Abbreviations xii

Introduction: Thought Experiments 1

1 Inside Excursions 17

2 Interest 73

3 Attention 125

4 Shadings 181

Conclusion: Greatnesses in the Brain 237

Notes 249
Index 273

ILLUSTRATIONS

Following the index.

2.1 Raphael, "The Transfiguration" (1520), oil on wood. Courtesy of Scala/Art Resource, New York
2.2 From *The Innocents Abroad* (Hartford: American Publishing Company, 1869), "Fifty-Two Distinct Repetitions" (p. 197)
3.1 From *The Adventures of Tom Sawyer* (Hartford: The American Publishing Company, 1876), "Tom at Home" (p. 1)
3.2 J. M. W. Turner, "The Slave Ship" (1840), oil on canvas. Photograph © 2017 Museum of Fine Arts, Boston
3.3 From *A Tramp Abroad* (Hartford: American Publishing Company, 1880), "Old Blue China" (p. 186)
3.4 From *A Tramp Abroad* (Hartford: American Publishing Company, 1880), "Piece of Sword" (p. 68)
4.1 "The Blue Rigi: Sample Study," 1841–42, by J. M. W. Turner (1775–1851). Photograph © Tate, London, 2016
4.2 From *A Connecticut Yankee in King Arthur's Court* (New York: Charles L. Webster and Company, 1889), "The Practical Joker's Joke" (p. 54)

PREFACE

This book begins an examination of Mark Twain's artistic preoccupations by assuming that he was, among many other things, an unusually perceptive student of his own mind and career, and that he undertook a review of that career—its methods and its pervasive interests—near the end of his life, just when many readers find him to be mired in a period of creative and emotional exhaustion. By the first decade of the twentieth century, he had every right to be exhausted, drained by the combination of disasters that struck his family between the collapse of his hopes for the Paige typesetting machine and the bankruptcy of his publishing company, both in 1894, and the death of his wife Olivia ten years later. The loss of their eldest daughter, Susy, to meningitis in 1896 was a blow from which neither Clemens parent entirely recovered.

But Twain had long come to accept a relentless, even merciless, vitality as part of his constitution: an inability to yield for very long to discouragement or despair. Albert Bigelow Paine, his first biographer, records a confession that Twain made shortly after his youngest daughter Jean had drowned in her bath, on Christmas Eve morning, 1909, apparently during an epileptic seizure. "Shall I ever be cheerful again, happy again?" Twain wondered, as he struggled to cope with this latest painful loss, and then quickly offered an answer as startling as the question itself is bitter: "Yes. And soon. For I know my temperament."[1] Like Ralph Waldo Emerson over sixty years earlier, Twain had found himself driven to acknowledge, in the final months of his life, that even profound suffering was evanescent—mere "scene-painting and counterfeit," Emerson had called it, a theatrical background for the essential drama of consciousness.

Where, Emerson wondered in the aftermath of the death of his five-year-old son, might one find "sharp peaks and ridges of truth," alpine extremities of awareness that were impervious to the terrible fluidity of existence? The psychological climax of his 1844 essay "Experience" turns on his recognition that "grief too will make us idealists":

> In the death of my son, now more than two years ago, I seem to have lost a beautiful estate,—no more. I cannot get it nearer to me. If tomorrow I should be informed of the bankruptcy of my principal debtors, the loss of my property would be a great inconvenience to me, perhaps, for many years; but it would leave me as it found me,—neither better nor worse. So it is with this calamity: it does not touch me: something which I fancied was a part of me, which could not be torn away without tearing me, nor enlarged without enriching me, falls off from me, and leaves no scar. It was caduceus. I grieve that grief can teach me nothing, nor carry me one step into real nature.[2]

Short of the extinction of consciousness itself, all calamities are peripheral events to the tyrannous "me" that brings Emerson's meditation to a close. Twain's haunting observation, after the death of his youngest child, points to a very similar realization. The irresistible momentum of "temperament"—one of the Lords of Life that Emerson addresses in his essay—propels Twain forward in an unbroken mental stream that even the most harrowing emotional trauma cannot balk for long—an attribute of consciousness that prompted Twain's lifelong struggle with guilt at the same time that it sustained the variety and vigor of his imagination. "All I know is reception," Emerson wrote as he reflected on the mysterious plenitude of his inner world.[3] The signal achievements of Mark Twain's career suggest that a similar introspective focus lies at the heart of his artistic legacy.

The following pages undertake to explore that legacy by tracing its inward excursions—the subterranean world of which McDougal's Cave in *The Adventures of Tom Sawyer* is the most memorable but far from the only emblem. The journey will begin by considering, at some length, the enigmatic dialogue *What Is Man?* that occupied Twain for much of his life but that he delayed putting in final form until the end of the nineteenth century and only published as an anonymous pamphlet in 1906. "Thought Experiments," the title to this book's introduction, points to the series of mental exercises that

Old Man devises for Young Man to conduct in order to illustrate the workings of the mind as their dialogue unfolds.

Our present use of "thought experiment," in itself an ancient concept, derives from the late nineteenth century's interest in harnessing the imagination as a tool of scientific inquiry.[4] For the purposes of the two speakers in *What Is Man?* consciousness itself is the object of study. Understanding the inner rather than the outer universe is their goal. The discussions that take place between them may seem, at first, to have very little in common with the exchanges that occur in Twain's fiction or in his travel books—the narratives on which his popularity and his fame are largely based. A patient reader of the dialogue, however, will have little difficulty detecting hints of the argumentative play in which Huck and Jim occasionally engage, echoes of the reflective intensity that fills *A Connecticut Yankee in King Arthur's Court*, or glimpses of Tom Sawyer's volatile mental world. *What Is Man?* recasts these familiar attributes of Twain's fiction into a strangely sober and serene "gospel" (as Twain sometimes called it) that underlies his imaginative life. To begin a book such as this one with *What Is Man?* risks discouraging many admirers of Twain's comic art and caustic political satire. But the risk is worth taking if it succeeds in alerting Twain's readers to a rich and neglected dimension of his achievement.

*   *   *

Haaris Naqvi and his colleagues at Bloomsbury Press oversaw the review and production of this book with exemplary care. Imaging staff at the Tate, at the Museum of Fine Arts in Boston, and at Art Resource in New York made obtaining illustrations and licenses virtually painless. I continue to be grateful to the University of Georgia for the generous support of the Sterling-Goodman Professorship over the past sixteen years.

ABBREVIATIONS

Parenthetical citations to works by Mark Twain refer to the following sources:

CA   "Chapters From My Autobiography" in *Mark Twain: Autobiographical Writings*, ed. R. Kent Rasmussen. New York: Penguin Books, 2012.

CY   Mark Twain, *A Connecticut Yankee in King Arthur's Court*, ed. Bernard L. Stein. Berkeley: University of California Press, 1984.

HF   Mark Twain, *Adventures of Huckleberry Finn*, eds. Victor Fischer and Lin Salamo. Berkeley: University of California Press, 2001.

IA   Mark Twain, *The Innocents Abroad*. New York: Penguin Books, 2002.

LM   Mark Twain, *Life on the Mississippi*. New York: Library of America, 1982.

MS   Mark Twain, *The Mysterious Stranger Manuscripts*, ed. William M. Gibson. Berkeley: University of California Press, 1969.

OM   "Old Times on the Mississippi" in seven numbered installments from *The Atlantic Monthly* 36 (January–June, August 1875).

PP   Mark Twain, *The Prince and the Pauper*. Berkeley: University of California Press, 1984.

PR   Mark Twain, *Personal Recollections of Joan of Arc*. New York: Oxford University Press, 1996.

RI   Mark Twain, *Roughing It*. New York: Penguin Books, 1981.

TA   Mark Twain, *A Tramp Abroad*. New York: Penguin Books, 1997.

TS   Mark Twain, *The Adventures of Tom Sawyer*. Berkeley: University of California Press, 1982.

WIM   Mark Twain, *What Is Man?* in *Mark Twain: Collected Tales, Sketches, Speeches, and Essays, 1891–1910*. New York: Library of America, 1992.

Introduction

Thought Experiments

In the brief preface that Mark Twain added in February 1905 to a collection of Socratic "papers" that he would not publish for another eighteen months, he claimed to have drafted studies for its pages as long as "twenty-five or twenty-seven years ago." That curiously inexact statement places the gestation of *What Is Man?* at the heart of Twain's artistic career: just after the publication of *The Adventures of Tom Sawyer* and "Old Times on the Mississippi," as he was finishing *A Tramp Abroad*, continuing work on *The Prince and the Pauper*, and puzzling over the manuscript fragments that would eventually knit themselves together in the story of Huckleberry Finn. By 1885 when *Adventures of Huckleberry Finn* finally appeared, two years after Twain had expanded his magazine articles on the "science" of piloting into *Life on the Mississippi*, most of the books on which his reputation rests were finished and, if his retrospective account of *What Is Man?* is accurate, he had begun to record the process of reflection that once led his precocious daughter Susy to remark that her father was, by nature, a philosopher (CA 211).

Between 1898 and 1904, Twain consolidated his drafts and completed his record of a protracted discussion between an Old Man and a Young Man in which the two debate Old Man's disquieting assertion "that the human being is merely a machine, and nothing more." Repeated rereadings of the finished dialogue, over several years, convinced Twain that this central assertion was not only true but had been tacitly accepted as such "by millions upon millions of men," generation after generation, and systematically concealed out of a fear of disapproval. "Why have I not published?" Twain asks himself. "The same reason has restrained me, I think. I can find no other" (WIM 731). On this introspective note *What Is Man?* begins by breaking into an ongoing conversation that subsequently drifts through a number of issues and phases, much as the dialogue itself had done during the years in which Twain worked through its initial versions: Does the mind originate its ideas or simply borrow them from outside sources? Is thinking really subject to our control? Are we capable of heroism and self-sacrifice or do we invariably seek personal contentment? Can training influence our inborn temperament for the better? Is animal instinct a lower form of intelligence or is it, too, a type of thought?[1]

As this list of topics should suggest, Twain's dialogue could easily be retitled "What Is Consciousness?" Though Old Man initially appears to take a discouragingly reductive view of human potential—man is "merely a machine"—as the dialogue unfolds, so does Twain's account of mental life, ultimately presenting it as a restless cacophony of thoughts, swarming about a mysterious interior "autocrat," or Master Passion as Old Man sometimes calls it, that selects its path through the cognitive swarm according to the shifting equilibrium of inner contentment that it seeks. When Old Man first introduces his view of the mental "mechanism," Young Man can scarcely bring himself to take the portrait seriously:

Y. M. You have arrived at man, now?

O. M. Yes. Man the machine—man, the impersonal engine. Whatsoever a man is, is due to his *make*, and to the *influences* brought to bear upon it by his heredities, his habitat, his associations. He is moved, directed, COMMANDED, by *exterior* influences *solely*. He *originates* nothing, himself—not even an opinion, not even a thought.

Y. M. Oh, come! Where did I get my opinion that this which you are talking is all foolishness?

O. M. It is a quite natural opinion—indeed an inevitable opinion—but *you* did not create the materials out of which it is formed. They are odds and ends of thoughts, impressions, feelings, gathered unconsciously from a thousand books, a thousand conversations, and from streams of thought and feeling which have flowed down into your heart and brain out of the hearts and brains of ten centuries of ancestors.

Personally you did not create even the smallest microscopic fragment of the materials out of which your opinion is made; and personally you cannot claim even the slender merit of *putting the borrowed materials together.* That was done—*automatically*—by your mental machinery, in strict accordance with the law of that machinery's construction. And you not only did not make that machinery yourself, but you have *not even any command over it.* (WIM 734; emphases in the original)

In response to Young Man's impatient objection, Old Man briefly but tellingly shifts his metaphorical focus from "man, the impersonal engine," to an elaborate system of exterior and interior streams coursing through the individual's mental machinery. Emotional or intellectual odds and ends, gleaned from a thousand books and conversations as well as from centuries of ancestral experience, all combine to form a cascade of inner materials out of which the mind weaves its conscious being. That being, in turn, is governed entirely by a single general law from which all variant, individual laws derive their force. "Will you put that law into words?" Young Man asks. Old Man promptly complies. "This is the law," he declares. "Keep it in your mind. *From his cradle to his grave a man never does a single thing which has any* FIRST AND FOREMOST *object but one—to secure peace of mind, spiritual comfort, for* HIMSELF" (WIM 741; emphases in the original). As these words imply, from the outset Old Man's doctrine is a curious hybrid of reductive and expansive elements: an iron-like constraint that shapes human behavior "from the cradle to the grave," coupled with the highly malleable and elusive ideal of "spiritual comfort," a kind of golden engine hidden in the mechanism.[2]

The mental apparatus that Old Man sketches in this opening stage of the discussion turns out to be quite an extraordinary agent: attentive even to the microscopic ingredients of its inner and outer worlds, an omnivorous collector indifferent to the barriers of time or space as it gathers its mental materials and, with astounding speed, forms them into thoughts and words. Young Man objects that his own opinions are personal, even original, or at the very least matters of individual choice, but Old Man asks him to undertake a simple thought experiment—one of a series of these that he incorporates into the conversation—in order to test Young

Man's belief. Try over the course of the next quarter hour, Old Man suggests, to change your opinion of man's mental independence and originality. If you are indeed a free agent, then you ought to be able to move freely in the world of thought. But the experiment proves otherwise. Young Man is unable to reshape his original reaction to Old Man's troubling claim. The conclusion would appear to be inescapable. You have no command over the "law" of your make, Old Man calmly repeats: "you see, yourself, that your mind is merely a machine, nothing more" (WIM 735).

Not all mental machines are alike, Old Man quickly concedes. He and his young friend are little better than sewing machines in their capacity to organize the fabric of consciousness in interesting shapes. By contrast Shakespeare was a Gobelin loom: equally dependent on outside influences for its working materials—the experiences and the books that Shakespeare absorbed—but capable of reconstructing and recombining those materials into "that pictured and gorgeous fabric which still compels the astonishment of the world." Another thought experiment seals Old Man's point. Imagine Shakespeare stripped of the stimulating cultural influences that he actually enjoyed, "born and bred on a barren unvisited rock in the ocean." In the absence of outside "teachings, mouldings, persuasions, inspirations" with which to work, Shakespeare's mind would have been as barren as his rocky home. Even Shakespeare, Old Man insists, "could not create," for he too was an automatic mechanism, however singular its make-up (WIM 736). Nor, as it turns out, does Old Man recognize the conventional value behind any of the heroic virtues or damning vices with which men have "ticketed" themselves over the millennia: "Love, Hate, Charity, Compassion, Avarice, Benevolence, and so on" (WIM 750). These words are all disguises for the operation of man's Sole Impulse: "the imperious necessity of securing his own approval, in every emergency and at all costs" (WIM 751). Self-contentment is the motive for all human effort, Old Man concludes. "Self-sacrifice" is a meaningless concept: "It describes a thing which does not exist."[3] Young Man resists what seems to him a deeply impoverishing view of life, but Old Man presses his case. The irreducible motive of self-contentment is the origin of civilization:

> To it we owe all that we are. It is our breath, our heart, our blood. It is our only spur, our whip, our goad, our only impelling

power; we have no other. Without it we should be mere inert images, corpses; no one would do anything, there would be no progress, the world would stand still. We ought to stand reverently uncovered when the name of that stupendous power is uttered.

Y. M. I am not convinced.
O. M. You will be, when you think. (WIM 751)

* * *

Old Man would be the first to admit that he too is a machine: the product of countless inherited streams of thought, all subjected to the stupendous power exerted by self-contentment. William Lecky, in his influential *History of European Morals* (1874), remained convinced that each individual possessed a reserve of "virtuous affections" that counteracted Old Man's view of universal selfishness. In surveying our collective ethical record "from Augustus to Charlemagne," Lecky argued strenuously for this redemptive moral psychology:

> The conception of pure disinterestedness is presupposed in our estimates of virtue. It is the root of all the emotions with which we contemplate acts of heroism. We feel that man is capable of pursuing what he believes to be right although pain and disaster and mental suffering and an early death be the consequence, and although no prospect of future reward lighten upon his tomb. This is the highest prerogative of our being, the point of contact between the human nature and the divine.[4]

Scholars have long recognized that Lecky's *History* was one of many exterior influences on the mental make-up of Mark Twain. "It is so noble a book, and so beautiful a book," Twain wistfully observed, "that I don't wish it to have even trivial faults in it.[5] But *What Is Man?* suggests that the faults he came to recognize in Lecky's pages were far from trivial. Self-interest always trumps self-sacrifice, Twain ultimately believed, a realization that Young Man declares to be a "desolating doctrine":

> It takes the glory out of man, it takes the pride out of him, it takes the heroism out of him, it denies him all personal credit, all applause; it not only degrades him to a machine, but allows him no control over the machine; makes a mere coffee-mill of him, and neither permits him to supply the coffee nor turn the crank; his sole and piteously humble function being to grind coarse or fine, according to his make, outside impulses doing all the rest. (WIM 800)

Old Man accepts this bald account as far as it goes, but at the same time he gently tries to turn his young friend's attention toward the exhilarating fluidity of thinking itself. Consciousness, as Twain portrays it in *What Is Man?* is infinitely more interesting than a coffee mill.[6]

The first instructive exercise that Old Man recommends involves Young Man's powers of critical analysis. "Whenever you read of a self-sacrificing act or hear of one, or of a duty done for *duty's sake*," Old Man suggests, "take it to pieces and look for the *real* motive" (WIM 754; emphases in the original). The result will be the discovery that a hunger for self-approval lies behind every instance of apparently benevolent behavior recorded in fact or fiction. Young Man ransacks romances and biographies, as well as his own memory, on this "degrading and exasperating quest" and finds himself repeatedly frustrated in his fondest hopes. As Old Man had predicted, self-approval is the hidden background, the ulterior motive, of all noble conduct. For the moment, it escapes Young Man's notice that he has found the quest itself "hatefully interesting," even "fascinating," as he reflects on the ingenuity with which man's Interior Master is able clothe its inherent selfishness in "golden deeds."

Indeed, Old Man will eagerly observe that the Interior Master is a kind of spiritual chameleon, able to assume any moral costume that its cultural circumstances require. Adaptation, not creation, is man's nature: a limitless aptitude for change to meet the needs of a changing spiritual habitat:

> But the impulse to do it must come from the *outside*—he cannot originate it himself, with that purpose in view. Sometimes a very small and accidental thing can furnish him the initiatory impulse and start him on a new road, with a new ideal. The

chance remark of a sweetheart, "I hear that you are a coward" may water a seed that shall sprout and bloom and flourish, and end in producing a surprising fruitage in the fields of war. The history of man is full of such accidents. The accident of a broken leg brought a profane and ribald soldier under religious influences and furnished him a new ideal. From that accident sprang the Order of the Jesuits, and it has been shaking thrones, changing policies, and doing other tremendous work for two hundred years—and will go on. The chance reading of a book or of a paragraph in a newspaper can start a man on a new track and make him renounce his old associations and seek new ones that are in sympathy with his new ideal; and the result, for that man, can be an entire change of his way of life. (WIM 761–2; emphasis in the original)

The cognitive machine that executes such extraordinary changes does much more than simply grind its experiences coarse or fine. Even a profane soldier like Ignatius Loyola can contain an unusually responsive "seed"—a type of inner potential that Old Man will ultimately characterize as "temperament"—which singles out some influences over others as possessing a particularly potent claim on attention. Accidents can give birth to tremendous results when the intervening consciousness is temperamentally disposed to make tremendous use of them.

Near the close of the dialogue Young Man suggests in passing that "conscience" is the name that common speech gives to the workings of this interior seed, but Old Man never accepts this label in the sense that Young Man uses it. Our fickle interior tyrant is in itself "a colorless force ... a blind, unreasoning instinct, which cannot and does not distinguish between good morals and bad ones, and cares nothing for results to the man provided its own contentment be secured" (WIM 797). Temperament helps direct the split-second movements of this unreasoning presence, but in the end it is a compound entity indifferent to all conscientious appeals, indifferent even to the integrity and consistency of that abject slave we customarily call the self, the "Me," or the "I." These familiar terms too have no meaning, Old Man believes, other than as vocal conveniences. "We all use the 'I' in this indeterminate fashion," Old Man observes, and "there is no help for it":

We imagine a Master and King over what you call The Whole Thing, and we speak of him as "I," but when we try to define him we find we cannot do it. The intellect and the feelings can act quite *independently* of each other; we recognize that, and we look around for a Ruler who is master over both ... but we have to give it up and confess that we cannot find him. To me, Man is a machine, made up of many mechanisms; the moral and mental ones acting automatically in accordance with the impulses of an Interior Master who is built out of born-temperament and an accumulation of multitudinous outside influences and trainings; a machine whose *one* function is to secure the spiritual contentment of the Master, be his desires good or be they evil; a machine whose Will is absolute and must be obeyed, and always *is* obeyed.

Y. M. Maybe the Me is the Soul?
O. M. Maybe it is. What is the Soul?
Y. M. I don't know.
O. M. Neither does any one else. (WIM 796–7; emphases in the original)

The traditional moral architecture to which Young Man pins his ideal of human nature—an ethical Self exerting its authority over the unreflective appetites and passions—is little more than a misleading metaphor in the dynamic account of our inner being that Old Man introduces and that forms the focus of Twain's final creative years.

"Letters from the Earth," an unpublished adaptation of biblical myth that Twain began writing late in 1909, is a half-playful, half-grim variation on the same cognitive drama that *What Is Man?* explores. It begins by replacing "Let there be light" with a much more introspective variation on Genesis. Against the splendid backdrop of heaven and "the black night of Space," God suddenly breaks a long meditative silence by declaring: "I have thought. Behold!"[7] A tremendous "fountain-spray" of suns instantly bursts from God's hand, at once puzzling and delighting the three archangel witnesses, Satan, Michael, and Gabriel, for whom the display has been staged. All three observers recognize almost immediately that it is not light so much as "law" that God has made, a "stupendous idea," Satan declares, far more intriguing than the material forms that it governs:

> Nothing approaching it has been evolved from the Master Intellect before. Law—*automatic* Law—exact and unvarying Law—requiring no watching, no correcting, no readjusting while the eternities endure! He said those countless vast bodies would plunge through the wastes of Space ages and ages, at unimaginable speed, around stupendous orbits, yet never collide, and never lengthen nor shorten their orbital periods by so much as the hundredth part of a second in two thousand years! That is the new miracle, and the greatest of all—*Automatic Law!* And He gave it a name—the LAW OF NATURE—and said Natural Law is the LAW OF GOD—interchangeable names for one and the same thing.[8]

Much like Thomas Paine, whose *Age of Reason* held a special place among Twain's mental influences, Satan is exhilarated by this Deistic spectacle. His subsequent letters to Michael and Gabriel, from one of the remote planets that God has "thought" into existence, attack some of the same episodes of biblical history that Paine singles out for special scorn.[9] But Twain's fable also has potent, introspective goals. "Letters from the Earth" contrasts the perfectly orchestrated energies of celestial space with the far less orderly profusion of Moral Qualities housed in human consciousness.

God's fountain spray of suns is little more than a preamble for a second, more ambitious exhibition to which He also summons his three angelic witnesses. This equally introspective exercise entails the making of animals as "an experiment in Morals and Conduct," followed by the introduction of Man, the "masterpiece" of animal creation, equipped with an interior nature as replete with mental energy as the countless celestial bodies plunging through the wastes of space. "What will you do with them, Divine One?" Satan asks of these enigmatic masterpieces:

> Put into each individual [God replies], in differing shades and degrees, all the various Moral Qualities, in mass, that have been distributed, a single distinguishing characteristic at a time, among the non-speaking animal world—courage, cowardice, ferocity,

gentleness, fairness, justice, cunning, treachery, magnanimity, cruelty, malice, malignity, lust, mercy, pity, purity, selfishness, sweetness, honor, love, hate, baseness, nobility, loyalty, falsity, veracity, untruthfulness—each human being shall have *all* of these in him, and they will constitute his nature. In some, there will be high and fine characteristics which will submerge the evil ones, and those will be called good men; in others the evil characteristics will have dominion, and those will be called bad men. Observe—behold—they vanish![10]

The human race "and all their fellow animals" are promptly dispatched to Earth, "a small globe" scarcely noticeable amid the celestial explosion which God's initiating thought had produced: "Time will show whether they were worth the trouble," the Master Intellect declares.

In *What Is Man?* Old Man concludes that they were, but not because he considers the contest for dominion between good and evil to be anymore important than God seems to do in "Letters from the Earth." Like the series of amoral mysterious strangers whose earthly adventures Twain was also drafting in his final years, Old Man's energies are engrossed by an experimental fascination with the properties of consciousness alone. A series of additional tests that he imposes demonstrates to Young Man's partial satisfaction that the Interior Master is intellectually adventurous and artistically gifted but marked, at the same time, by a formidable vitality that is "as independent of me as it could be if it were in some one else's skull." This conclusion emerges from one of the last thought experiments that Old Man devises in order to illustrate that "the waking mind and the dreaming-mind are the same machine." Choose a good opportunity, Old Man suggests, and carefully observe what your mind will do when left "to its own devices." Young Man complies and offers a detailed account of the results:

I was shaving. I had slept well, and my mind was very lively, even gay and frisky. It was reveling in a fantastic and joyful episode of my remote boyhood which had suddenly flashed up in my memory,—moved to this by the spectacle of a yellow cat picking its way carefully along the top of the garden wall. The color of this cat brought the bygone cat before me, and I saw her walking along a side-step of the pulpit; saw her walk onto a large sheet of sticky flypaper and get all her feet involved; saw her struggle and fall down, helpless and dissatisfied; saw her go on struggling, on her back and getting more and more dissatisfied, more and more urgent, more and more unreconciled, more and more mutely profane; saw the silent congregation quivering like jelly, and the tears running down their faces. I saw it all. The sight of the tears whisked my mind to a far distant and a sadder scene—in Tierra del Fuego—and with Darwin's eyes I saw a naked great savage hurl his little boy against the rocks for a trifling fault; saw the poor mother gather up her dying child and hug it to her breast and weep, uttering no word. Did my mind stop to mourn with that nude black sister of mine? No—it was far away from that scene in an instant, and was busying itself with an ever-recurring and disagreeable dream of mine. In this dream I always find myself, stripped to my shirt, cringing and dodging about in the midst of a great drawingroom throng of finely dressed ladies and gentlemen, and wondering how I got there. And so on and so on, picture after picture, incident after incident, a drifting panorama of ever-changing, ever-dissolving views manufactured by my mind without any help from me—why, it would take me two hours to merely name the multitude of things my mind tallied off and photographed in fifteen minutes, let alone describe them to you. (WIM 777–8)

This hodge-podge of images serves Old Man's point in more ways than one. Young Man's extraordinary inner tour depicts the volatility of the Interior Master as it seizes on a chain of associations so unpredictable in scope that it is able to link a yellow cat on a garden wall, a passage from *The Descent of Man*, and a stubbornly humiliating dream with a drifting panorama of mental photographs too numerous to catalog. This fifteen-minute spectacle would seem to confirm Old Man's account of the mind's complete indifference to consistency or control. We are, in effect, always dreaming, even during a morning shave.

But the waking dream that Young Man describes also resembles an elaborate chamber of mirrors, capturing different facets of itself in a sequence of provocative reflections. The mind and the yellow cat, for instance, are equally "frisky" entities, sharing exquisite powers of agility that a piece of sticky flypaper briefly arrests, during the first stage of Young Man's introspective experiment, much as

Darwin's book arrests the reading mind with its disturbing images. The photograph, like the page, is a sticky surface that can entangle the viewer in its untallied complexity. A congregation in its Sunday best and a drawing room full of finely dressed ladies and gentlemen are analogous incitements to the same cringing sense of nakedness that Tierra del Fuego evokes. The savage father's murderous rage captures the capacity of trifles to ignite uncontrollable mental forces, just as the innocuous yellow cat does at the outset of these visions. The Interior Master, in short, responds to a range of interests that are not always reducible to simple self-gratification or associational accident. It is given to contemplating its mix of strengths and weaknesses beneath the vast array of disguises that it employs.

Old Man underscores this point when he recommends that Young Man exercise the disciplines of speech and writing to harness the mind's reflective power. Once one latches on to some particularly intriguing thought or subject tossed up by the mental stream, the Interior Master "will take full charge" of the mind's verbal tools "and furnish the words itself" in an irresistible (if brief) creative flood (WIM 778). Even these celebrated creative gifts, however, depend on mental processes that men share with rats, cows, birds, elephants, ants—the full panoply of "unrevealed" minds that science has yet to investigate completely or to appreciate fully in the plenum of consciousness that life displays. Surely, Young Man complains, the Moral Sense still lifts human nature far above the lower forms of animal life. But Old Man points out the flaw in this invidious view: "The fact that man knows right from wrong proves his *intellectual* superiority to the other creatures; but the fact that he can *do* wrong proves his *moral* inferiority to any creature that *cannot*. It is my belief that this position is not assailable" (WIM 791; emphases in the original).

"What is left for the moralist to do?" a discouraged Young Man had asked his friend at an earlier stage in Old Man's performance (WIM 770). The first "Admonition" that Old Man provides is little more than a trick. Train your ideals "upward," he suggests, so that in the process of securing your own approval—the goal that is your "chiefest pleasure"—you will simultaneously "confer benefits upon your neighbor and the community" (WIM 767). Ideals, in other words, are simply bait, a high-minded means of hoodwinking the Interior Master into seeking socially useful sources of spiritual contentment. But it is never entirely clear how

Old Man's manipulative result is to be achieved in the face of the mind's capricious independence, nor is Young Man at all convinced, by the end of their long conversation, that life will be worth living without the comforting delusion that Man is "the supreme marvel of the Creation" (WIM 801). Old Man has no patience with such delusions both because he considers them a cultural humbug, and because he thinks they overrate the power of belief. "Beliefs? Mere beliefs? Mere convictions?" Old Man scoffs: "They strive in vain against inborn temperament" (WIM 802).

As this sharply dismissive rejoinder suggests, the refinement of our ideals or the perfection of our beliefs plays no role in the closing portion of Twain's dialogue.[11] Despite a certain, temporary willingness to appease Young Man's anxieties, Old Man is not particularly drawn to framing moral admonitions that temperament will invariably ignore. Such tactics are at best simply forms of ethical engineering—a kind of consciousness factory not unlike the Man-factories that one of Twain's late narrators will attempt to insert into sixth-century England, only to discover that his efforts to engineer progress are futile. Like the ethical tags and noble traits with which people strive to ornament the fictitious self or the soul, "progress" (in Old Man's view) is a name for a thing that does not exist. But this realization seems to exhilarate rather than discourage him. The stupendous energies of the mental chameleon are unimpaired by the discovery that those energies alone are real. "I have thought. Behold!" God announces in "Letters from the Earth" before launching his fountain spray of suns. That announcement is the catalyst of Mark Twain's artistic life, as well as the key to Old Man's sublime contentment at the end of his Socratic performance.

* * *

"Open your mouth and begin to talk," Old Man had gently advised his disillusioned young friend, "or take your pen and use that" (WIM 778). With luck, the Interior Master will pour out the sentences that embody your mental world, generating a portrait of consciousness as vivid as the cascade of images that filled Young Man's internal mirror during Old Man's final thought experiment. The misleading artistic values of closure or control would give way to an unexpected overlapping of fresh interests that perpetually rejuvenate creative life. Twain himself was systematically applying this advice to the work of his last years, but its lessons were evident even at the outset of his career. Between 1875 and 1883, as the preliminary drafts for *What Is Man?* slowly evolved, he worked with particular intensity on a fountain spray of books that overlap and diverge in much the same way that the inquisitive energies of the Interior Master repeatedly do in the course of his Socratic dialogue. *The Adventures of Tom Sawyer, A Tramp Abroad, Life on the Mississippi,* and *The Prince and the Pauper* ultimately form a striking matrix of highly varied but closely integrated work within which the *Adventures of Huckleberry Finn* gradually took shape and the initial impetus for *A Connecticut Yankee in King Arthur's Court* first attracted Twain's attention. Though he famously complained of his struggles with writer's block, his imaginative tank was never empty, anymore than Young Man's mind was ever blank as he watched its infinite gyrations in his shaving mirror.

The pages that follow work backward from the end of Twain's career to its beginning, when he first formulated and explored the account of mental life to which Old Man gives sustained expression. Chapter 1, "Inside Excursions," begins by focusing on the samples from Twain's autobiographical dictations that he agreed to publish, late in his life, in the *North American Review*. This effort to exploit the disorderly flow of his memory, as a basis for the *Review*'s sequential "Chapters," repeatedly results in a far more potent, and more complex, account of mental experience than association alone would lead one to expect. The three distinct stories that form *The Mysterious Stranger Manuscripts* celebrate the same unpredictable, but malleable, imaginative fertility that the autobiographical dictations exploit. Both artistic enterprises from Twain's final decade dramatize the impact that his increasingly detailed account of the Interior Master exerted on his narrative practices.

"Interest," the title of this book's second chapter, springs directly from the extraordinary propensity to be interested that characterizes Twain's two Mysterious Stranger narrators, Theodor Fischer and August Feldner. Selective interest and its close relative, focalized attention, form what William James once called the joint "keel" of contemporary psychology: a vital but inherently inexplicable feature of mental life. Together they play formative roles in a cluster of Twain's earliest work as well: "Jim Smiley and His Jumping Frog," *The Innocents Abroad,* and *Roughing It*. The inexhaustible powers of transfiguration and of mental repletion that characterize his first two ambitious travel memoirs anticipate key features of Old Man's portrait of consciousness. Chapter 3, "Attention," begins by exploring Twain's fascination with the complex cognitive demands involved in the "science" of steamboat piloting that he treated at some length in "Old Times on the Mississippi." The seven magazine pieces in the "Old Times" series link the circumstantial world of Twain's Missouri boyhood with an inquiry into the processes of consciousness that preoccupies the third of his major travel books, *A Tramp Abroad*. This book's final chapter, "Shadings," focuses on the fine gradations of interior life that animate *Life on the Mississippi*, *Adventures of Huckleberry Finn*, and *A Connecticut Yankee in King Arthur's Court*. The close engagement with language that all four sections employ reflects Twain's own interest in the acute powers of discrimination that the term "shadings" implies and that his most famous narrator both practices and exemplifies.

1

Inside Excursions

In April 1904, two months before the death of his wife, Mark Twain dictated an embarrassing confession about an act of unconscious plagiarism that he claimed to have committed nearly forty years earlier in his dedication to *The Innocents Abroad*. He and his family were living in a rented villa near Florence, Italy, following the advice of Olivia's doctors, who hoped that the mild climate might help her recover her health. For much of the time, Twain was at loose ends, prohibited from seeing Olivia for more than a few minutes a day, and often reduced to writing her brief notes when his physical presence seemed likely to drain her rapidly failing strength. Meanwhile he continued to work on a handful of magazine articles and, for the first time, to experiment with the practice of dictating autobiographical vignettes to his secretary, Isabel Lyon, a working method that he would soon recommend to William Dean Howells in glowing terms. The dictation experience was a revelation, Twain wrote his old friend. Its results had a "woodsy freshness" about them, a spontaneous coherence and vitality that captured "the subtle something which makes good talk so much better than the best imitation of it that can be done with a pen."[1]

Ultimately good talk proves to be the catalyst for Twain's embarrassing confession. A few months after writing Howells, he began dictating his memory of a conversation that he had in 1872 with Joseph Goodman, an old comrade from his Nevada days who was visiting New York at the time. During a walk down Broadway, Goodman suddenly asked how Twain had come to steal the dedication to *The Innocents Abroad* from the collected poems of Oliver Wendell Holmes: "I'm not discussing the question of whether you stole it or didn't," Goodman insists, "I am only asking you *how* you came to steal it, for that is where my curiosity is focalized" (CA 227; emphasis in the original). This unexpected assertion of mental focus at first takes Twain by surprise, but a quick visit to a nearby bookstore soon convinces him that Goodman is right. Both dedications pay tribute to the author's mother in fairly conventional terms: the "most indulgent of readers, the kindest of critics," Holmes had called his "beloved mother"; "my most patient reader and most charitable critic," Twain had called his "aged" one.[2] The two men are juggling nearly identical clichés in a tightly scripted format that is bound to produce a measure of verbal overlap. But Goodman's gleeful accusation instantly fills Twain with shame. He is completely unable to account for the unsettling resemblance in wording until a chance letter that he receives a few months later from another old Virginia City friend triggers a series of interwoven memories that explain what happened. "The natural way provided by nature and the construction of the human mind for the discovery of a forgotten event," Twain observes in the 1904 dictation, "is to employ another forgotten event for its resurrection" (CA 227).

The letter indirectly reminds Twain of the two weeks he spent in his room at the Honolulu Hotel, in 1865, recovering from a case of saddle sores that he had developed while collecting material for his newspaper correspondence on the Sandwich Islands. He spent the time mostly "unclothed, and in persistent pain," leafing through the sole book in the hotel, a small volume of Holmes's poems. "Of course I read them almost constantly," Twain remembers, "I read them from beginning to end, then read them backwards, then began in the middle and read them both ways, then read them wrong end first and upside down. In a word, I read the book to rags, and was infinitely grateful to the hand that wrote it" (CA 228). The result (he concludes) was that Holmes's dedication lay dormant in his mind until he was in search of a dedication for his own book, when it miraculously "came forward ... and was promptly mistaken by me as a child of my own happy fancy."

Twain quickly wrote Holmes to apologize and received a gracious reply that echoes Old Man's account of our mental machinery from *What Is Man?* In his letter:

> Dr. Holmes laughed the kindest and healingest laugh over the whole matter, and at considerable length and in happy phrase assured me that there was no crime in unconscious

plagiarism; that I committed it every day, that he committed it every day, that every man alive on the earth who writes or speaks commits it every day and not merely once or twice but every time he opens his mouth; that all our phrasings are spiritualized shadows cast multitudinously from our readings; that no happy phrase of ours is ever quite original with us, there is nothing of our own in it except some slight change born of our temperament, character, environment, teachings and associations; that this slight change differentiates it from another man's manner of saying it, stamps it with our special style, and makes it our own for the time being; all the rest of it being old, moldy, antique, and smelling of the breath of a thousand generations of them that have passed it over their teeth before! (CA 228–9)

Twain's memory attributes to Holmes a milder version of Old Man's stark claim that our minds are incapable of originality, but the resemblance between the positions is striking. Even the healing laugh that Twain detects in the letter suggests Old Man's constitutional cheerfulness, in the face of Young Man's wounded vanity.[3]

By the spring of 1904 *What Is Man?* was nearly finished. Twain had compiled its early drafts into a typescript when his family was living in Vienna in 1898. This text was the basis of a second typescript prepared in 1902 that he would use to complete the dialogue's final version three years later.[4] With each stage in the process, Twain seems to have grown increasingly committed to Old Man's account of consciousness, though each stage also carried him farther from the dramatic immediacy of "good talk" that the dialogue form exploits and deeper into the imitative artifice of the pen. Holmes's healing laughter highlights the same distinction, since a written page can only "laugh" in the vivifying imagination of its reader. Twain's Old Man and Dr. Holmes agree on a central fact of mental life: though each of us may be deeply conditioned by training, we remain a subtle blend of the spiritualized shadows that flow over us from without and the peculiar, inward stamp, the "special style," that distinguishes the individual temperament. Originality and plagiarism, Holmes implies, are hopelessly imperfect concepts. Each is a distortion of the complex engagements that characterize the mental world.

"In the thirty-odd years that have come and gone since then," Twain concludes, "I have satisfied myself that what Dr. Holmes said was true" (CA 229). The stream of ideas and reminiscences has a life of its own as heedless of control as the Interior Master whose elusive vitality pervades Old Man's thought experiments. Twain grapples with the challenge of describing this mental vitality on a number of occasions as the autobiographical dictations unfold. In a reminiscence dated January 6, 1907, he compares it to the unregulated traffic between two concurrent mental swarms: a "commerce of association" between the ceaseless activity of thought and a pervasive cloud of "reminders" that "almost continuously" stimulate the memory. The work of writing, Old Man had observed, could impose a degree of control on this inner tumult, focalizing the mind's attention on a segment of the shifting array long enough to identify the links that compose it, but the array itself was beyond the reach of our deliberative powers. The discovery of Twain's unconscious plagiarism captures the entire process in action.

Joe Goodman's abrupt remark on the streets of New York cuts through the stimulating distractions of Broadway to "focalize" on a strictly interior point of interest. A visit to a nearby bookstore appears to confirm Goodman's intuition, but despite Twain's considerable chagrin, he cannot account for the disquieting similarity between the two dedications. The incident had stirred his mind, however, and prepared it to make unexpected use of some details in a letter that arrived months later. The memory of his desperate reading, along with the vivid recollections of bodily pain, unbearable tedium, and infinite gratitude, flow into familiar channels and complete the resurrection that Twain set out to illustrate. When Holmes's generous letter arrives, it replicates the healing impact of his poems. The kinetic complexity of the episode beautifully illustrates what William James calls the "fantastic laws of clinging" that weave together the kaleidoscopic bits of our mental experience.[5] None of his philosophic or scientific predecessors, James believes, had adequately characterized the richness and subtlety of the neural networks that James undertakes to describe in *The Principles of Psychology*.

"The manner in which trains of imagery and consideration follow each other through our thinking," James observes,

> the restless flight of one idea before the next, the transitions our minds make between things wide as the poles asunder, transitions

which at first sight startle us by their abruptness, but which, when scrutinized closely, often reveal intermediating links of perfect naturalness and propriety—all this magical, imponderable streaming has from time immemorial excited the admiration of all whose attention happened to be caught by its omnipresent mystery.[6]

How are these intermediating links preserved in the physical makeup of the brain, James wonders? What forces influence the capricious activity of "attention" as it traverses the imponderable stream, temporarily pursuing one train of imagery only to diverge with startling speed along another? Thomas Hobbes had illustrated the continuity of mental association by comparing its movement to the way water "upon a plain Table is drawn which way any one part of it is guided by the finger," but for James each point on the cerebral cortex resembled a neural water drop susceptible to the influence of countless guiding "fingers" originating in every corner of the brain.[7] The result was a shimmering "tract of conduction," a perpetually unstable labyrinth of neural pathways. Once established, these pathways remained in highly variable states of latency within the brain, James reasoned, susceptible to momentary renewal much like a piece of paper always "remembers" where it has been folded.[8]

Some pathways both reflect and respond to the simple contiguity of experiences. Mental events that occur together tend to cohere in neural matrices with many different points of entry or recall, like Holmes's volume of poems and Twain's Honolulu hotel. Others reflect the forces of recency, vividness, or emotional "congruence" that form their own mutually competing associative webs. Concentrated interest, like Joe Goodman's focalized curiosity, could influence neural tension for comparatively brief periods, but only until some succeeding mental interest superseded it in the shifting equilibrium of inner life. Reason, James continues,

> is only one out of a thousand possibilities in the thinking of each of us. Who can count all the silly fancies, the grotesque suppositions, the utterly irrelevant reflections he makes in the course of a day? Who can swear that his prejudices and irrational beliefs constitute a less bulky part of his mental furniture than his clarified opinions? It is true that a presiding arbiter seems to sit aloft in the mind, and emphasize the better suggestions

into permanence, while it ends by dropping out and leaving unrecorded the confusion. But this is all the difference. The *mode of genesis* of the worthy and the worthless seems the same. The laws of our actual thinking, of the *cogitatum*, must account alike for the bad and the good materials on which the arbiter has to decide, for wisdom and for folly.[9]

Old Man would insist that James's presiding arbiter is simply an additional participant in the omnipresent mystery of mental experience. Reason has no intrinsic claim on the Interior Master's loyalties. Indeed, James's inventory of our mental furniture—its fancies, opinions, prejudices, and suppositions—constitutes a fabric of "inward iridescences," as he once called them, an intoxicating psychic world to which James and Twain found themselves equally attracted as the nineteenth century drew to a close and the twentieth began.[10]

* * *

The Florentine Dictations were not the first of Twain's attempts to impose literary form on his autobiographical meditations, nor would they be the last. Over the final decade of his life he dramatically expanded the dictation experiments, completed his anonymous dialogue on what William James had called the "magical, imponderable streaming" of mental life, and wrote three interlinked tales of angelic visitation that tried to sum up his account of consciousness. These final products of Twain's artistic life, published and unpublished, suggest the intense interest that he took in bringing to bear what Holmes had termed the special stamp of his individual temperament on the multitudinous shadows of our inner world.

In August 1906, the same month that *What Is Man?* appeared, Mark Twain agreed to let George Harvey, the owner-editor of the *North American Review*, run a series of magazine installments drawn from the increasingly unwieldy mass of Twain's autobiographical dictations.[11] Since the preceding January, with the help of a stenographer, Twain had already compiled a typescript memoir of around a quarter of a million words, a fraction of what he would ultimately produce. Harvey's late summer visit to Twain's Dublin, New Hampshire, retreat was the culmination of several years of assiduous effort to get access to this growing trove of work.¹² After a three-day immersion in Twain's typescript, Harvey left Dublin carrying a full set of the existing dictations in order to consult William Dean Howells on the final shape of the magazine installments. Twain revised the published "chapters" apparently without altering the narrative sequences that Harvey and Howells helped create. Beginning with the eighth *Review* installment, the printed text incorporates the dates of each dictation, exposing the erratic jumble of years that these editorial collaborations produced and mimicking the method of the dictations themselves. Throughout the series, Twain depicts himself selectively cutting and rearranging passages from a biography of her father that his daughter, Susy, had begun to write in 1885, when she was thirteen years old. The result of this compositional entanglement is an elaborate hybrid of associative and narrative paths, formed on different principles, at different times, and by different hands.[13]

The first excerpt to appear, in the September 7, 1906, issue of the *North American Review*, begins with a dictation from the previous March:

> I intend that this autobiography shall become a model for all future autobiographies when it is published, after my death, and I also intend that it shall be read and admired a good many centuries because of its form and method—a form and method whereby the past and the present are constantly brought face to face, resulting in contrasts which newly fire up the interest all along, like contact of flint with steel. Moreover, this autobiography of mine does not select from my life its showy episodes, but deals mainly in the common experiences which go to make up the life of the average human being, because these episodes are of a sort which he is familiar with in his own life, and in which he sees his own life reflected and set down in print. The usual, conventional autobiographer seems to particularly hunt out those occasions in his career when he came into contact with celebrated persons, whereas his contacts with the uncelebrated were just as interesting to him, and would be to his reader, and were vastly more numerous than his collisions with the famous. (CA 3–4)

The dictation scheme itself set out to harness the fleeting energies of contact, collision, and interest, much as Old Man's thought experiments strove to do as they exposed Young Man to the erratic plentitude of consciousness.[14] "If I should talk to the stenographer two hours a day for a hundred years," Twain insisted, "I should still never be able to set down a tenth part of the things which have interested me in my lifetime." His reminiscences will offer no probing confessional insights, Twain suggests, and no summation of the meaning of his times. Henry Adams, who dates the preface to his *Education* five months after the appearance of Twain's first *North American Review* installment, shares Twain's concern with setting aside generic conventions, but Adams also singles out Rousseau, Franklin, and Carlyle as models for his self-portrait. The *Education* would follow the chronological stages of its hero's life, if only to dramatize the narrator's theme of existential confusion as history lost its reassuring predictive value. "For him alone," Adams wrote of himself, "the old universe was thrown into the ash-heap and a new one created," marked by a clash of temperaments and technologies that Adams would spend his adult life trying to master.[15]

By contrast, Twain's account of autobiographical form and method invokes no ambitions beyond the desire to mirror the intrinsic disorder of the reader's ordinary experience. By March 1906 the old universe had been thrown onto the ash heap for Twain as well as for Henry Adams, but the tremendous personal and national cataclysms that he had witnessed in his life did not diminish his appetite for new interests, new collisions between the present and the past, provided that these events could be left free to establish their own order in the flow of Twain's dictations. A cradle-to-grave narrative, he complained, would exclude all "side-excursions," and the unpredictable intrusion of side-excursions, Twain believed, constituted "the life of our life-voyage."[16] The key to Twain's dictation method is its commitment to a degree of introspective freedom capable of responding to those instants when consciousness ignites in the iridescent sensation of the "interesting."

Subject matter in itself is by nature as static as the term implies. But this inner readiness to be interested—to plunge, however briefly, into the panoramic flow of consciousness wherever the attention might happen to "focalize" itself—participated directly in the endless streaming of the mental world. "What a wee little part of a person's life are his acts and his words!" Twain wrote as he considered the astonishing growth of his dictations:

His real life is led in his head, and is known to none but himself. All day long, and every day, the mill of his brain is grinding, and his *thoughts*, (which are but the mute articulation of his *feelings*,) not those other things, are his history. His *acts* and his *words* are merely the visible thin crust of his world, with its scattered snow summits and its vacant wastes of water—and they are so trifling a part of his bulk! a mere skin enveloping it. The mass of him is hidden—it and its volcanic fires that toss and boil, and never rest, night nor day. *These are his life*, and they are not written, cannot be written. Every day would make a whole book of eighty thousand words—three hundred and sixty-five books a year. Biographies are but the clothes and buttons of the man—the biography of the man himself cannot be written.[17]

The glittering web of association that William James describes is only in part, or only by fits and starts, an orderly mental "commerce." To Twain it resembles a grinding mill, a volcanic cauldron, and an inexhaustible verbal deluge that corresponds directly to the formidable energies of the Interior Master, as Young Man had observed them in the closing pages of *What Is Man?* A century of steady dictation, Twain knew, would fall hopelessly short of disclosing the scope of the tumult within.

But even the most sweeping inventory of ideas, images, and interests would amount to little more than an inert collection of mental furniture rather than a portrait of the elusive agent that had assembled the collection during the erratic course of its thought. Capturing that mysterious entity in action was a representational challenge that William James compared to catching the motion of a spinning top by grabbing it or turning up the gas lamp quickly in order to see what darkness looked like.[18] James devoted most of his attention, in the essays and articles that he published between 1878 and 1884, to the dynamism that he detected in the bird-like "flights and perchings" of mental experience. A focus on resting places, he argued, had blinded his contemporaries to the importance of what he called "the transitive parts" in thought's stream, the relational network of ideas or images partly reflected in the fluidity of syntax or the shifts in vocal inflection through which written and spoken language tried to embody the mind's transitive life:

There is not a conjunction or a preposition, and hardly an adverbial phrase, syntactic form, or inflection of voice, in human speech, that does not express some shading or other of relation which we at some moment actually feel to exist between the larger objects of our thought. If we speak objectively, it is the real relations that appear revealed; if we speak subjectively, it is the stream of consciousness that matches each of them by an inward colouring of its own. In either case the relations are numberless, and no existing language is capable of doing justice to all their shades.[19]

The misleading stability of verbalized ideas, James believed, could not hope to capture the "delicate idiosyncrasies" of feeling that characterize the mind's transitive nature. Twain's dictations hope to dramatize those delicate idiosyncrasies in action.

The first of the chapters to appear in the *North American Review*, on September 7, 1906, begins by bragging about the "hardened and perfected" judgmental instincts that Twain claims to have inherited from his Clemens ancestors, a legacy that encourages him to embarrass an American diplomat named William Walter Phelps, who was hosting a Berlin dinner in Twain's honor during the winter of 1891. On this occasion, both Twain and Phelps were eager to impress a third dinner guest, "Count S.," with their own claims of distinguished (if untitled) lineage. When Phelps took the party on a tour of his drawing room, he pointed to an engraving on the wall and remarked "with exulting indifference" that one of its figures—a secretary seated before the judge's bench at the trial of Charles I—was his ancestor. Twain immediately responded by pointing to one of Charles's judges in the same engraving and repeating, "with scathing languidness," one of the Clemens family traditions: "Ancestor of mine. But it is a small matter. I have others" (CA 6).

The exquisitely calculated verbal impressions that the two men are trying to convey capture the "inward colouring" that William James associates with the dynamism of transitive life. Twain's scathing languidness trumps Phelps's exulting indifference and almost immediately casts a subtle shadow of regret over the memory: "I wonder how he felt?" A mix of trivial and profound emotional inflexions shapes Twain's account of this outwardly ceremonial occasion. As the evening drags on, Count S. postpones appearing at the bedside of a dying colleague and Twain suffers in silence with an uncomfortable pair of new shoes, waiting for some indefinite signal that the time to leave had arrived. "At last," Twain recalled, "we all rose by one blessed impulse and went down to the street door without explanations—in a pile, and no precedence; and so, parted" (CA 7). Aristocratic prestige itself seems to recede into the semi-anonymity of "Count S." and the impending nonentity of the "dying official" at whose bedside he is expected to attend. The *Review* series as whole repeatedly responds, with exquisite sensitivity, to the invisible presence of inexplicable impulses that are anything but hardened and perfected.

Immediately after describing the outcome of the Phelps dinner, for instance, Twain turns to a description of the obscure Tennessee village of Jamestown where his father and mother had first set up housekeeping before eventually moving to Twain's Florida, Missouri, birthplace. The seventy-five thousand acres of land that John Marshall Clemens had purchased while the family was living in Jamestown would prove to be his only material legacy. "Cling to the land and wait," he urged his wife and children, as he lay on his deathbed, twelve years after leaving Tennessee for what he had hoped would be a more prosperous life across the Mississippi. This poignant blend of optimism and desperation links him, in Twain's dictation, to James Lampton, a cousin of Twain's mother and the original of Colonel Sellers, a Micawber-like figure whom Twain had introduced in *The Gilded Age*. "I merely put him on paper as he was," Twain claimed, but when a well-known comic actor named John T. Raymond tried to play Sellers in Twain's stage adaptation of the book, he missed the emotional nuances that Twain associated with James Lampton's actual nature. Raymond captured the comic dimensions of the role, Twain remembered in his dictation, but he could not convey its pathos (CA 10). In "humorous portrayal," Twain conceded, Raymond "was superb, he was wonderful—in a word, great; in all things else he was a pigmy of the pigmies."[20] Raymond could carry off an "effect," Twain concluded, but not a character. He could not convey the "tinted mist of magnificent dreams" which had enabled Lampton to sustain a lifetime of relentless failure—the inward iridescence that shallow comedy failed to touch. As the dictation project continues, Twain quickly realizes that its implicit subject has become this striking contrast between the intangible delicacy of interior life and the superficiality of "effects," or the fixity of death.

The second installment of *Review* "Chapters" compresses the rich emotional weave of this first reminiscence into a single, startling account of a conversation that Twain had with Robert Louis Stevenson on a park bench in Washington Square. The passage is part of Twain's initial 1904 Florentine dictations, ten years after Stevenson's death, in which Twain recalls the only meeting between the two men in the spring of 1888. The *Review* installment decouples Twain's description both from its placement in the larger dictation enterprise and in the biographical sequence of both men's lives. The result casts into sharp relief the emotional impact produced by Stevenson's haggard appearance. "His business in the Square," Twain remembered, "was to absorb the sunshine":

> He was most scantily furnished with flesh, his clothes seemed to fall into hollows as if there might be nothing inside but the frame for a sculptor's statue. His long face and lank hair and dark complexion and musing and melancholy expression seemed to fit these details justly and harmoniously, and the altogether of it seemed especially planned to gather the rays of your observation and focalize them upon Stevenson's special distinction and commanding feature, his splendid eyes. They burned with a smouldering rich fire under the penthouse of his brows, and they made him beautiful. (CA 22)

Cutting these words off from their 1904 context prevents the reader of the *Review* from tying Twain's intently focalized concentration on Stevenson's face to Joseph Goodman's "focalized" curiosity about the dedication to *The Innocents Abroad*, a passage that the *Review* won't print for another year. Instead a different kind of impression arrests Twain's attention, the "altogether of it" that he senses in the mortal extremity of Stevenson's appearance and strives to capture in the striking contrast between the great mental vitality expressed in Stevenson's eyes and the ravages of the disease that is killing him.

Despite his companion's haunting presence, or perhaps because of it, Twain begins chattering away about the limited talents of Bret Harte in contrast to the dazzling conversational abilities of Thomas Bailey Aldrich. He dictates, as if from memory, a strangely insensitive tribute to Aldrich's verbal powers that fuses the rich fire of Stevenson's appearance with a grim forecast of his fate. Twain's awkward attempt to retrieve the situation with a joke only tightens the transfigurative interplay that underlies the passage, hinting at the acute sensation of psychological distress that Twain is trying to depict. As a conversationalist, he begins, Aldrich was in a class by himself, "always witty, always brilliant, if there was anybody present capable of striking his flint at the right angle":

> I added—
> "Aldrich has never had his peer for prompt and pithy and witty and humorous sayings. None has equalled him, certainly none has surpassed him, in the felicity of phrasing with which he clothed these children of his fancy. Aldrich was always brilliant, he couldn't help it, he is a fire-opal set round with rose diamonds; when he is not speaking, you know that his dainty fancies are twinkling and glimmering around in him; when he speaks the diamonds flash. Yes, he was always brilliant, he will always be brilliant; he will be brilliant in hell—you will see."
> Stevenson, smiling a chuckly smile, "I hope not."
> "Well, you will, and he will dim even those ruddy fires and look like a transfigured Adonis backed against a pink sunset." (CA 22-3)

Aldrich was still alive when this passage appeared in the *North American Review*, but Stevenson's gaunt presence casts a shadow over Twain's reconstructed speech, twice pushing Aldrich's living brilliance into the past tense, as if Twain's verbs register the same collision between social surfaces and existential depths that the Phelps dinner had displayed. The "chuckly smile" and complexly shaded reply to Twain's manic outburst suggest that Stevenson recognizes in Twain's words the kind of nervous noise that the healthy often find themselves making in the presence of profound illness.

At this point the conversation with Stevenson unexpectedly shifts to the topic of "submerged renown." Though Twain cannot recall which of the two men coins the expression, it springs from a conversation that Stevenson had recently held with the proprietor of an Albany, New York, bookshop, who explained to his famous customer the extraordinary popularity of a series of cheap anthologies compiled by a man named Davis whom neither Stevenson nor Twain had ever heard of. Stevenson then embarks on a performance of his own, as Twain reconstructs their discussion, adopting the bookseller's voice as he explains the difference between superficial and submerged reputations. "Nobody has heard of Davis," Stevenson's informant begins:

> "You never see his name mentioned in print, not even in advertisement; these things are of no use to Davis, not any more than they are to the wind and the sea. You never see one of Davis's books floating on top of the United States, but put on your diving armor and get yourself lowered away down and down and down till you strike the dense region, the sunless region of eternal drudgery and starvation wages—there you'll find them by the million. The man that gets that market, his fortune is made, his bread and butter are safe, for those people will never go back on him. An author may have a reputation which is confined to the surface, and lose it and become pitied, then despised, then forgotten, entirely forgotten ... But it is a different matter with the submerged reputation—down in the deep water; once a favorite there, always a favorite; once beloved, always beloved; once respected, always respected, honored, and believed in. For, what the reviewer says never finds its way down into those placid deeps; nor the newspaper sneers, nor any breath of the winds of slander blowing above. Down there they never hear of these things. Their idol may be painted clay, up there at the surface, and fade and waste and crumble and blow away, there being much weather there; but down below he is gold and adamant and indestructible." (CA 24)

The ruddy fires and verbal brilliance that formed Twain's playful vision of Aldrich in hell are inadequate imaginative diving armor for a visit to the sunless depths where Davis finds his audience—a zone of drudgery and starvation that hungers, all the same, for the immaterial forms of nourishment that Davis's little collections provide. This dense region of changeless esteem, beneath the unstable whirlwind of the popular press, is both a refuge and a grave. It recasts the contrast between the two writers who have met for the first and last time in Washington Square, one poised at the volatile crest of his career and the other on the verge of death, not as a showy encounter between celebrated persons but as an exploration of the subtle network of transitive relations subsisting beneath the brittle veneer of reputation.[21]

* * *

The fantastic laws of clinging at play in the mental world are more easily recognized and labeled than controlled. Stevenson's passive presence in the spring sunshine of Washington Square asserts a subtle agency in Twain's memory, linking sight with elusive forms of outer and inner warmth that organize and briefly stabilize the image that the passage evokes. Davis's obscure anthologies acquire an evocative power, in Stevenson's monologue, that temporarily reverses the polarities of fame and obscurity, life and death, as it echoes the very different psychological postures that Twain and Stevenson embody. Each posture, in turn, is a matter of shadings and colorings, as William James might suggest, that occur almost on the spot, turning the materials at hand into exquisite meditative vignettes.

The dictation method itself is partly responsible for creating a verbal matrix that permits Twain to span the considerable gap between Aldrich's gem-like surfaces and Stevenson's existential depths, but Twain and his editors collaborate on a chapter arrangement, in the pages of the *North American Review*, that links the serio-comic street door plunge of William Walter Phelps's weary dinner guests to the placid deeps where Davis's readers preserve their miraculous indifference to the superficial storms of precedence. An artistic arbiter does, in fact, preside over the apparent narrative disorder, much like the deliberative presence that William James had envisioned presiding over the associative confusion of human thought. But the mind's astonishing agility remains at the heart of Twain's dictation experiments. Thomas Bailey Aldrich's "dainty fancies" may be negligible mental products, but Twain evidently relishes their spark-like brilliance, even as he shifts his focus to the deeper shadows that Stevenson's commanding presence evokes.

Variations on this striking range of interior capacities recur throughout the dictations, repeating the juxtaposition between glittering surfaces and sunless depths that Aldrich and Stevenson introduce. In the December 7, 1906, issue of the *Review*, for instance, Twain transcribes a brief, obsequious note that he sent to

Grover Cleveland the previous March, on Cleveland's sixty-ninth birthday, ranking the ex-president's "unassailable" character with that of George Washington. Immediately following this extravagant reminder of the attraction that worldly precedence always held for Twain, the installment includes a remarkable paragraph describing the dementia from which Harriet Beecher Stowe had suffered in the last years of her life:

> In a diary which Mrs. Clemens kept for a little while, a great many years ago, I find various mentions of Mrs. Harriet Beecher Stowe, who was a near neighbor of ours in Hartford, with no fences between. And in those days she made as much use of our grounds as of her own, in pleasant weather. Her mind had decayed, and she was a pathetic figure. She wandered about all the day long in the care of a muscular Irish-woman. Among the colonists of our neighborhood the doors always stood open in pleasant weather. Mrs. Stowe entered them at her own free will, and as she was always softly slippered and generally full of animal spirits, she was able to deal in surprises, and she liked to do it. She would slip up behind a person who was deep in dreams and musings and fetch a war-whoop that would jump that person out of his clothes. And she had other moods. Sometimes we would hear gentle music in the drawing-room and would find her there at the piano singing ancient and melancholy songs with infinitely touching effect. (CA 87)

The text of this dictation imposes no typographic fences between Twain's egregious flattery of Cleveland and this carefully muted account of Stowe's mental decay. The childish mischief and infinite grief that compose her "moods" have an incongruous emotional richness that makes Twain's self-serving deference to conventional success seem all the more ridiculous, much like Stowe's startled neighbors must have appeared, when her war-whoops abruptly broke into their musings. The confident cultural immunities that Twain and Cleveland embody are ephemeral, at best, subject to disquieting surprises. Mrs. Clemens's slender diary and the memory of Stowe's "melancholy songs" seem the more durable expressions of feeling, human aptitudes closely linked to the psychic deeps where Davis's anonymous readers subsist.

The purposed jumble that Twain had set out to achieve in his autobiographical dictations, as presented in its magazine installments, turns out to be far more carefully "purposed" than it seems. The unpredictable, shifting iridescences that William James detected in the mental stream are themselves susceptible to a kind of shifting that is responsible for the juxtaposition of Twain's pompous birthday letter with his suggestive description of Stowe's decline. Seen through the selectively capricious lens of attention, political prominence or literary fame seem little more than variations on James Lampton's tinted mist: delusions that Stevenson's splendid eyes or Stowe's haunting melodies dispel, offering in their place suggestive glimpses of more profound emotional registers. Those deeper registers shape the long *Review* installment for March 1, 1907, in which Twain painstakingly recreates the boyhood months that he regularly spent at the farm of his uncle, John Quarles, outside Florida, Missouri (CA 142–54). The fifteen or twenty Negro slaves whom Quarles owned provided Twain with his earliest and in many ways most intimate exposure to slavery. At first the 1907 dictation barely glances at the racial makeup of the Quarles household before launching into an elaborate list of the many "sumptuous" dishes that comprised the family's old-fashioned country meals. But after a brief survey of the Quarles farmyard, Twain's focus shifts to "a little log cabin" near the main house where a hill "fell sharply away" toward a buried landscape that fractures his superficially bucolic account, much as a page break fractures a narrative or the steep slope of this hillside breaks his mental topography into incompatible worlds.[22]

The descent behind the cabin leads to "a limpid brook which sang along over its gravelly bed ... in the deep shade of overhanging foliage and vines," an inviting refuge concealing a number of forbidden swimming holes where the Quarles children and their Clemens relative often played. The memory of the prohibited swimming pools dissolves other imaginative prohibitions as well, once the course of the reminiscence enters this deeply shaded underworld where Twain and his cousins "had early been taught the value of forbidden fruit" (CA 143). The next sentence introduces detailed descriptions of two Quarles family slaves, Aunt Hannah and Uncle Dan'l, the first a bed-ridden old woman and the second a middle-aged man, both of whom Twain had been able to weave into his fiction. But he recalls without naming the slave children with whom he played, "comrades, and yet not comrades" of his eight cousins and himself. The racial barrier between them "rendered complete fusion impossible" (CA 144).

Throughout his "schoolboy days," Twain continues, nothing in his immediate surroundings had challenged the legitimacy of slavery. The pulpit, the papers, and the Bible formed what amounted to a seamless front of approval: "In Hannibal we seldom saw a slave misused," Twain insisted, "on the farm never." But when this deceptive veneer inevitably breaks, it leaves an indelible mark on Twain's memory:

> There was, however, one small incident of my boyhood days which touched this matter, and it must have meant a good deal to me or it would not have stayed in my memory, clear and sharp, vivid and shadowless, all these slow-drifting years. We had a little slave boy whom we had hired from some one, there in Hannibal. He was from the Eastern Shore of Maryland, and had been brought away from his family and his friends, half-way across the American continent, and sold. He was a cheery spirit, innocent and gentle, and the noisiest creature that ever was, perhaps. All day long he was singing, whistling, yelling, whooping, laughing—it was maddening, devastating, unendurable. At last, one day, I lost all my temper, and went raging to my mother, and said Sandy had been singing for an hour without a single break, and I couldn't stand it, and wouldn't she please shut him up. The tears came into her eyes, and her lip trembled, and she said something like this—
>
> "Poor thing, when he sings it shows that he is not remembering, and that comforts me; but when he is still, I am afraid he is thinking, and I cannot bear it. He will never see his mother again; if he can sing, I must not hinder it, but be thankful for it. If you were older, you would understand me; then that friendless child's noise would make you glad." (CA 145)

Sandy's vocal energy mimics the lively brook on the Quarles farm; his stillness mimics its forbidden pools. The fantastic laws of clinging beneath the surface of Twain's reminiscence construct this resemblance out of the paradoxically shadowless sounds that he recalls. Jane Clemens's alertness to the signals of Sandy's hidden nature prompts a similar alertness, on Twain's part, in the last several pages of the March 1907 *Review* installment, highlighting their latent psychological contours.[23] From this point forward Twain's account of the Quarles farm grows more attentive to the clash of mental states that Sandy's example represents.

"I can see the farm yet, with perfect clearness," Twain declares as he resumes the broken thread of the dictation, but the clarity of what follows is far from perfect. The "rising and falling wail" of a spinning-wheel in the Quarles parlor, Twain remembers, "was the mournfulest of all sounds to me" (CA 146). Its emotional cadence draws a procession of ambivalent images in its wake: hot coals dying "a leisurely death" on the oak floor near the hearth; rattlesnakes and adders sunning themselves on a country road where the Quarles children easily kill them; a vast limestone cavern near the river where Twain and a companion were once nearly hopelessly lost; the terrible shame he felt at the age of seven when a "strapping" schoolgirl mocked him for being unable to chew tobacco. "I realized that I was a degraded object," Twain remembers, an imagistic compression of the mixed world that the Quarles farm embodies: "Children have but little charity for each other's defects" (CA 150).

Such memories repeatedly disrupt the *Review* installment's nostalgic flow, preventing its perfect fusion even at moments that seem fully saturated with sentiment. Long catalogs like the following passage only appear to be unreflective immersions in sensory pleasure:

> I know the look of green apples and peaches and pears on the trees, and I know how entertaining they are when they are inside of a person. I know how ripe ones look when they are piled in pyramids under the trees, and how pretty they are and how vivid their colors. I know how a frozen apple looks, in a barrel down cellar in the winter-time, and how hard it is to bite, and how the frost makes the teeth ache, and yet how good it is, notwithstanding. I know the disposition of elderly people to select the specked apples for the children, and I once knew ways to beat the game. I know the look of an apple that is roasting and sizzling on a hearth on a winter's evening, and I know the comfort that comes of eating it hot, along with some sugar and a drench of cream. I know the delicate art and mystery of so cracking hickory-nuts and walnuts on a flatiron with a hammer

that the kernels will be delivered whole, and I know how the nuts, taken in conjunction with winter apples, cider and doughnuts, make old people's tales and old jokes sound fresh and crisp and enchanting, and juggle an evening away before you know what went with the time. (CA 152)

These words exercise their own delicate mystery, juggling time in order to suggest the alluring ways in which old people implicate the young in a tedious and repetitive human tale, a form of forbidden knowledge fused by Twain's reiterative "I know" into an accumulation that resists mental sweetening. Nothing in these pages of the *Review* installment is delivered whole.

A final reminiscence of life on the Quarles farm extends the eerie reciprocity of light and darkness that the previous *Review* chapters had explored:

I remember the pigeon seasons, when the birds would come in millions, and cover the trees, and by their weight break down the branches. They were clubbed to death with sticks; guns were not necessary, and were not used. I remember the squirrel hunts, and the prairie-chicken hunts, and the wild turkey hunts, and all that; and how we turned out, mornings, while it was still dark, to go on these expeditions, and how chilly and dismal it was, and how often I regretted that I was well enough to go. A toot on a tin horn brought twice as many dogs as were needed, and in their happiness they raced and scampered about, and knocked small people down, and made no end of unnecessary noise. At the word, they vanished away toward the woods, and we drifted silently after them in the melancholy gloom. But presently the gray dawn stole over the world, the birds piped up, then the sun rose and poured light and comfort all around, everything was fresh and dewy and fragrant, and life was a boon again. (CA 154)

This passage describes a tentative ascent from the mind's sunless places, a journey that incorporates with the memory of these "dismal" hunts a brief glimpse of Twain's sickly childhood and the psychological vulnerability that had partly shaped it. Even on the Quarles farm, the boon of existence was at best an unstable gift, a comforting and a brutalizing mix of experiences to which the mind of a child struggled to accommodate itself. This interchange between luminous surfaces and nearly impenetrable depths forms the underlying mental rhythm of the *Review* installments as a whole—a rhythm that depends on Twain's facility at mingling his rising and falling psychological cadences, presenting them as a single interior event despite the competing emotional forces that they contain.

* * *

Twain's serialized memoir repeatedly exploits the subtle mental flux that the dictations evoke, adapting the stream of sensations and images to a measure of control, just as Old Man had recommended Young Man try to do with the tools that speech and writing could provide. The mysterious neural "streaming" that William James compared to an aurora's flickering energy formed a hybrid of transience and beauty that responded with extraordinary suppleness to the exercise of artistic choice. Twain and his editorial collaborators are able to shape this elusive material into its successive magazine chapters by teasing its representational variety into high relief, focusing it on aspects of Twain's Hartford years that he revisits through the medium of his daughter's 1885 family memoir. The fourth autobiographical installment to appear in the *Review*, on October 19, 1906, takes up Susy's manuscript for the first time. Nearly every installment that follows touches on her words as a catalyst for Twain's own, scissoring up Susy's pages in precisely the same way that George Harvey cut up her father's unwieldy typescript into pieces that he could subsequently reassemble in his magazine. As Twain reflected on this interleaving process, he called attention to some features of his daughter's working method that echo his own: the orderly disorder of her expressive record, an "accumulation" that gradually discloses its own fantastic laws of clinging. "I think a great deal of her work," Twain wrote:

> Her canvases are on their easels, and her brush flies about in a care-free and random way, delivering a dash here, a dash there and another yonder, and one might suppose that there would be no definite result; on the contrary I think that an intelligent reader of her little book must find that by the time he has finished it he has somehow accumulated a pretty clear and nicely shaded idea

of the several members of this family—including Susy herself—and that the random dashes on the canvases have developed into portraits. I feel that my own portrait, with some of the defects fined down and others left out, is here; and I am sure that any who knew the mother will recognize her without difficulty, and will say that the lines are drawn with a just judgment and a sure hand. (CA 206)

The penetrating artistic distinctions that Susy achieves belie the chaotic energy with which she seems to have worked, guided by a "sure" hand that is, at the same time, as impetuous as the Interior Master whose movements Young Man finds himself helpless to chart.

A similar interplay of psychological shadings characterizes Twain's account of Susy's nature. On the easel that his pages provide, she resembles a strange combination of the same implacable darkness and iridescent delight that Twain often imposed upon the memories of his Missouri childhood. "Like other children," he remembered, Susy "was blithe and happy, fond of play," but she also displayed a grasp of life's disappointments far beyond her years, "much given to retiring within herself to search out the hidden meanings of the deep things that make the puzzle and pathos of human existence" (CA 34). From the beginning of her life, Twain recalled, she was equipped with the kind of emotional diving armor that Stevenson's bookshop owner had described. The October 5, 1906, *Review* installment pinpoints the circumstances in which Twain first learned that his eldest daughter was dead. Olivia and Clara, Susy's younger sister, had accompanied Twain on the world lecture tour that he began in July 1895 to repay his creditors and recover from bankruptcy. Susy and fifteen-year-old Jean remained behind with relatives. The three travelers had just arrived in England, the last stop on the tour, when they received a letter reporting what would prove to be Susy's fatal illness.

Within a few days, Olivia and Clara were halfway across the Atlantic, having sailed to America expecting to assist at what a subsequent cable had assured them would be Susy's "long, but certain" recovery. Twain remained behind in Guilford, England, where the family hoped to reunite once Susy could travel, and was standing in his rented dining room "thinking of nothing in particular, when a cablegram was put into my hand. It said,

'Susy was peacefully released to-day'" (CA 32). The cable's trite euphemism for Susy's death—a platitude as empty of emotional resonance as the state of mind in which Twain receives it—sharpens the contrast that the passage ultimately presents between the brittle formulations of convention and the extraordinary psychological struggle that follows, a nightmarish interior journey through which Twain strives to describe how the mind grapples with such a catastrophic, blow:

> The intellect is stunned by the shock, and but gropingly gathers the meaning of the words. The power to realize their full import is mercifully wanting. The mind has a dumb sense of vast loss— that is all. It will take mind and memory months, and possibly years, to gather together the details, and thus learn and know the whole extent of the loss. A man's house burns down. The smoking wreckage represents only a ruined home that was dear through years of use and pleasant associations. By and by, as the days and weeks go on, first he misses this, then that, then the other thing. And, when he casts about for it, he finds that it was in that house. Always it is an essential—there was but one of its kind. It cannot be replaced. It was in that house. It is irrevocably lost. He did not realize that it was an essential when he had it; he only discovers it now when he finds himself balked, hampered, by its absence. It will be years before the tale of lost essentials is complete, and not till then can he truly know the magnitude of his disaster. (CA 32)

The house of memory is an ancient trope for the mind and its contents, an image perfectly adapted to the ruin that Susy's death would make of the Clemens family's Hartford home. The litany of neutral pronouns that Twain employs—"it was in that house," "there was but one of its kind," "it is irrevocably lost"—signals the unbroken grip of emotional homelessness that lasted from Susy's death to the end of his life. His daughter had "died at the right time, the fortunate time of life," Twain concluded, before "the cares, the sorrows, and the inevitable tragedy" of existence could blight her spirit: "For her mother's sake I would have brought her back from the grave if I could," he concluded, "but I would not have done it for my own" (CA 73).

Along with Susy, Orion Clemens is the only other figure whose complete existence Twain tries to incorporate into the pages of the *North American Review*, but unlike his daughter, Twain's older brother far outlives the fortunate time of life. Orion emerges from the pages of the autobiographical dictations as both a caricature and a victim of the furious succession of interests that drive the restless stream of consciousness. His defining trait, as Twain remembered it, "was eagerness":

> He woke with an eagerness about some matter or other every morning; it consumed him all day; it perished in the night and he was on fire with a fresh new interest next morning before he could get his clothes on. He exploited in this way three hundred and sixty-five red-hot new eagernesses every year of his life. But I am forgetting another characteristic, a very pronounced one. That was his deep glooms, his despondencies, his despairs; these had their place in each and every day along with the eagernesses. Thus his day was divided—no, not divided, mottled—from sunrise to midnight with alternating brilliant sunshine and black cloud. Every day he was the most joyous and hopeful man that ever was, I think, and also every day he was the most miserable man that ever was. (CA 113)

It is not difficult to detect the resemblances between this passage and Twain's account of Susy's complex mental world or his description of the extraordinary "volcanic fires" of thought and feeling that the ceaseless mill of consciousness generated in himself. Indeed, Orion's mental vacillations echo almost perfectly the brash confidence with which the *Review* installments themselves embrace the ceaseless flux of Twain's red-hot eagernesses. "Everything he did," Twain wrote of his brother, "he did with conviction and enthusiasm and with a vainglorious pride in the thing he was doing" (CA 114). But unlike the case with Twain's resilient ego, Orion's vainglory would give way to "sackcloth and ashes" every twenty-four hours, not in a neat or symmetrical division of temperamental phases but in a "mottled" blend, a subtle interior entanglement that persists nearly moment by moment, feeling by feeling, across the span of Orion's life. "I think he was the only person I have ever known," Twain wrote, "in whom pessimism and optimism were lodged in exactly equal proportions" and in the same mental rooms.

Every printing house, small-town newspaper, or law practice that Orion tried to establish throughout his checkered career, by Twain's account, invariably failed as a direct result of his impractical generosity: "He was never able to comprehend that work done on a profitless basis deteriorates and is presently not worth anything" (CA 124). His tenure as secretary of the Nevada Territory represented the zenith of Orion's fortunes, but even then he managed to come to grief: "at the critical moment," his brother observed, "the inborn capriciousness of his character rose up without warning, and disaster followed" (CA 128). In a spasm of virtue, when Nevada was about to become a state, and Orion had every reason to expect a lucrative post in the newly constituted government, he suddenly declined on principle to campaign for office on the grounds that to do so would taint the electorate's "unspotted gift." When a simple visit to a saloon might have swayed the necessary votes in his favor, Orion abruptly embraced teetotalism and was left out in the cold.[24] A brief spate of success as an editor on the Hartford *Evening Post* came to an end when a group of politicians enticed Orion away from this "easy berth" to edit a new daily and then summarily fired him, an outcome that Twain claims to have predicted in a bitter speech to Orion that reads like a painful confession of his own insecurities, as well as an indictment of his brother's failings:

> "You are as weak as water. Those people will find it out right away. They will easily see that you have no backbone; that they can deal with you as they would deal with a slave. You may last six months, but not longer. Then they will not dismiss you as they would dismiss a gentleman: they will fling you out as they would fling out an intruding tramp." (CA 133)

These harsh words about Orion's weakness of character mirror Twain's own ill-fated flirtation with fabulous wealth during the flush times of the Comstock Lode, as well as the anxieties that occasionally led him to think of his own improbable success story as that of a tramp thrusting himself into the company of eastern gentlemen.

As the Clemens brothers' lives diverged, Twain repeatedly loaned Orion money that Orion, just as regularly, vowed to repay through a variety of publishing projects or implausible inventions over a span of thirty years. In all that time he frequently assumed "offices of trust where other people's money had to be taken care of," opportunities that sprang from the general respect which his personal integrity never failed to inspire in others. But none of these offices ever paid a salary. Orion "never lost a cent for anybody," Twain noted with a mix of pride and exasperation, "and never made one for himself" (CA 135). A faithfulness to "grounded principle" was the single, unwavering feature of his character. His antislavery convictions, his sincerity, and his truthfulness never faltered. In all other matters, Twain concluded, his brother was "unstable as water": "he never acquired a conviction that could survive a disapproving remark from a cat" (CA 115).

Orion, Twain concluded, was "the strangest compound that ever got mixed in a human mould," but it was a compound clearly built out of many of the same elements that Twain recognized in himself: an extraordinary need for the approval of others; a propensity to swing between emotional extremes of great delight and deep gloom; a fondness for improbable economic schemes or for nurturing ingenious but ultimately useless inventions. The cablegram announcing Orion's death arrived while the Clemens family was living in Vienna in 1898, during their period of self-imposed exile after Susy's death had made the Hartford house uninhabitable. Orion and his wife had been struggling to make a success of a boarding house in Keokuk, Iowa. "He was seventy-two years old," Twain remembers in a long dictation dated April 5, 1906: "He had gone down to the kitchen in the early hours of a bitter December morning; he had built the fire, and had then sat down at a table to write something; and there he died, with the pencil in his hand and resting against the paper in the middle of an unfinished word" (CA 137). These details express with stark economy the mixed sense of futility and hope, of beginnings and endings, that Twain singles out as the central ingredients of his brother's portrait. Like Susy's random dashes on her biographical canvas, they capture the interchange between transience and permanence in written form.

* * *

The last three *North American Review* installments appear in the closing months of 1907. Each is a collage of dictations that Twain had made over the previous two years, mixed with a pair of final extracts from Susy's family memoir, along with the entire newspaper transcription of the speech that Twain had delivered on December 17, 1877, at John Greenleaf Whittier's seventieth birthday dinner. Together these reminiscences span Twain's entire life, from his schoolboy days in Hannibal through the celebration of his Oxford University honorary degree in June 1907. The painfully mixed memory of the Whittier birthday speech falls almost precisely in the middle of this closing sequence, underscoring Twain's candid acknowledgment of the hunger for "emotional attention" that had been the shaping force of his life. That hunger is the psychic link that ties his nearly fatal bout with measles in 1845 to his rapture at Oxford's lavish academic ceremonies over six decades later where he, Sidney Lee, and Rudyard Kipling were made doctors of literature. "It makes me proud to read it," Twain remarked of the oration delivered in his honor when he received his degree:

> as proud as I was in that old day, sixty-two years ago, when I lay dying, the centre of attraction, with one eye piously closed upon the fleeting vanities of this life—an excellent effect—and the other open a crack to observe the tears, the sorrow, the admiration—all for me—all for me! (CA 274)

Between these two exuberant experiences falls the chill of the Whittier dinner, but it too reflects the same insatiable emotional need that erupts in the cathartic "all for me" with which the above passage ends.

In the course of revisiting this complex memory, Twain reaffirms the pervasive impurity of our mental and verbal worlds. In preparation for his ceremonial role at the Whittier dinner, he had carefully memorized an elaborate anecdote about a lonely miner in the California gold country who is visited, one evening, by three drunken imposters claiming to be Ralph Waldo Emerson, Henry Wadsworth Longfellow, and Oliver Wendell Holmes. Together they embody the system of spiritualized shadows to which Holmes's letter had referred, only a few years earlier, when he reassured Twain about the wording of his dedication to *The Innocents Abroad*. At the Whittier dinner, some of the dignified "phrasings" of New England's literary idols would reemerge in Twain's speech, smelling of the breath of three anonymous vagabonds. Emerson,

Longfellow, and Holmes, along with Whittier, were guests of honor at the dinner. These four were "seated at the grand table," Twain recalled, facing an audience of "shadowy figures" only a few of whom he claims to remember after the lapse of thirty years. The other speakers and birthday guests are "ghosts now to me, and nameless forever more," swallowed up in the same human pile with which the *Review* installments had begun.[25]

Immediately before Twain rose to deliver his western anecdote, a New York dramatic editor named Willie Winter recited a "dainty" poem that sounded "exactly as if it was pouring unprepared out of heart and brain," Twain remembered, a sure sign of Winter's glib familiarity with the prevailing social expectations. Twain's frontier background and reputation imposed more complex burdens on his own performance:

> Mr. Chairman—This is an occasion peculiarly meet for the digging up of pleasant reminiscences concerning literary folk; therefore I will drop lightly into history myself. Standing here on the shore of the Atlantic and contemplating certain of its largest literary billows, I am reminded of a thing which happened to me thirteen years ago, when I had just succeeded in stirring up a little Nevadian literary puddle myself, whose spume-flakes were beginning to blow thinly Californiawards. (CA 290)

The following day's *Boston Evening Transcript* printed the full text of the speech, the source from which Twain is able to retrieve it for the final *Review* installment in order to reconstruct his painful impressions of the event. The audience response stunned him. When he was barely two hundred words into his playful yarn, Twain recalled, their faces "turned to a sort of black frost," instantly blighting the dainty impact of Winter's poem, as Twain adapts the metaphorical weather of his preamble into a vivid account of his social disgrace. Boston's literary luminaries and the rest of the birthday guests sat through the entire speech as if "turned to stone" with horror at Twain's comic indiscretion. Howells, who was also present, immediately grasped the extent of the disaster. The speaker who followed Twain—an inexperienced young novelist named Bishop—was so paralyzed by the grim mood of the room that his words "began to waste away and disappear out of his head like the rags breaking from the edge of a fog ... and at last he slumped down in a limp and mushy pile," a forlorn successor to the literary puddle where Twain claimed his own career had begun. The episode "nearly killed me with shame," he remembered, "during that first year or two whenever it forced its way into my mind" (CA 298).

For nearly three decades he tried to avoid thinking about the Whittier speech altogether, until a letter from an admirer in 1906 suddenly focalized his memory, just as Joe Goodman's thoughts three decades earlier were abruptly focalized on the dedication to *The Innocents Abroad*. Twain sent to Boston for a copy of the text from the *Transcript* archives:

> As I said, it arrived this morning, from Boston. I have read it twice, and unless I am an idiot, it hasn't a single defect in it from the first word to the last. It is just as good as good can be. It is smart; it is saturated with humor. There isn't a suggestion of coarseness or vulgarity in it anywhere. What could have been the matter with that house? It is amazing, it is incredible, that they didn't shout with laughter, and those deities the loudest of them all. Could the fault have been with me? Did I lose courage when I saw those great men up there whom I was going to describe in such a strange fashion? If that happened, if I showed doubt, that can account for it, for you can't be successfully funny if you show that you are afraid of it. Well, I can't account for it, but if I had those beloved and revered old literary immortals back here now on the platform at Carnegie Hall I would take that same old speech, deliver it, word for word, and melt them till they'd run all over that stage. Oh, the fault must have been with *me*, it is not in the speech at all. (CA 299)

The psychological complexities of this episode are far richer than those surrounding the gratifications of Twain's Oxford honorary degree or his boyhood struggle with measles, just as the speech itself draws upon a more elaborate complex of mental energies than either of those incidents calls into play. Saturation is precisely the right figure of speech to evoke the highly unstable equilibrium of verbal acuity, humor, courage, self-doubt, bewilderment, confidence, and resentment that swirls through these pages. Twain's fluid states of feeling are intensified rather than blunted by the passage of time, much as they are in his accounts of his daughter's subtle intelligence or his brother's baffling blend of firm virtues and watery weaknesses. Three decades after the fact, Twain is able to reconstitute the extraordinary emotional flux that lay at the center of his artistic consciousness. That insight in turn plays a decisive role in the three interrelated stories that compose the final inside excursion of Twain's career.

* * *

Off and on for a period of ten years, beginning in the fall of 1897, Twain worked on a series of three loosely linked narratives exploring the idea of miraculous visitation. He began writing the earliest of the three, "The Chronicle of Young Satan," shortly after his family had settled in Vienna, during their long, self-imposed exile from America after Susy Clemens's death. The story takes place in Austria, early in the eighteenth century, and revolves around the effect that Satan's nephew has on a sleepy Austrian village and on the three village boys whom he befriends, before assuming the disguise of a travelling gentleman-student, Philip Traum, in order to study village life. While this plot was still developing, Twain set it aside late in 1898 to write six brief chapters of a second tale that he called "Schoolhouse Hill," transporting a version of his young Satan figure to the Mississippi River town of St. Petersburg during the boyhood years of Tom Sawyer and Huckleberry Finn, though neither of those well-worn characters plays a significant role in the new story.

By the summer of 1899 he had returned to the first manuscript, doubling its length by August 1900, when he seemed to lose interest in both of these unfinished experiments shortly before the Clemens family began to make arrangements to return to the United States. Two years later, however, working first in New York City, then in Florence, Italy, Twain adapted the opening paragraphs of "The Chronicle of Young Satan" to the beginning of the third and longest of what his editors now call "The Mysterious Stranger" manuscripts. This final effort offered the most resistance to Twain's imagination, in large part because of the emotional disruption associated with Olivia's death in June 1904. When he finally took up the story once more, during the summer of 1905 in Dublin, New Hampshire, he destroyed thirty thousand words of the manuscript and began to reconstruct nearly half of the remaining book from scratch, a process that ended in 1908 when Twain took six pages that he had originally written four years earlier and tacked them on to the end of the third "Mysterious Stranger" tale, titling this last brief section the "Conclusion of the Book."[26]

Unlike its two predecessors, this final story dispenses entirely with the nephew or the child of Satan as its central figure, substituting instead an enigmatic visitant to a late-fifteenth-century Austrian print shop who is identified only by a serial number: "Number 44, New Series 864,962" (MS 238). The other inhabitants of the print shop—its owner, his family, and his staff of journeymen and apprentices—are bewildered and ultimately angered by their visitor's quiet answer to the shop master's request for his name, but Twain is almost certainly thinking of the long string of stops and starts, revisions and cancellations, variants and adaptations, lying behind the serial narrative that he was once again about to undertake. The several stories and their author had all covered a great deal of physical and psychological territory since 1897, an experience that this improbable numerical name partly acknowledges and partly mocks.

Twain's last miraculous visitant is emphatically "made," or produced, not born into the family lineage of a fallen archangel. He is the forty-fourth copy of the latest modification in a sequence of nearly one million prototypes or predecessors that collectively compose the "new," not the first or the final, serial outpouring of the exuberant transformational energies that they embody. The central figures Twain creates for all three versions of the mysterious stranger story share a preeminent eagerness for "making" matched only by their comparative indifference to possessing or preserving what they make. This indiscriminate appetite for production both delights and alarms their closest human companions. Each stranger, in turn, is beautifully adapted to the corporeal possibilities of the manufactured worlds in which they find themselves, worlds largely populated with maladaptive human beings.

Each of the Mysterious Stranger narratives is set in a small community dominated by a petty tyrant whose influence is abetted by the superstition or the complacency of the surrounding population. The drunken priest, Father Adolf, browbeats his neighbors in both Austrian versions of the story, though he plays a lesser role in Number 44's tale, where a collection of print shop workers, along with their master's wife, combine to persecute the oddly named young wanderer whom the master tries to shelter. In

"Schoolhouse Hill" the new, "surprisingly handsome," and well-dressed boy who appears one winter morning at the schoolhouse door must first vanquish the school's reigning bully, the spoiled son of the town slave trader, before he can gain a fleeting acceptance among the other boys.[27]

Striking beauty, along with great muscular and mental gifts, characterize the mysterious visitors in all three stories, traits that seem concentrated in, though not confined to, the hypnotic power of their eyes. Number 44 appears to take a "high joy" in exerting "his strange and enduring strength" to supply wood and water for the inmates of the print shop or to subdue one of the apprentices who tries to taunt him into a fight. Despite the contemptuous reception that his offer receives, he is prepared to take an equal pleasure in soothing his defeated antagonist's injuries: "if you will let me I will stroke your arms for you and get the stiffness and the pain out" (MS 243). Erotic potency and receptivity are key ingredients in the completely commensurate humanity that Twain attaches to his miraculous visitants. To be in love with any of these remarkable beings, as many of the characters who encounter them ultimately are, is to be in love with the finest inner and outer capacities of corporeal life.[28]

As Number 44's name suggests, however, the possibilities of embodiment are infinite rather than individual in scale. Creative profusion and creative indifference permeate the worlds in which Twain situates each of his miraculous visitors, an improbable compound of opposing energies that he captures in the remarkable picture of the great blizzard that settles over St. Petersburg in the middle of the "Schoolhouse Hill" narrative. "It was this storm's mission," Twain wrote, "to bury the farms and villages of a long, narrow strip of country for ten days, and do it as compactly and thoroughly as the mud and ashes had buried Pompeii nearly eighteen centuries before" (MS 200). In the uncanny description that Twain soon provides for these overlapping forms of burial—by snow, ash, and time—he draws attention to many of the personal attributes that the mysterious strangers themselves will come to exercise: their ingratiating modesty, artistic gifts, and disorienting power.

> The Great Storm began its work modestly, deceptively. It made no display, there was no wind and no noise; whoever was abroad and crossed the lamp-glares flung from uncurtained windows

noticed that the snow came straight down, and that it laid its delicate white carpet softly, smoothly, artistically, thickening the substance swiftly and equably; the passenger noticed also that this snow was of an unusual sort, it not coming in an airy cloud of great feathery flakes, but in a fog of white dust-forms—mere powder; just powder; the strangest snow imaginable. By 8 in the evening this snow-fog had become so dense that lamp-glares four steps away were not visible, and without the help of artificial light a passenger could see no object till he was near enough to touch it with his hand. Whosoever was abroad now was practically doomed, unless he could soon stumble upon somebody's house. Orientation was impossible; to be abroad was to be lost. A man could not leave his own door, walk ten steps and find his way back again. (MS 200)

A surreal fatality, as beautiful as it is deadly, links the acts of creation and extinction that this language evokes, the soundless "thickening" of the snow calling to mind the accumulation of words on a fresh sheet of paper, in the bright "lamp-glare" of a writer's desk, much as Susy's scattered insights slowly cohered into the family portraits of her journal. The "fog of white dust-forms" generated by the storm seems both skeletal and ghostly, a "thick mask" or an "on-coming wall" (Twain calls it) smothering the insignificant particularity of the present (MS 201).

The chronicle of human history to which Young Satan eventually introduces his three Eseldorf friends, in the first version of Twain's three-part series, is an equally disorienting blizzard: a monotonously repetitive sequence of bodily propagation and destruction, building up layers of "dull nonsense" and civilized hypocrisy a million years in the making—an utterly meaningless cultural incrustation. Yet when Satan detects the pain and despair that this relentless vision causes in his young companions, he gently invites them to drink their health from a set of "shapely and beautiful goblets" that he conjures up out of the surrounding atmosphere: "They were very brilliant and sparkling," the astonished narrator recalls, "and of every tint, and they were never still, but flowed to and fro in rich tides which met and broke and flashed out dainty explosions of enchanting color" (MS 138). Like the delicate carpet of snow-forms in "Schoolhouse Hill," these uncanny vessels too descend from the sky, carrying an unearthly wine that produces "a strange and witching ecstasy" before they disappear like "a triplet of radiant sundogs." Extinction and exaltation are close neighbors in these narratives, like the delicate fusion of beginnings and endings that the *Review* installments capture in the beautiful iridescence of Susy's nature or the details of Orion's death.

A deep-seated ambivalence toward bodily experience underlies all three Mysterious Stranger stories, but it is rooted in the potential for high joy that Number 44 most vividly represents. Twain is careful to introduce this key feature of his magical visitants into the earliest versions of the plot. When the narrator's family in "The Chronicle of Young Satan" gather to discuss some of the remarkable opinions and accomplishments of the attractive young tourist who has suddenly appeared in their midst, both parents express misgivings about his behavior. Theodor Fischer—one of the three boys to whom Satan reveals his true identity when he first meets them outside their home village of Eseldorf—is looking back on these events many years later, remembering among other things the stir that "Philip Traum" immediately created with two of the town's young women, one of whom is Theodor's sister Lilly. Despite her mother's disapproval, Lilly finds herself irresistibly drawn to Traum's "beautiful nature." "He is ever so kind-hearted, mother," she exclaims in his defense, immediately adding the unhelpful remark that Traum even admires rattlesnakes:

"Ad—mires rattlesnakes! Is he insane?"
"No. But he has read all about them, and admires their noble character."
"Their noble character—the most infamous beast that crawls! What rubbish is this you are talking?"
"But mother, it is not so unreasonable when he explains it. He says this, to the credit of the rattlesnake: that he never takes advantage of any one, and has none of the instincts of an assassin; that he never strikes without first giving warning, and then does not strike if the enemy will keep his distance and not attack him. Isn't that true of the rattlesnake, papa?"
"Well—yes, it is. I had not thought of it before. The truth is, it is better morals than some men have."
"I am so glad you think so, papa; it is what *he* says." (MS 98; emphasis in the original)

Finding herself outnumbered, Theodor's mother changes the subject to an elaborate embroidery project that her daughter had barely begun and had only one month to finish, when Lilly blurts out that the painstaking work is already done, "a little picture, wrought in threads of silk and gold" that Philip Traum had completed for her in twenty minutes. "My mother was astonished again," Theodor wrote, but after examining the picture for herself in every possible light, "her eyes speaking her wondering and worshiping delight," she too succumbs to this gifted stranger. "Marvelous creature, amazing creature," she mutters to herself before announcing out loud that Traum is "a most singular creature, take him how you will. Embroiders like an angel, and admires rattlesnakes; a most unaccountable mixture in the matter of tastes" (MS 99).

This scene is the third instance in Theodor's narrative that depicts the extraordinary creative powers of this singular "creature," all of which highlight the vague sense of unaccountable mixture that his conduct presents. Though Traum/Satan clearly possesses superhuman powers, they just as clearly fall within the range of human appreciation. He completes Lilly's embroidered scene not exclusively by magic but by magical dexterity, working the rich threads into their pattern with stunning speed, yet still consuming time in the exercise of his craft. Theodor's mother takes a "worshiping delight" in the mastery of a complex skill carried to a spectacular degree of perfection, perhaps, but admirable rather than frightening in its results. Her horror at Traum's respect for rattlesnakes completely dissipates when matched against the pleasure that she takes in the "exquisite delicacy" of his workmanship. Traum shows an equally exquisite gift for reason in his defense of the rattlesnake's noble character, though that knowledge too is continuous with, not different from, human aptitudes that Traum has enhanced through reading. According to Lilly, he has been researching the world that he has decided to study, apparently visiting the library of the future to consult Benjamin Franklin's famous mid-eighteenth-century comparison of rattlesnakes to transported felons, a novel idea to the Eseldorf villagers of 1702, but one that Mark Twain probably counted on his contemporaries to recognize: "it is what *he* says."[29]

Words, like embroidery, are an expressive medium with which Twain's mysterious visitors are entirely comfortable. In the long opening scene from "Schoolhouse Hill," the new boy in St.

Petersburg incites the joy of the schoolteacher and the wonder of his classmates with a series of extraordinary verbal feats, beginning with his perfect recall of the rules of English grammar after having heard them recited only once, by the school's grammar class, in a language that he doesn't understand. French, it so happens, is the native language of Hell, and though the Scottish schoolmaster, Archibald Ferguson, is delighted to hear his new pupil speak a tongue that Ferguson enjoys, he doesn't expect him to be fluent in English for some time. In a matter of minutes, however, the new boy is able to skim an entire English dictionary simply by giving each page "a lick from top to bottom with his eye," before reciting the contents:

> It was another miracle. The boy poured out, in a rushing stream, the words, the definitions, the accompanying illustrative phrases and sentences, the signs indicating the parts of speech—everything; he skipped nothing, he put in all the details, and he even got the pronunciations substantially right, since it was a pronouncing dictionary. Teacher and school sat in a soundless and motionless spell of awe and admiration, unconscious of the flight of time, unconscious of everything but the beautiful stranger and his stupendous performance. (MS 181)

Missouri idioms and much of the heavily accented Scottish verse that schoolmaster Ferguson uses at moments of excitement still puzzle the new pupil, but a grasp of those details, Ferguson assures him, will come with practice. It takes their visitor only twenty minutes to acquire this rushing stream of knowledge—exactly the interval that Philip Traum's embroidery consumes—though no one in the school pays attention to the clock once the fantastic recitation begins. Twain makes clear, however, that time is the common medium on which the entire experience depends, from the beautifully swift "lick" of the stranger's eye to the spellbound awe and comic delight of his audience when the new boy proves capable of imitating their teacher's colorful classroom exasperation with a "deep gravity and sincerity" that reduce the entire school to "screams and throes and explosions" of cathartic laughter (MS 180).

Meanwhile the schoolmaster cannot resist the urge to investigate this wonderful cognitive instrument. "Let me experiment a little—for the pure joy of it," Ferguson had exclaimed when he got his initial glimpse of the new boy's mental abilities and put the English dictionary in his hands to test their extent. The same experiment and the same results follow with Latin, Greek, and an English shorthand instruction book, all of which the new pupil masters in the space of a morning, while the rest of the school "droned and buzzed along" with its ordinary work, at its ordinary pace, while keeping "the bulk of its mind and its interest" focused on the uncanny intellectual machinery of their visitor. "How do you manage these things?" the teacher finally asks: "What is your method? You do not read the page, you only skim it down with your eye, as one wipes a column of sums from a slate" (MS 182). In fact, the boy explains, he does absorb the contents of what he reads, but he simply sees each page as a whole rather than as a sequence of characters. He does not "skim it down" but takes it in at a glance, like single picture: "Why shall I glance twice?" He does glance once, however, exercising a skill that the school, in turn, is instantly capable of appreciating.

Ferguson's experiments continue with blackboard exercises in grammar and geometry, followed by a test in which he pits the new boy's powers of mental addition against the speed of "the famous lightning-calculator." The boy completes his sums in a few seconds, and Ferguson dismisses school for the day, smitten with wonder at "the excitements and bewilderments of this intellectual conflagration" (MS 184). He and the rest of his pupils may be "dull moles" in comparison to the capacities of their new companion, but sheer delight in the capacities themselves is the overriding emotion that he feels.

Delight is the reaction that Theodor Fisher's mother feels, too, at Philip Traum's miraculous facility for embroidery, a skill that partly explains her daughter's attraction to their mysterious visitor. A different exhibit of Traum's accomplishments had a similar effect on the heart of another Eseldorf girl, in the pages immediately preceding the discussion in the Fischer household. Marget is the niece of a suspended priest who has fallen into a mix of religious and legal difficulties in which Traum will eventually intervene. Meanwhile he has arranged for her old housekeeper to receive magical supplies of food while her uncle is in prison awaiting trial. During a visit to Marget's house, Traum's presence alone lifts her spirits, an effect it repeatedly has whenever he appears among groups of villagers, but when he tries to entertain her suitor, Willhelm Meidling, by agreeing to some games of chess, Traum's skill is so daunting that his young opponent loses his composure. Traum offers to play without his knights, and then without his queen, but the outcome is the same. "I think he could have beaten him with a pawn," Theodor remarks, obviously impressed by this display, but Satan too takes pleasure in his skill. A few moments after the last chess game has concluded, the course of the conversation leads Marget to ask if Traum can play music. "Oh certainly," Satan replies, "I am a good player" (MS 92). The remark seemed no more conceited in him, Theodor remembered, "than it would seem conceited in a fish to say 'Yes, I am a good swimmer.'"

In order to soothe Willhelm's wounded pride after his chess defeats, Traum takes up a poem that the young man had written and improvises a melody to its words on Marget's old spinet. Theodor thought the poem a "very stirring tale" about a young hero who rescues his beloved from bandits after a stormy, night-long pursuit, only to die of his wounds at the end of a climactic battle, "as the morning sun was brightening the world with hope and happiness." None of the listeners in Marget's house is prepared for the effect of Traum's performance of Willhelm's poem:

> For this was no music such as they had ever heard before. It was not one instrument talking, it was a whole vague, dreamy, far-off orchestra—flutes, and violins, and silver horns, and drums, and cymbals, and all manner of other instruments, blending their soft tones in one rich stream of harmony. And it was mournful and touching; for this was the lover realizing his loss. Then Satan began to chant the words of that poor fellow's lament—gentle and low; and the water rose in those two people's eyes, for they had heard no voice like that before, nor had any one heard the like of it except in heaven, where it came from. (MS 93)

When the storms, the battle, and the death scene are all concluded, Theodor, Willhelm, and Marget are dazed in ecstasy. Traum has disappeared, and when Marget approaches the spinet and strikes a key "she got only the old effeminate tinkle-tankle the thing was born with." Theodor's concluding remark quietly underscores the limitations of mere mechanisms and the brittle materials from which they are made. Satan's powers of "making," however, are limitless and fluid, an integrative artistic "stream" which awakens a response in his listeners that differs in scale, but not in kind, from his own.[30]

Theodor and his two friends, Nikolaus Baumann and Seppi Wohlmeyer, are unable to explain Traum's amazing abilities to the other inhabitants of Eseldorf because Satan has imposed a magical prohibition on their powers of speech that prevents the boys from revealing his identity. But after Lilly hints at her growing romantic attachment to this inaccessible being, Theodor feels compelled to try to reason her out of her dreams and revive her interest in Joseph Fuchs, the town brewer's son and "the best catch in the region" despite some of what Theodor calls the "tinselings of his character." Fuchs is callow and vain, but he is also "honest and clean and true," Theodor concedes, "and had warm affections and deep feelings," another of the many instances of "unaccountable mixture" with which Twain fills all three of the Mysterious Stranger tales. Not the least of these unaccountable phenomena is Theodor's continuing fondness for Satan, despite Theodor's belief that the Eseldorf villagers were all "bugs" in Satan's eyes, and "by his nature he seemed unable to take a bug seriously" (MS 100).

He takes Theodor and his friends very seriously indeed, however, seeking out their companionship and soothing their initial fears out of a sincere yearning for social contact that is among the first unaccountable notes in Satan's makeup. His attitude toward human nature is far more complicated than the analogy to bugs implies. "He likes to rough a person up," Theodor notes much later in the story, thinking of Satan's caustic view of sacred institutions or the follies of human history, "but he likes to smooth him down again just as well" (MS 168). Both of those aptitudes are on dramatic display in the opening pages of the "Chronicle" where Satan gives the most deeply unsettling evidence of his creative gifts. Twain read these episodes to his wife in Vienna, shortly after abandoning the "Schoolhouse Hill" chapters and returning to Theodor Fischer's narrative as the more promising of the two drafts. "It is perfectly horrible—and perfectly beautiful," Olivia remarked after hearing the account of Satan's first exchanges with Theodor and his friends in the woods outside Eseldorf. This wonderfully concise judgment, Twain wrote Howells, exactly matched his own.[31]

The three boys were resting in a favorite shady place "away up into the hills," talking over some impressive ghost stories, when a friendly stranger approached through the trees and joined them. He had "a winning face and a pleasant voice," Theodor noted, and before long was able to make up for the boys' carelessness in forgetting their flint and steel by lighting their tobacco pipes with his breath. "We jumped up and were going to run," Theodor recalled, but their visitor's "soft persuasive way" lured them back: "it was not long before we were content and comfortable and chatty" (MS 45). Other miraculous tricks follow, but when in response to a question from Theodor, the stranger calmly answers that he is an angel, their fear returns, though not their urge to run away:

> He went on chatting as simply and unaffectedly as ever; and while he talked he made a crowd of little men and women the size of your finger, and they went diligently to work and cleared and leveled off a space a couple of yards square in the grass and began to build a cunning little castle in it, the women mixing the mortar and carrying it up the scaffoldings in pails on their heads, just as our work-women have always done, and the men laying the courses of masonry—five hundred of those toy people swarming briskly about and working diligently and wiping the sweat off their faces as natural as life. In the absorbing interest of watching those five hundred little people make the castle grow step by step and course by course and take shape and symmetry, that feeling of awe soon passed away, and we were quite comfortable and at home again. (MS 47)

The intricate scaffolding that leads up to this passage may have contributed to Olivia Clemens's appreciation for the beauty of the story's early pages. Ever since this engaging stranger first emerged from the woods, his friendly overtures had accumulated like courses of masonry, beginning with his primal ability to generate both fire and ice with his breath, then to make all kinds of fruits and snacks appear in the boys' pockets, then to construct a toy squirrel and a tiny dog out of clay, along with small birds that fly away into the forest when he claps his hands. These wonderful creative feats are a prelude to the miniature world they introduce: a rescaled version of Genesis that ascends from the elemental energies of creation, a *spiritus* of fire and ice, through plants and animals to an entire community of people who are already diligently at work in the sweat of their brows building a "cunning little castle."

    This is the moment in the "Chronicle" when the mysterious visitor identifies himself as Satan, an unfallen nephew of the notorious uncle for whom he has been named: "He said it placidly, but it took our breath, for a moment, and made our hearts beat hard" (MS 48). Theodor's visceral response to this knowledge is the prelude to a remarkable blend of erotic feelings that anticipate his sister's infatuation with Philip Traum, an inner "quiver" prompted by the encounter with "something that is so strange and enchanting and wonderful that it is just a fearful joy to be alive." The passages from Twain's autobiography that focus on his brother emphasize the wild oscillations of feeling that characterized Orion's daily existence. Every twenty-four hours, Twain wrote, would find Orion swinging between extremes of ecstasy and despondency, mornings of red-hot eagerness succeeded by evenings of deep despair that made him both the most joyous and "the most miserable man that ever was." Satan's appearance in Eseldorf puts Theodor Fischer and his friends through a similar cycle of emotions: a wary reserve yields to friendly feelings, fear yields to wonder, awe recedes into familiarity and comfort, followed once again by a paralytic terror that precedes an insatiable desire for intimacy. "You wouldn't be anywhere but there," Theodor concluded about this latest phase in his emotional response to Satan's presence, "not for the world."[32]

Man as a whole, Satan will explain to Theodor much later in the story, is a global extension of the same emotional volatility that the boys experience when they first meet him in the Eseldorf woods, a projection of the interior makeup of Orion Clemens (MS 112). "Every man is a suffering machine and a happiness machine combined," Satan observes, a conclusion that he will dramatize in pantomime in the story's opening pages, using the cunning little castle and its busy human community to make an unforgettable impression on his new friends. Without warning a quarrel breaks out between two of the tiny workmen whom Satan had recently created. "In buzzing little bumble-bee voices they were cursing and swearing at each other," Theodor remembers, capturing the discordant outbreak of passion in an uncanny clash of sounds: "now came blows and blood, then they locked themselves together in a life-and-death struggle" (MS 49). In retrospect the fight seems almost inevitable. Satan had hardly finished making his little cluster of men and women before they had immediately set out to build a castle, as if their first concerns were the impending acts of aggression and the need for defense that their nature simply instructs them to expect, as automatically as tiny dogs chase tiny squirrels, or birds molded out of clay one moment fly away singing the next.

Much to the horror of Theodor and his friends, Satan puts an abrupt end to the struggle by crushing the little antagonists between his fingers, wiping the blood off on his handkerchief, and blithely declaring that angels such as himself "cannot do wrong; neither have we any disposition to do it, for we do not know what it is" (MS 49). Shocked though they are by this gratuitous murder, the boys are also "miserable," on Satan's behalf as well as on their own, "for we loved him," Theodor admitted, "and had thought him so noble and beautiful and gracious, and had honestly *believed* he was an angel; and to have him do this cruel thing—ah, it lowered him so, and we had had such pride in him" (emphasis in the original). These feelings form a paralyzing emotional entanglement that echoes the erratic trajectory of feeling—the dramatic swings between joy and misery, tenderness and bitter exasperation—Twain had associated with the memory of his brother. But the experience gets worse when Satan detects the sounds of grief produced by the friends and family of the little workmen whom he has destroyed:

> For the wives of the little dead men had found the crushed and shapeless bodies and were crying over them and sobbing and lamenting, and a priest was kneeling there with his hands crossed upon his breast praying, and crowds and crowds of pitying friends were massed about them, reverently uncovered, with their bare heads bowed, and many with the tears running down—a scene which Satan paid no attention to until the small noise of the weeping and praying began to annoy him, then he reached out and took the heavy board seat out of our swing and brought it down and mashed all those people into the earth just as if they had been flies, and went on talking just the same. (MS 50)

"It made us sick to see that awful deed," Theodor remembers, but before long Satan's enchanting voice and the extraordinary stories he tells reassert their intoxicating claim on the boys' attention, even though by annihilating this small crowd of mourners, Satan has also killed their miniature priest, reminding the boys that none of these little people had been able to take the sacraments and prepare for death.

In the course of reestablishing his profound erotic influence, making the boys "drunk with the joy of being with him, and of looking into the heaven of his eyes," Satan makes plain that the cunning little castle actually embodies all the forms of cultural cunning that the little funeral service had invoked, the customs and rituals which these tiny builders scarcely bothered to construct before deploying them out of the same reflexive piety that drives Theodor and his friends to lament their deaths. All history, in fact, is just such a reflexive spectacle in Satan's eyes, one to which he promptly introduces his three new friends, taking them on a whirlwind tour of the religious universe that includes a glimpse of Samson burying his enemies in their temple, much like Satan had buried the little funeral ceremony, and a terrifying vision of hell that leaves their angelic tutor completely unmoved: "those poor babes and women and girls and lads and men shrieking and supplicating in anguish," Theodor remembers, "why, we could hardly bear it, but he was as bland about it as if it had been so many imitation rats in an artificial fire" (MS 50). Lilly's romantic interests seem to have affixed themselves to a monster.

In fact, Satan implies, the fires are indeed artificial, a kind of "fiction" (in his words) like the cult of good manners that constrains Theodor's criticism of Satan's behavior or the annoying funeral rites that seem to augment the aggressive and defensive instincts that the little castle represents (MS 51). This "quite matter-of-course" dismissal of human feeling and human customs startles Theodor. Satan's extraordinary artistic gifts have not entirely eclipsed the boy's memory or his sympathy. But neither is Satan as dismissive of human life as Theodor implies. He has decided to visit Eseldorf out of interest rather than contempt, drawn by the strange mixture of the worthless and the sublime that he uncovers in earthly "doings." That unaccountable mixture too lies behind the blend of creation and destruction that the episode of the little castle brings to a close in an apocalyptic storm that Satan brews in order to swallow the castle itself and all of its remaining inhabitants, a miniature world of "innocent life," as Theodor mistakenly calls it, though innocence seems never to have formed a part of its makeup.

"Don't cry," Satan tells his friends, when the castle's magazine of powder explodes and an earthquake consumes the ruins. "Our hearts were broken," Theodor recalls, but Satan casually remarks that these marvelous little people were of no value: "we can make more." For his part, he was "as gay as if this were a wedding instead of a fiendish massacre." This is the third instance in the story's opening pages where Satan seems to signal his scorn for the inconsequential flies or imitation rats whose "marvelous" community he has just obliterated, but the sensational language Theodor uses to describe these horrific episodes is entirely his own. Satan shows even less evidence of fiendish gaiety than he does of grief. Delight in the company of his new companions and in his own creative powers is the most prominent ingredient in his nature. Soon he has the three boys dancing on the castle's grave to the music that he makes on "a strange sweet instrument which he took out of his pocket" (MS 52).

As the story unfolds, Satan's contempt is ultimately reserved for the perverse operations of what he terms the Moral Sense and its unaccountable cultural products: hatred, prayers, castles, and gunpowder among them, the constituent ingredients of the miniature world he had just destroyed. This mental feature of human beings is by far the worst exhibit in what Satan considers the "museum of disgusting diseases" to which they are subject—the source of the endless conflict between human tigers and human housecats to which Old Man reduces all of history at the conclusion of *What Is Man?* Pure consciousness, however, is a strange, sweet instrument, a fluent vehicle for the intense pleasures that Satan repeatedly elicits from the three boys even when he decides to "dissolve" himself before their eyes at the end of their first meeting in a conclusive display of his creative and destructive gifts:

> He stood up, and it was quickly finished. He thinned away and thinned away until he was a soap-bubble, except that he kept his shape. You could see the bushes through him as clearly as you see things through a soap-bubble, and all over him played and flashed the delicate iridescent colors of the bubble, and along with them was that thing shaped like a window-sash which you always see on the globe of the bubble. You have seen a bubble strike the carpet and lightly bound along two or three times before it bursts. He did that. He sprang—touched the grass—bounded—floated along—touched again—and so on, and presently exploded,–*puff*! and in his place was vacancy. (MS 56)

A nearly identical scene from "No. 44, The Mysterious Stranger" emphasizes extinction rather than transcendence when the narrator's dream self, or duplicate, is finally allowed to escape the loathsome bodily cage that Number 44 had devised for him, his clothes, flesh, and bones slowly thinning away until only a filmy statue is left, "perfect and beautiful, made out of the delicatest soap-bubble stuff" that quickly bursts (MS 381). From August Feldner's point of view, the "distinctly handsome, distinctly trim and shapely" being who disappears in this memorable way is the mirror image of his "peachy, bloomy" self. To his duplicate, however, this corporeal creature is "odious" (MS 370).

Like Theodor Fischer, who narrates the first of the Mysterious Stranger tales, August Feldner is recording a series of miraculous events that took place many years earlier, after Number 44's sudden appearance amid the "mixed family" of his master's fifteenth-century print shop, lodged in part of a ruined castle above Eseldorf, "like a swallow's nest in a cliff" (MS 229). Those events ultimately include the creation of a complete set of duplicate printers and apprentices who (much to Number 44's delight) throw the shop into turmoil, thwart the workers' plans for a strike, and disrupt their love lives. August's duplicate, Emil Schwarz, is on the point of marrying Marget Regen, the master's niece and the object of August's own romantic interest, when Schwarz suddenly confesses his complete disgust for earthly bodies and his desperate wish to resume his place in the transcendent realm of his fellow "dream-creatures," an expansive erotic paradise completely free of the "crazy tissues" and the "little globe" that imprison human beings. These transcendent bodies, however, still remain bound to the sensory and psychological extremes of human consciousness.

Dream-sprites, Schwarz explains to August, travel at "thought-speed" through a timeless, cosmic ether: a weary void of "black gloom and thick darkness" that periodically explodes into "spirit-cheering archipelagoes of suns which rise sparkling far in front of you, and swiftly grow and swell, and burst into blinding glories of light" before receding into "a twinkling archipelago" again that is soon "blotted out in darkness" (MS 377). This description is a celestial projection of the cathartic laughter in "Schoolhouse Hill" or of Orion Clemens's mental world, a succession of emotional depths and heights that August Feldner too experiences as Number 44's spirit-cheering presence alternately appears and disappears from the seemingly infinite chambers and gloomy hallways of the ruined castle where he and his fellow printers live. The castle itself is yet another architectural surrogate for the mind, like the cunning little structure that Young Satan exhibits and destroys or the devastated house of memory that Twain invokes to try to explain the disastrous impact of Susy Clemens's death.[33]

The volatility of the Interior Master from *What Is Man?* lies behind Emil Schwarz's description of the restless energy generated by billions of dream-sprites encountering one another in their "unending flight":

> coming from a billion worlds, bound for a billion others; always friendly, always glad to meet up with you, always full of where they'd been and what they'd seen, and dying to tell you about it; doing it in a million foreign languages, which sometimes you understood and sometimes you didn't and the tongue you understood to-day you forgot to-morrow, there being *nothing* permanent about a dream-sprite's character, constitution, beliefs, opinions, intentions, likes, dislikes, or anything else; all he cares for is to travel, and talk, and see wonderful things and have a good time. Schwarz said dream-sprites are well-disposed toward their fleshly brothers, and did what they could to make them partakers of the wonders of their travels, but it couldn't be managed except on a poor and not-worth-while scale, because they had to communicate through the flesh-brothers' Waking-Self imagination, and *that* medium—oh, well, it was like "emptying rainbows down a rat-hole." (MS 377–8; emphases in the original)

The dream-sprite's amoral zest for movement, its indifference to consistency or permanence, its complete imaginative independence of the Waking Self—all conform very closely to the ungovernable associative behavior of Young Man's mind when he tries to observe the activity of his Interior Master during one of the introspective experiments that Old Man asks him to conduct. These billions of fleeting intersections and exchanges depict almost perfectly the ceaseless neural streaming that William James envisioned at the heart of the mind's transitive life. Schwarz's contemptuous reference to rainbows and rat-holes, however, recalls the bewildering clash of feelings that Theodor Fischer describes as he studies Young Satan's nature and worries about his sister's infatuation with Philip Traum, "a wanderer of the skies, an object as unattainable as a comet" who could never "meet her on her own human level" and make her happy (MS 101).

When Theodor tries to act on his concerns and warn Lilly of her danger, he receives a sharp rebuke that is partly deluded and partly sublime, both petty and grand, a concise expression of the unaccountable human compound. Lilly refuses to acknowledge any parallel whatever between her own capricious behavior and that of her rival, Marget, though both girls have mistreated deserving young suitors after being exposed to the magnetic appeal of Philip Traum. Once "a love matter" takes hold of a woman's mind, Theodor concludes, she "isn't any more moveable by argument than a stump is" (MS 109). But when he takes another tack and tries to explain to Lilly that Traum is not capable of human love, the results that he elicits are far from stump-like: "Storm-fires began to gather in her eyes, and she rose and sat up in the bed and looked me over, much as a comet looks a little dog over that has been trying to help it conduct its excursion in the safest way" (MS 110).

In a swift series of questions, vaguely reminiscent of the biblical cross-examination of Job, Lilly challenges Theodor's pretense of superior reason and experience, summing up Traum's stunning creative displays and pulling the remarkable embroidery picture "from under her pillow" to undermine her brother's claims to an intimate understanding of Traum's mind: "Come—infer me an inference," she insists, "What do you infer from these things?" When Theodor can offer only a fumbling reply, she closes her case in triumph. Traum, she quite rightly proclaims, "is governed by laws that are not the laws which govern other people's actions." Theodor believes that he has a better grasp of those laws than Lilly does, but he cannot reveal Satan's identity, nor would that knowledge be at all likely to disturb his sister's faith that her loving sympathy and perception have given her a privileged insight into Traum's nature. Both blinded and exalted by her feelings, she is at once generous and selfish in her own defense. Traum is a law unto himself, she declares, but "[h]e will love me yet, and only me" (MS 110). Even in defeat, Theodor recognizes the transfiguring energy of Lilly's experience. "There was a glory in her eyes that made her beautiful," he recalled, as she clung to her "golden hope."

Satan's zeal for involving himself in the life of Eseldorf has introduced a "whole wide wreck and desolation" into village affairs, Theodor concludes, "[a]nd he, the author of all the trouble, was the only person concerned that got any rapture out of it." For the moment Theodor has forgotten the rapture in his sister's eyes, but he is entirely correct in his belief that Satan is enjoying his earthly sojourn, "grateful to be alive and improving things" (MS 111). The most exuberant advocate for the rich possibilities of earthly existence in all three Mysterious Stranger tales is the last of Twain's visitants, Number 44, whose appearance in an Eseldorf print shop in 1490 prompts an unexpected mental awakening in August Feldner far greater in scope than the awakening of Theodor Fischer's sister in "The Chronicle of Young Satan" or Archibald Ferguson's intellectual conflagration in "Schoolhouse Hill." The complex intelligence of Twain's final narrator asserts itself almost immediately with his engrossing review of the "mixed family" that inhabits the deserted castle where the press is hidden. This human inventory begins with the master, Heinrich Stein, a portly and dignified figure "with a large and benevolent face and calm deep eyes" that immediately link him with Number 44's most salient physical feature. Though the head of the household, Stein is a dreamer, not an artisan or a craftsman, "who would have submerged his mind all the days and nights in his books and been pleasantly and peacefully unconscious of his surroundings, if God had been willing" (MS 230).

Each individual that follows in August's survey of the personalities around him is far less submerged than this one, presenting different mixtures of inner and outer attributes that combine to form a remarkable composite portrait of human nature: avaricious and bigoted (Stein's wife), fatuous and vain (her personal astrologer), venomous but incandescently beautiful (Stein's stepdaughter), soldierly and loyal but superstitious (his cook), and innocent and winning (his niece). The printing force mingle genuine learning and "lightning bug" flashes of wit that August is compelled to admire with a range of disabilities that make the only cripple among them seem the healthiest spirit:

> Adam Binks, sixty years old, learnèd bachelor, proof-reader, poor, disappointed, surly.
> Hans Katzenyammer, 36, printer, huge, strong, freckled, red-headed, rough. When drunk, quarrelsome. Drunk when opportunity offered.
> Moses Haas, 28, printer; a looker-out for himself; liable to say acid things about people and to people; take him all around, not a pleasant character.

Barty Langbein, 15; cripple; general-utility lad; sunny spirit; affectionate; could play the fiddle.

Ernest Wasserman, 17, apprentice; braggart, malicious, hateful, coward, liar, cruel, underhanded, treacherous. He and Moses had a sort of half fondness for each other, which was natural, they having one or more traits in common, down among the lower grades of traits. (MS 233)

A final member of the printing force, Gustav Fischer, has strength, courage, and "a good disposition," August observes, but these virtues only make him the more vulnerable in such a volatile community. Like Marget Regen, the master's niece, he is "a kitten in a menagerie."

The procession of characters ends with the tale's narrator: "Last of all comes August Feldner, 16, 'prentice. This is myself" (MS 234). The first of these two statements could easily absorb the second— "Last of all comes myself, August Feldner"—but by splitting the information, Twain appears to anticipate dividing his narrator into two versions: the work-a-day apprentice and the formidable dream-sprite, Emil Schwarz, who is his duplicate. "This is myself" seems in fact to encapsulate the entire human inventory that precedes it, rather than simply repeating the preceding sentence. It invites the reader to view August Feldner, from the beginning, as an aggregate being: a compound of the many traits that compose the different members of the printing force, a composite of various human grades, far richer in mental resources than the sixteen-year-old "girl-boy" (another form of split being) that he contemptuously represents himself to be. "I am the entire human race compacted together," Twain had declared in an autobiographical dictation from October 12, 1906, a "duplicate" in miniature of the species (CA 283). This sense of inner variety marks August Feldner's nature as well, a limitless receptivity to thought and feeling that gradually supersedes even the formidable mental attributes of Number 44 as the story unfolds.[34]

At first August seems a typical product of his time and place, sharing completely in the "solemn and awful respect" that his Eseldorf neighbors accord their brutal priest. But his story quickly abandons Eseldorf and its vestigial subplots in favor of the life of the print shop and the transformative presence of Number 44. From the instant that the mysterious waif first appears, his coarse clothes "lightly powdered with snow" and his feet wrapped in rags, asking for food and shelter, the lower human grades of character predominate. The "war of talk" among the printing force briefly falls still at Number 44's unexpected plea, but it quickly reasserts its sway in the cacophony of screams and shrieks, jeers and cruel laughter, that largely substitute for speech among the castle's residents. August himself is drawn to the stranger out of an ignoble mixture of wonder and envy, believing that Number 44 might help him gain favor with Frau Stein's all-powerful astrologer and magician, to whom the household in general ascribes the marvels that Number 44 is able to perform. "I was one of 44's enviers," August admits: "If I hadn't been, I should have been no natural boy" (MS 246).

Fear, shame, and intense interest, however, quickly succeed these initial feelings. When Heinrich Stein abruptly states his determination to take Number 44 into his shop as an apprentice, August is exhilarated by the prospect but wary of the results, weighing with considerable psychological acuity the attitude of the printing force to this assault on their privileges and watchful of their simmering resentment. When the bully of the shop, Ernest Wasserman, threatens to expose August's growing intimacy with Number 44, August defends himself with unexpected ferocity but almost instantly lapses into a mix of depression and unhappiness as he anticipates the "sorrow in store for me" (MS 254). He sends telepathic cues to his new friend that help Number 44 survive the rough reception that the printing force gives him when he joins them in the press room to assume his new status. But this secret collaboration only deepens August's vulnerability: "I had saved 44, unsuspected and without damage or danger to myself," he notes, "and it made me lean toward him more than ever" (MS 259). "I never saw a man with so much variety of feeling as papa has," Susy Clemens had written of her mercurial father, an observation that Twain preserved in his autobiographical dictations (CA 30). The same extraordinary complexity and depth of feeling quickly become the central features of August Feldner's makeup.

Music helps to underscore his inner richness. In "The Chronicle of Young Satan" Philip Traum's virtuoso vocal performance partly dilutes the impact of the beautiful sounds that he elicits from Marget's old spinet. Number 44 will eventually demonstrate equal musical skills with the Jew's harp and the banjo, but August's receptivity to music is completely independent of, and not always congruent with, Number 44's tastes. Supernatural influences are completely absent from a long church scene in August Feldner's tale when a pipe organ makes its debut performance. No one in the castle had ever heard this new invention before, but once it begins to play an overture for the procession of nuns who are about to consecrate their new chapel, all vestiges of August's psychologically stunted world dissolve:

> Presently it began to softly rumble and moan, and the people held their breath for wonder at the adorable sounds, and their faces were alight with ecstasy. And I—I had never heard anything so plaintive, so sweet, so charged with the deep and consoling spirit of religion. And oh, so dreamily it moaned, and wept, and sighed and sang, on and on, gently rising, gently falling, fading and fainting, retreating to dim distances and reviving and returning, healing our hurts, soothing our griefs, steeping us deeper and deeper in its unutterable peace—then suddenly it burst into breath-taking rich thunders of triumph and rejoicing, and the consecrated ones came filing in! You will believe that all worldly thoughts, all ungentle thoughts, were gone from that place, now; you will believe that these uplifted and yearning souls were as a garden thirsting for the fructifying dew of truth, and prepared to receive it and hold it precious and give it husbandry. (MS 271)

A mixture of miracle tales and priestly fund-raising follows this extraordinary immersion in the floods of subjective experience, restoring the status quo of superstitious ignorance, hard-hearted self-interest, and sheer terror that appears to dominate life in Eseldorf, but Twain captures a range of emotional possibilities and constraints in this portion of August's narrative that represents the core of the mysterious stranger tales.

Number 44 echoes, in slightly less pejorative terms, Emil Schwarz's disparaging comparison between rainbows and rat holes when he tries to explain to August some of the differences between his own unearthly mental capacities and those of human beings. Mere words, however, are ultimately useless as vehicles for this explanation, since "the difference between a human being and me is as the difference between a drop of water and the sea, a rushlight and the sun, the difference between the infinitely trivial and the infinitely sublime!" (MS 319). Some pages later he resorts to a more colloquial comparison. The attempt to enlighten a human mind, Number 44 exclaims, is hopeless: "If it only had *some* capacity, some depth, or breadth, or—or—but you see it doesn't *hold* anything; one cannot pour the starred and shoreless expanses of the universe into a jug!" (MS 332; emphases in the original).

But the jug is a far more impressive vessel than Number 44 takes it to be. August listens to his friend's exasperated dismissal of the human mind "in frozen and insulted silence"—an unspoken response that for once Number 44 seems unable to detect as readily as he had the quick succession of reverence, wounded pride, pleasure, forgiveness, stunned bitterness, and icy scorn that August had felt in earlier scenes. The infinitely trivial human intelligence, as August embodies it, is as supple as the church organ in its affective and contemplative range. His brain can "whirl" with incomprehension as he tries to contemplate eternity, just as swiftly as Number 44 spins in midair and buzzes with delight at the sound of the Jew's harp. Each response reflects an ineffable mental state as different as it could possibly be from cognitive emptiness. When Number 44 gratuitously insults the human race, August can repress his angry replies out of charity or politeness, though he quickly shifts his mental focus away from these fleeting resentments in response to an acute desire to ask questions that Number 44 periodically, and capriciously, stifles before August can ask them. This deeply human hunger to know is unavailable to Number 44. To savor it he has to suspend his power of instant foreknowledge as mechanically as he does August's urgent questions (MS 386). Ignorance, curiosity, and surprise form the rich dramatic medium in which August's intelligence must operate at every moment in the story. "You have a quality which I do not possess," Number 44 once observes of August's ability to feel fear (MS 302). In fact August has a stunning range of qualities that Number 44 does not possess, all of which are distributed across the three facets of his consciousness that August learns to call the Workaday-Self, the Dream-Self, and the Soul.[35]

The first two of these mental dimensions are responsible for Number 44's introduction of the Duplicates. Emil Schwarz and his fellow dream-selves are "fictions," Number 44 explains to August, but only insofar as they appear to be separate beings from their living hosts:

"The way of it is this," he said. "You know, of course, that you are not one person, but two. One is your Workaday-Self, and 'tends to business, the other is your Dream-Self, and has no responsibilities, and cares only for romance and excursions and adventure. It sleeps when your other self is awake; when your other self sleeps, your Dream-Self has full control, and does as it pleases. It has far more imagination than has the Workaday-Self, therefore its pains and pleasures are far more real and intense than are those of the other self, and its adventures correspondingly picturesque and extraordinary.... The Workaday-self has a harder lot and a duller time; it can't get away from the flesh, and is clogged and hindered by it; and also by the low grade of its own imagination." (MS 315)

Both of the imaginative grades that Number 44 describes inhabit a single mind, housed in the same brain, despite the sharp contrast in the pains and pleasures that they perceive (MS 343). As the story nears its conclusion, August lays claim to a third interior entity that Number 44 has also explained to him: a collection of "tremendously effective" forces and feelings known as the Soul. The cognitive capacities of this last mental entity are more than a match for the affective and sensory gifts of the Dream-Self. They combine "passions, emotions, sensations, and the arts and graces of persuasion" in a productive blend that is as free of bodily limitation, yet as full of bodily potency, as the components of Heinrich Stein's press prove to be when they unexpectedly embark on the "complex and beautiful work" of completing a large order of printed Bibles, just as Philip Traum had completed Lilly Fischer's elaborate embroidery task, operating at superhuman speed and in absolute silence.

This extraordinary spectacle is among the earliest of the wonders brought about by Number 44's presence in Stein's print shop. Unlike many of his more sensational miracles, however, it is completely mediated by human gifts, employing an elaborate pantomime of carefully synchronized and sophisticated skills representing the higher grades of dexterity and intelligence in action (MS 282). Like the "rushing stream" of language that pours from the "beautiful stranger" in "Schoolhouse Hill," while he demonstrates his complete mastery of English grammar to his rapt teacher and classmates, it is a "stupendous performance," an exercise in the perpetual making and remaking of "forms," a term that describes both the matrix of lead type that is the foundation of the printed page and the profusion of miraculous beings and events that fill all three versions of Twain's story.[36]

August and his stalwart ally, the wandering compositor who calls himself Doangiveadamn, were on the point of locking Stein's rebellious workforce in the shop until they agreed to resume their duties, when the bully Ernest Wasserman, "swaying and tottering" in fear, alerts them to a dreadful development in the press room that he is too terrified to explain. When the men rush to the shop, the spectacle of the whirling press paralyzes them with wonder as it spins off "printed sheets faster than a person could count them—just *snowing* them onto the pile" without the presence of a single printer in the room:

> Yes, all the different kinds of work were racing along like Sam Hill—*and all in a sepulchral stillness.* The way the press was carrying on, you would think it was making noise enough for an insurrection, but in a minute you would find it was only your fancy, it wasn't producing a sound—then you would have that sick and chilly feeling a person always has when he recognizes that he is in the presence of creatures and forces not of this world. The invisibles were making up forms, locking up forms, unlocking forms, carrying new signatures to the press and removing the old: abundance of movement, you see, plenty of tramping to and fro, yet you couldn't hear a footfall; there wasn't a spoken word, there wasn't a whisper, there wasn't a sigh—oh, the saddest, uncanniest silence that ever was. (MS 282; emphases in the original)

For once the deeply flawed members of Stein's household are struck dumb, as these disembodied skills enact their craftsmen's "mystery" unencumbered by the petty jealousies and vindictive suspicions of corporeal existence. In effect, the scene is an exemplary inside excursion, a celebration of the potent "invisibles" of consciousness, depicting the impersonal cascade of language to which Oliver Wendell Holmes had attributed the universal plagiarism of verbal life. As the press's moving parts gradually come to a stop with the printing of the last sheets, the scraping of composing rules breaks the "ghostly hush," a journeyman's traditional expression of contempt that August compares to "the dry and crackly laughter of the dead" (MS 283). Like the flowing cadences and rich thunders of the pipe organ that had brought August "unutterable peace" only a handful of pages earlier, this scene too is an index to introspective depths, an emblem of the eagerness for "making" to which the Mysterious Stranger series repeatedly returns in its journey to incompletion.

2

Interest

When the invisibles take command of Heinrich Stein's print shop, the "dead matter" of the press comes to life. Lead type seems to leap of its own accord out of a freshly washed galley, "scattering itself like lightning into the boxes" where clean letters are stored. New words arrange themselves on composing sticks, framing new sentences and setting new pages into place "in the time it takes a person to snap his fingers." The miraculous fulfillment of Stein's weighty contract—two hundred printed Bibles for the University of Prague that the wildcat strike of his workers has sought to block—unfolds within the primal chaos of the print shop in such perfection that the finished product called for no correcting of proofs. Gazing at this inexplicable display on the part of an inert cluster of tools and machines, August Feldner and his companions are paralyzed with wonder. The scene "was so terrifyingly fascinating that we had to look and keep on looking, we couldn't help it" (MS 283). Five duplicate beings resembling members of Stein's workforce load the carefully packed pages onto a wagon when his customers finally arrive to collect their books.

The infuriated members of the household blame Frau Stein's magician for the disruption of their strike, but the magician quickly directs their anger toward Number 44 and puts the boy under a terrible curse, an "enchantment" that "shall slowly consume him to ashes before your eyes!" if he should ever again interfere in print shop affairs. "Well, to my mind," August Feldner observes, "there is nothing that makes a person interesting like his being about to get burnt up":

> We had to take 44 to the sick lady's room and let her gaze at him, and shudder, and shrivel, and wonder how he would look

when he was done; she hadn't had such a stirring up for years, and it acted on her kidneys and her spine and her livers and all those things and her other works, and started up her flywheel and her circulation, and she said, herself, it had done her more good than any bucketful of medicine she had taken that week. (MS 297)

Before long the potency of interest affects all the servants of the castle, filling them with sympathy for Number 44's predicament and bringing tears to their eyes when they think of his peril, though they "had taken hardly any interest in him before." Even Stein's vindictive wife and her self-absorbed daughter "were full of interest in him ... and said a lot of things to him that came nearer to being kind, than anything they were used to saying, by a good deal."

This outpouring of attention leaves Number 44 himself completely unaffected, "it being one of his wooden times, you know," August observes. Soon, however, he throws himself into what August dismissively calls "temporal interests," including "a most extravagant and stirring and heathen performance" with a Jew's harp that leaves the pious August both heartbroken and disgusted with his friend's shallow nature. But their misunderstanding is short-lived. Number 44 soon teaches August how to become invisible, so that he can move about the castle free of fear, and both boys briefly forget about the magician's menacing curse: "It was an interesting time, of course," August concludes, "for it was the nature of 44 to be interesting" (MS 301).

Within the space of a few pages in the last of his Mysterious Stranger narratives, Twain singles out the pervasive role of "interest" in the psychological make-up of nearly every character in the story, just as he did in describing the Interior Master's cascade of successive eagernesses in *What Is Man?* Our human "chameleonship," Old Man insists, is a direct result of the mind's exquisite sensitivity to the blend of outer and inner attractions that compose its world, each "initiatory impulse" that it meets propelling it along a "new track" of urgent pursuits or new ideals, once the intelligence has seized upon them and identified them as life's overriding interest. Lying just beneath the mechanistic metaphors that Old Man applies to the mind is "the problem of Discrimination," as William James once put it, "and he who will have thoroughly answered it will have laid the keel of psychology."[1]

It is the nature of consciousness to be interested. This slight adjustment in August Feldner's summary of Number 44's impact reflects a constellation of key insights into the operations of the mind that gradually came to define James's understanding of mental life in the decade preceding the publication of *The Principles of Psychology*. Between 1878 and 1880, as James was formulating his account of the streaming aurora that constituted our inner experience, he published a cluster of articles outlining the critical roles played by "interest" and "attention" in the formation of a navigable mental world.[2] The concept of the association of ideas, James recognized, had only recently begun to incorporate "the teleological factor of interest" as an agent of selection, an insight that James credited to S. H. Hodgson's "masterly" 1865 book *Time and Space*.[3] What could explain the mind's ceaseless acts of choice among the competing sources of stimulation to which it was exposed: the bombardment of feelings and images generated every second by the senses and their inner concomitants of thought and memory? How does consciousness avoid drowning in what James called the "undistinguishable, swarming *continuum*" in which it found itself immersed?[4] Some principle of discrimination had to be involved:

> Millions of items of the outward order are present to my senses which never properly enter into my experience. Why? Because they have no interest for me. My experience is what I agree to attend to. Only those items which I notice shape my mind—without selective interest, experience is an utter chaos. Interest alone gives accent and emphasis, light and shade, background and foreground—intelligible perspective, in a word. It varies in every creature, but without it the consciousness of every creature would be a gray chaotic uniformity, impossible for us even to conceive.[5]

The mysterious process of inner consent produces different intelligible results in different creatures, just as accent and emphasis, light and shade, differ from artist to artist and painting to painting—an exhilarating escape from gray uniformity that James's early aesthetic apprenticeship had stressed.[6]

In an 1878 essay entitled "Brute and Human Intellect" James concluded that most animals inhabited mental worlds built out of very few, but very intense, interests. A dog that spent its life in the Vatican Museum, he remarked, would never develop a sophisticated appreciation for art, though its appreciation for the museum's various smells would be inexhaustible and far more detailed than that of any human tourist. A tourist, by contrast, would bring to bear on his Vatican visit a continually expanding array of "aesthetic and practical interests" vastly more complex than those of the dog. And those interests, in turn, would continually busy themselves in attending to different features of the surrounding environment: comparing, choosing, concentrating on and then changing the objects of concentration in a split second, depending on subtle shifts in the relative urgency with which different mental combinations exerted a claim on attention. What these interests "lay their accent on," James wrote, "that we notice; but what they are in themselves we cannot say. We must content ourselves here with simply accepting them as irreducible ultimate factors in determining the way our knowledge grows."[7]

A few months later, in an 1879 article entitled "Are We Automata?" James underscored his point: "Whoever studies consciousness, from any point of view whatever," he wrote, "is ultimately brought up against the mystery of *interest* and *selective attention*."[8] The swarming *continuum*—the gray, chaotic uniformity of the unmediated neural world—presented the mind with limitless opportunities for choice: for singling out from the "theatre of simultaneous possibilities" some images for "focalized" attention (as James termed it), while suppressing others, much as Joseph Goodman had focalized his mind on the introduction to *The Innocents Abroad* and briefly suppressed the allurements of a walk on Broadway. When not focalized we are scatterbrained, James wryly noted, "but, when thoroughly impassioned we never wander from the point." The mental disarray of "ordinary languid times" gives way to formidable selective powers when these passions are engaged until, inevitably, a new center of focalized interest emerges and the processes of concentration, suppression, and inhibition begin once more to refine and direct our attention.[9]

The "accentuating finger of consciousness," James insisted, was never still for very long, never entirely free from the competing appeal of fresh mental attractions on the fringes of its present thought.

Consciousness, in turn, employs all the tools of association and memory to weave its shimmering interests together, forming the mental aurora of inner life. Heinrich Stein's whirling press in *The Mysterious Stranger* (though apparently a type of automaton) is a remarkably complete picture of this psychic energy in action: dividing, selecting, arranging, remembering, and dismembering at lightning speed, as it casts its printed sheets into the air like snowflakes, all in obedience to a complex of invisible teleological interests. Near the end of "Are We Automata?" James sets aside "Automaton-theory" altogether, along with its contention that our conscious minds are no more than "impotently paralytic spectators" of experience. Scientific materialism (James believed) had overlooked the unpredictable but indisputable shaping power of interest. Even amid the "meteoric showers of images and suggestions" that make up our dreams, James insists, "the watchful eye of consciousness" is making choices that can have far-reaching results:

> The world as a Goethe feels and knows it all lay embedded in the primordial chaos of sensation, and into these elements we may analyze back every thought of the poet. We may even, by our reasonings, unwind things back to that black and jointless continuity of space and moving clouds of swarming atoms which science calls the only real world. But all the while the world we feel and live in, will be that which our ancestors and we, by slowly cumulative strokes of choice, have extricated out of this, as the sculptor extracts his statue by simply rejecting the other portions of the stone. Other sculptors, other statues from the same stone! Other minds, other worlds from the same chaos![10]

The mind is a builder, a chooser, James elsewhere insists. It has a "vote" in the construction of its universe, much as Oliver Wendell Holmes had observed, in the letter absolving Twain of plagiarism, that an individual temperament could mingle its own special stamp with the multitudinous flow of "spiritualized shadows" that compose our mental world.[11]

At the heart of James's early treatments of consciousness lay a critique of Herbert Spencer's work that James published in the January 1878 issue of the *Journal of Speculative Philosophy*. According to James, Spencer had reduced "the entire process of mental evolution" to a mechanism not so very different from the least palatable features of Old Man's position in *What Is Man?* The mind, Spencer suggested, was little more than a highly refined tool for adjusting the inner world of the nervous system to the outer conditions in which it found itself, its sole evolutionary end being its own survival. James was appalled at the moral implications of Spencer's view, but his scientific instincts rejected the possibility that natural selection would have produced "a creature of superb cognitive endowments" whose single, overriding passion was "survival at any price."[12] Common opinion, James believed, refused to endorse this narrow portrait of our mental nature. Spencer's stark existential imperative had to strive for our attention amid an infinite array of competing mental claims and urgent interests to which consciousness found itself drawn:

> What are these interests? Most men would reply that they are all that makes survival worth securing. The social affections, all the various forms of play, the thrilling intimations of art, the delights of philosophic contemplation, the rest of religious emotion, the joy of moral self-approbation, the charm of fancy and of wit—some or all of these are absolutely required to make the notion of mere existence tolerable; and individuals who, by their special powers, satisfy these desires are protected by their fellows and enabled to survive, though their mental constitution should in other respects be lamentably ill-"adjusted" to the outward world.[13]

The artistic and the philosophic constitutions—ill-adjusted though they might be—exerted a powerful claim on human desire, securing a place for artists and thinkers in the "outward world." "All the luxuriant foliage of ideal interests" (as James put it) represented too great a commitment of mental resources to be treated as a subsidiary effect of the impetus to mere survival.

In the end James brushed aside Spencer's focus on survival with an extraordinary analogy that anticipates the eccentric thought experiments from *What Is Man?* In place of Old Man's mechanistic metaphors for consciousness, James offers a pair of industrial ones:

> A furnace which should produce along with its metal fifty different varieties of ash and slag, a planing-mill whose daily

yield in shavings far exceeded that in boards, would rightly be pronounced inferior to one of the usual sort, even though more energy should be displayed in its working, and at moments some of that energy be directly effective. If ministry to survival be the sole criterion of mental excellence, then luxury and amusement, Shakespeare, Beethoven, Plato, and Marcus Aurelius, stellar spectroscopy, diatom markings and nebular hypotheses are by-products on too wasteful a scale. The slag-heap is too big—it abstracts more energy than it contributes to the ends of the machine; and every serious evolutionist ought resolutely to bend his attention henceforward to the reduction in number and amount of these outlying interests and the diversion of the energy they absorb into purely prudential channels.[14]

No thoughtful evolutionist, of course, would propose such a diversion of energy—none, at least, who had given serious consideration to the frequency with which consciousness chose to ignore prudential channels. Outlying interests, like the side-excursions that Mark Twain prized in his autobiographical dictations, were the life of the life narrative that most people strove to pursue. An acute sensitivity to the presence of these fresh initiatory impulses, and a corresponding responsiveness to their appeal, were critical ingredients in Twain's early literary success. They were, in fact, the recurring subject of his career.

The story that launched that career is built around a comic collision involving several species of consciousness, all of which touch on the distinction between the purely prudential and the luxuriant products of mental life. "Jim Smiley and His Jumping Frog," Twain's 1865 title for the story that first brought him to the attention of a national audience, makes Smiley himself the center of the plot. Dan'l Webster, the "celebrated" jumping frog of the story's later title, is only one exhibit in the extensive menagerie Smiley assembles in the Sierra mining camp that Twain calls Boomerang in the original version of the tale. Smiley had collected rat terriers, "chicken cocks," and tomcats, along with a bull-pup named Andrew Jackson and a racing mare that his fellow miners called "the fifteen-minute nag" in an obscene allusion that probably contributed to Twain's reputation among Eastern readers as a "wild humorist" with roots in the red-light district of San Francisco. All of these creatures were instrumental to the overriding passion of Smiley's existence: making bets.

The story's narrator, the citified newspaper correspondent "Mark Twain," is the victim of a practical joke aimed at exposing him to the relentless memory of old Simon Wheeler, a fixture in the barroom of Boomerang's ancient tavern, who if properly prompted would automatically proceed to bore his unsuspecting visitor with an endless and "infernal reminiscence" of Jim Smiley's obsessive life, "as long and tedious as it should be useless to me."[15] Both Wheeler and Smiley seem initially to be little more than mental mechanisms, the first a narrating and the second a betting machine, neither of which has much appeal for the prudential mind of a newspaper writer interested in meeting a deadline. But even before Twain stirs his informant out of a nap, he notes that he was "fat and baldheaded" with "an expression of winning gentleness and simplicity upon his tranquil countenance," qualities that had clearly led his fellow citizens of Boomerang to value him long after his active mining days had ended. Wheeler, in short, is interesting even in his sleep.[16]

An additional, invisible virtue seems to have encouraged Twain's Eastern friend, Artemus Ward, to ask a favor that involves paying Wheeler a visit. The instant Twain awakens him to inquire about Leonidas W. Smiley, the old man launches into a monologue in which he loses none of the tranquil simplicity that forms the core of his nature:

> Simon Wheeler backed me into a corner and blockaded me there with his chair—and then sat down and reeled off the monotonous narrative which follows this paragraph. He never smiled, he never frowned, he never changed his voice from the quiet, gently-flowing key to which he tuned the initial sentence, he never betrayed the slightest suspicion of enthusiasm—but all through the interminable narrative there ran a vein of impressive earnestness and sincerity, which showed me plainly that so far from his imagining that there was anything ridiculous or funny about his story, he regarded it as a really important matter, and admired its two heroes as men of transcendent genius in finesse.[17]

To Twain's mind, Wheeler's performance is so "exquisitely absurd" that for the moment he suppresses his reporter's impatience: "I let him go on in his own way, and never interrupted him once." The charm only ceases when Wheeler hears someone call his name from outside the bar and briefly leaves his chair, breaking the narrative flow and allowing his captive listener to escape, much as the characters in his story had done moments before.[18]

Wheeler had been describing, at some length, Jim Smiley's frantic need to stir up interest among the citizens of Boomerang by filling life with bets. He tended to be lucky in his wagers, Wheeler remembered, but winning or losing was the least of Smiley's concerns: "there couldn't be no solitry thing mentioned but that feller'd offer to bet on it, and take any side you please." The wager was an end in itself, a mechanism that Smiley employed to infuse his world with what William James might have called intelligible perspective. Races and animal fights of all kinds never failed to get Smiley's attention, but he was also willing to bet on predictions of Parson Walker's success in getting converts at a revival or on guessing which of two birds perched on a nearby fence would fly off first:

> If he even seen a straddle-bug start to go anywhere, he would bet you how long it would take him to get wherever he was going to, and if you took him up, he would foller that straddle-bug to Mexico but what he would find out where he was bound for and how long he was on the road.[19]

In the generous imaginative climate of Twain's story, even a straddle-bug can have an inner life that sometimes calls for extraordinary outward exertions. Wheeler and Smiley clearly belong to the human slag heap left in the wake of a mining boom, remnants of the swift reversal of fortune for which Boomerang was evidently named. But Smiley seems to have been especially determined to fill life's vacancy with a profusion of interests that might make it tolerable, becoming in turn a source of interest to Simon Wheeler, another ill-adjusted survivor of flush times, straddling the gap between different worlds.

The most remarkable addition to Smiley's menagerie of betting animals was the painstakingly educated frog, Dan'l Webster, whom Smiley trained to jump on command, much like the nimble politician for whom he was named. Constant practice had made Dan'l unbeatable at a jumping competition, so Smiley would occasionally carry his pet to town "in a little lattice box" and try to set up a bet. In the longest episode of Wheeler's story, he describes

Smiley's successful effort to entice a nameless stranger into betting against Dan'l Webster, only to lose the wager when his prudential opponent takes advantage of Smiley's brief absence in search of a second frog competitor to fill Dan'l with several teaspoons of quail shot that weigh him down "solid as an anvil."[20]

As the stranger takes Smiley's money and prepares to leave, he repeats the insult that he had directed at Dan'l Webster to instigate the bet: "Well, *I* don't see no p'ints about that frog that's any better'n any other frog."[21] Smiley was "monstrous proud" of his gifted pet and this parting slur only exacerbates his anger when he discovers the quail-shot ruse "and took out after that feller." But the stranger had an uncanny agility of his own, Wheeler observes, and Smiley "never ketched him." At that moment the old man hears his own name called and briefly abandons his narrative blockade, disappearing as quickly as Smiley and the stranger had done, in answer to a new configuration of his mental focus. Twain himself will do the same, before the sociable old man is able to resume his survey of Smiley's wonderful menagerie. Nearly all of the characters in the tale, human and animal alike, have minds that respond to the blend of prudential and outlying interests with which they impose accent and emphasis, light and shade, on existence.[22] The luxuriant foliage of our inner world flourishes even in Boomerang, just as it does in the Vatican museum of consciousness to which William James had compared the restless profusion of interests competing for attention in the mind's primordial chaos. The first extended narrative that Twain would attempt took him, both literally and figuratively, to the Vatican Museum of human interests, where the imponderable, magic stream of mental life would prove to be the most engrossing exhibit.

* * *

The preface to *The Innocents Abroad* makes clear that its author plans to focus on the keel of psychology: to grapple with the swarming *continuum* of experience that William James would link to the problem of discrimination. Ultimately Twain's account of the *Quaker City*'s 1867 Mediterranean tour has introspective rather than prospective goals. Despite the celebrated cities, famous works of art, and ancient ruins that fill his pages, he is not trying to draft an iconoclastic guide book but to reproduce the experience of seeing "with impartial eyes" as he sorts through "objects of interest beyond the sea," navigating the exotic sensory swarms that threaten to engulf him. Twain confronts this navigational challenge in several stages when he begins to recast his newspaper correspondence as an extended narrative. The carnivalesque outburst entitled "The Story of the Cruise" which he published in the New York *Herald* the day after the ship returned to the United States was, at best, an impulsive outburst. Once Twain had agreed to produce a book based on the voyage, he began to supplement his original letters with new details from his journals, along with anecdotes extracted from the handful of *Quaker City* passengers with whom he still remained on good terms. This textual hodgepodge would undergo careful revision during the months that Twain struggled to meet his publisher's deadline, but he insisted that it remained "only a record of a picnic," not the satiric assault on his fellow tourists that he gave to the *Herald* or the report of a solemn scientific expedition.[23]

Twain's picnic is more ambitious than it seems. His exuberant imaginary prospectus for the *Quaker City*'s voyage, in the opening pages of *The Innocents Abroad*, highlights the psychological distinction that William James will ultimately draw between the luxuriant foliage of conscious life and the prudential constraints of mere physical existence. Advance publicity for the trip, Twain reports, had unleashed pent-up reserves of speculation around "countless firesides" where the excursion's novelty promised to break with the tedious vacancy of the present. Twain had immersed himself in the turmoil of post–Civil War politics as he began drafting *The Innocents Abroad* in a Washington, DC, boarding house, but even the venal spectacle of Andrew Johnson's impeachment could not compete with the exhilarating catalogue of outlying interests that Twain set out to explore as he recreated the *Quaker City*'s lavish, months-long tour of Europe and the Holy Land.[24]

He frames his expectations in language that anticipates Emil Schwartz's ecstatic account of a dream-sprite's cosmic voyage in the *Mysterious Stranger*'s final version:

> They were to sail for months over the breezy Atlantic and the sunny Mediterranean; they were to scamper about the decks by day, filling the ship with shouts and laughter—or read novels and poetry in the shade of the smoke-stacks, or watch for the jelly-fish and the nautilus, over the side, and the shark, the whale, and

other strange monsters of the deep; and at night they were to dance in the open air, on the upper deck, in the midst of a ballroom that stretched from horizon to horizon, and was domed by the bending heavens and lighted by no meaner lamps than the stars and the magnificent moon—dance, and promenade, and smoke, and sing, and make love, and search the skies for constellations that never associate with the "Big Dipper" they were so tired of; and they were to see the ships of twenty navies—the customs and costumes of twenty curious peoples—the great cities of half a world—they were to hob-nob with nobility and hold friendly converse with kings and princes, Grand Moguls, and the anointed lords of mighty empires! (IA 221)

By contrast with this restless cascade of gratification, the official voyage "programme" that Twain reprints in the opening chapter of the book is little more than a dutiful list of tourist attractions, from Gibraltar to the Pyramids, that the passengers can expect to visit, mixed with reassuring endorsements of the ship's comfort and safety. No lovemaking, no new constellations, and no curious peoples enliven its prudential pages.[25]

The "finite mind" (Twain admits) could discover no flaw in the *Quaker City*'s cautious official itinerary. It was, he slyly noted, "almost as good a map." Once the ship gets under way, monotony and variety quickly begin to collide with one another like the shuffleboard discs with which the passengers strive to entertain themselves. Life at sea, Twain soon realized, had "a good deal of sameness about it." In an effort to amuse themselves the passengers start a debating club, but the ship has no talented orators aboard and few talented musicians. Those who could play an instrument "made good music," Twain reported, "but we always played the same old tune" (IA 25). Reading doesn't offer the combustible delights that he had anticipated before the voyage began, and even the monsters of the deep become matters of course: "We saw the usual," Twain blandly observes, "the regular list of sea wonders" (IA 28). Filling the pages of a journal under these conditions proves a hopeless enterprise. The motion of the sea itself offers the only relief by throwing deck games into laughable disarray or converting starlight dances into exhilarating adventures. The couples found themselves tossed back and forth between the ship's rails, as the swell threatened to spill them overboard: "The Virginia reel, as performed on board the *Quaker City*," Twain noted, "had more genuine reel about it than any reel I ever saw before, and was as full of interest to the spectator as it was full of desperate chances and hairbreadth escapes to the participant" (IA 24). But this perilous form of interest was a risky exception to the prevailing sameness. Even the moon seemed to remain stationary in the sky, day after day, as the ship's eastward progress appeared to neutralize the passage of time.[26]

The appearance of the Azores, midway across the Atlantic, encapsulates this clash of psychic experiences. As the ship approaches the islands in the predawn hours, the crew stir up the passengers to witness the first landfall of the trip, but Twain is simply annoyed at the disturbance: "I did not take any interest in islands at three o'clock in the morning" (IA 28). Eventually he succumbs to "the general enthusiasm" and goes on deck, where a sequence of perceptual events replicates the mental rhythm of the opening chapters. "The island in sight was Flores," Twain noted:

> It seemed only a mountain of mud standing up out of the dull mists of the sea. But as we bore down upon it, the sun came out and made it a beautiful picture—a mass of green farms and meadows that swelled up to a height of fifteen hundred feet, and mingled its upper outlines with the clouds. It was ribbed with sharp, steep ridges, and cloven with narrow canons, and here and there on the heights, rocky upheavals shaped themselves into mimic battlements and castles; and out of rifted clouds came broad shafts of sunlight, that painted summit, and slope, and glen, with bands of fire, and left belts of somber shade between. It was the aurora borealis of the frozen pole exiled to a summer land! (IA 29)

This vision for the moment reawakens the slumbering zeal with which Twain had initially greeted the brave conception of the *Quaker City* tour. Despite "the pitiless gale and the drenching spray," the passengers bring out their opera glasses while the ship skirts the coast, trying to distinguish objects of interest on shore, but when they change course for San Miguel, the chief island in the group, Flores quickly "became a dome of mud again, and sank down among the mists and disappeared," much like the nebular archipelagoes that sink into blackness during a dream-sprite's interstellar voyage, or Jim Smiley's frog when it reverts to a glob of amphibious mud after performing its wonderful jumping feats.

This brief transfiguration of Flores, from mud mountain to terrestrial aurora and back again, is a forecast of the complicated mix of experiences that Twain presents when the *Quaker City* stops at Horta on the island of Fayal. At first the town seems to be a cultural backwater. The inhabitants cultivate their rich volcanic soil "after the fashion prevalent in the time of Methuselah." They share living quarters with their livestock, venerate the images and relics of a battered old Jesuit cathedral, and show a very limited interest in the doings of the outside world. "Nobody comes here, and nobody goes away," Twain writes, "News is a thing unknown in Fayal" (IA 34). Once the passengers debark, however, the population quickly proves to be an energetic human swarm, "all ragged, and barefoot, uncombed and unclean," who instantly convert their visitors into a circus parade "just as village boys do when they accompany the elephant on his advertising trip from street to street."

The news vacuum on the island is not so complete as Twain suggests. One of the citizens belatedly asks the travelers if the American Civil War had ended, a not unreasonable question in light of Reconstruction's ongoing hostilities and the Plains Indian wars that had kept General Sherman from joining the excursion. The frantic muleteers who conduct Twain and his companions on a tour over the island's stone roads entertain themselves by singing "John Brown's Body" in "ruinous" English while urging the nimble little donkeys that the tourists are riding into a barely controlled stampede. "It was fun," Twain concluded, "scurrying around the breezy hills and through the beautiful canyons. There was that rare thing, novelty, about it; it was a fresh, new, exhilarating sensation, this donkey riding, and worth a hundred worn and threadbare home pleasures" (IA 36). The roads themselves are a "wonder," he admits, paved and guttered, "neat and true as a floor," bordered by lava walls "which will last a thousand years in this land where frost is unknown" (IA 37). Even the Catholic Church, for all its "gilt gimcracks" and "humbuggery," contains an "elegantly wrought" chancel wall of painted porcelain that Twain and his friends admire. The island, in short, is a paradoxical blend of the inert and the energetic, of filth and elegance, the first of many lessons in the complexities of transfiguration that *The Innocents Abroad* ultimately sets out to explore.[27]

The mangled version of "John Brown's Body" that Horta's muleteers sing, along with the stampede over which they preside, is to some degree a joyful parody of the moral and political disorder from which these American excursionists hope to escape. When one *Quaker City* passenger hosts a dinner in Horta's main hotel, his horror when he gets a bill expressed in the inflated local currency mirrors, in a similar way, the economic chaos that will mark the onset of the Gilded Age. "Go—leave me to my misery, boys," the stricken host declares, "I am a ruined community" (IA 31). But even this extravagant declaration of mock misery forms part of the pervasive mental luxuriance of the Horta visit. It is a reminder of the forms of inward wealth that William James would associate with the inexhaustible surfeit of conscious life: the play of social affections, of charm and wit, the vivid emotional flux that confers interest on the gray uniformity of material existence.

Examples of genuine misery recur in *The Innocents Abroad* but these too disclose mental reserves capable of making the most extreme conditions of deprivation tolerable. Twain and his companions encounter just such a clash of extremes once the *Quaker City* steams into the Mediterranean world. During their stop in Marseille, before taking a train to Paris, they pay a visit to the celebrated dungeons of Castle d'If in the city harbor in order to inspect the "sad epitaphs" left behind on the prison walls by generations of prisoners. "How thick the names were!" Twain exclaims: "And their long-departed owners seemed to throng the gloomy cells and corridors with their phantom shapes" (IA 70). To preserve his sanity, one captive had spent decades inscribing the images of his mental life onto the stone surfaces of his cell, reproducing in clusters of "intricate designs" an exacting museum depicting his lost world. But such physical remnants were not essential to the transformation of this grim environment. Twain and his companions respond to their memories of the legend of the Iron Mask when they visit this nameless victim's cell. "Mystery!" Twain declared: "That was the charm.... These dank walls had known the man whose dolorous story is a sealed book forever! There was fascination in the spot" (IA 71).

When the party passes through Florence on their way toward rejoining the ship in Naples, they encounter an exquisite variation on the dungeon carvings of Castle d'If: a depiction of mental intricacy captured in the elaborate beauty of the anonymous Florentine mosaics. Using bits of colored glass or stone, these unknown craftsmen were capable of producing lifelike "counterfeits" of flowers or insects, even a picture of Rome's ruined Coliseum, "within the cramped circle of a breastpin," much as the Marseille prisoner had produced a counterfeit world on the walls of his cell. One "little trifle of a centre table," Twain noted, depicted the inlaid image of a flute, complete with its "mazy complication of keys":

> No painting in the world could have been softer or richer; no shading out of one tint into another could have been more faultless than this flute, and yet to count the multitude of little fragments of stone of which they swore it was formed would bankrupt any man's arithmetic! I do not think one could have seen where two particles joined each other with eyes of ordinary shrewdness. Certainly *we* could detect no such blemish. This table-top cost the labor of one man for ten long years, so they said, and it was for sale for thirty-five thousand dollars. (IA 176–7)

Eyes of ordinary shrewdness, though, can readily discern through the crude monetary calculus that the passage highlights, a richly shaded figure for the mazy complication of feeling and skill that produced this faultless design.

By the end of the *Quaker City* excursion Twain will present all of Palestine as a geographic projection of this striking clash between a hard and intractable reality—the bankrupt arithmetic of the era— and the intricate aptitudes of the imagination. Though the Holy Land is steeped in religious dreams, Twain admits, the Palestine of the present is an arid wasteland utterly devoid of the soft tints that he admired in the Florentine mosaics. This dismal setting is home to a degraded population whose suffering seldom awakens the same sympathy that Twain expresses for the long-dead prisoners of Castle d'If: "It is," he concludes, "a hopeless, dreary, heart-broken land."[28] By night the Sea of Galilee reclaims a measure of its ancient aura, but even then the mystical impression is chiefly an introspective construct of "dreamy influences" and "secret noises" that cannot sustain the same durable fascination that Twain and his companions felt in the Marseille dungeons. By day Galilee remains a scene of "repulsive" incongruities (IA 385). The overland journey to Jerusalem had taken Twain and his companions up the slopes of Mt. Tabor, the traditional site of the biblical transfiguration where Christ had briefly appeared to a handful of his startled disciples, bathed in light and accompanied by Moses and Elijah. The only lasting inspiration that the travelers find on the summit of Tabor now is a pile of old ruins and a Greek convent that offers good coffee (IA 393). The Syrian village at the mountain's base is a replica of every other Syrian village that the tourists had seen, Twain wrote: squalid collections of cramped houses, shaped like dry-goods boxes, topped with dried disks of camel dung (IA 377).

"Old Tabor," he concludes, is a "tiresome" subject that not even the imagination can coax into life. The view from its summit takes in the ancient battlefield of Esdraelon on the plain below, inviting the mind to reconstruct a "phantom pageant" of all the armies that had fought there from the time of Joshua through Napoleon. Twain briefly tries to evoke this fantastic vision: a vast host "sweeping down the plain, splendid with plumes and banners and glittering lances," in an exotic amplification of the great military reviews that celebrated the end of the American Civil War (IA 394). But not even moonlight, he insists, could coax this visionary pageant to materialize. What the climb up the mountain does accomplish, however, is to remind Twain's reader of the hunger for transfiguration that the biblical story captures and that Twain too has been systematically exploring since the visual metamorphosis of Flores in his opening chapters. Raphael's painting of the transfiguration scenes from Matthew 17 formed a high point of Twain's visit to the Vatican Museum, midway through the book. Even so his imperfect recollection of the painting underscores the transient nature of mental ecstasy. Amid the Vatican's dizzying "wilderness" of art, Twain noted, only Raphael's huge panel juxtaposing the scene on Mt. Tabor with the simultaneous failure of the disciples to heal an epileptic boy had left a distinct image in his memory (see Figure 2.1). In contrast to the "crazy chaos" of the galleries—a kind of institutional seizure—it was set apart in a room almost entirely its own (IA 221). But this favorable isolation does not keep Twain from dramatically understating the painting's size, or abruptly comparing its rejuvenating impact to his schoolboy experience of buying a new pocketknife.[29]

Nearly forty years later, he revisits this inverse form of transfiguration in "The Chronicle of Young Satan," as Theodore Fischer and his friends watch their angelic companion float above the grass, for a few moments, like a lovely soap bubble just before he bursts—a half-whimsical allusion to Raphael's pictorial design that underscores the psychological clash between surfeit and emptiness pervading Twain's career. Like the role that Twain assigns himself in recalling his childhood bout with measles, the epileptic boy whom the disciples are trying to cure basks in the whirlwind of adult emotion that he awakens, just as Tom Sawyer repeatedly will. *The Innocents Abroad* is particularly rich in the abrupt interchange of mental states that Twain recognizes in Raphael's panel and that he experiences amid the ruins on Mt. Tabor's summit. When the Rock of Gibraltar first "swung magnificently into view," as the *Quaker City* approached the Mediterranean, Twain and his companions "needed no tedious traveled parrot" to identify such a sublime object: "There could not be two rocks like that in one kingdom," Twain declared. But tedious guides thrive there parroting mindless anecdotes for the tourist trade (IA 41–3).

The same psychological interplay that Twain explored in the fleeting transfiguration of Flores, the dungeons of Marseille, or the exquisite Florentine mosaics lends itself to the alternating experiences of fatigue and wonder that mark every stage of the *Quaker City* tour. After spending some days admiring the art and architecture of Milan, Twain and his companions begin to find the relentless routine of sightseeing intolerable. On the advice of their guide, they decide to visit the famous echoing courtyard of the Palazzo Simonetti (IA 139). Troops of peasant girls on their way home from work "hooted at us, shouted at us, made all manner of game with us" as the travelers set out from the city, expecting to encounter only another obligatory "wonder." But the old palazzo lives up to its reputation, producing an "astonishing clatter of reverberations" from a variety of test sounds, including a single "Ha" from a lovely young guide that produces "a rollicking convulsion of the jolliest laughter that could be imagined" in the echoing courtyard. Everyone in Twain's jaded party finds the comical effect irresistible and joins in, echoing in the process the hoots of delight that the peasant girls had expressed on seeing yet another group of genteel tourists pass their way.

Twain tries to capture the extraordinary profusion of echoes at Simonetti by making pencil marks in his notebook as fast as the echoes recur, but he cannot dot his page quickly enough to keep up. The text of *The Innocents Abroad* reproduces Twain's entry to illustrate his experimental effort, side by side with a notebook page describing a picture by Titian in Milan's cathedral that a canny priest claimed had been painted in the dark, not unlike the intricate images that Twain and his friends had discovered on Castle d'If's dungeon walls (see Figure 2.2). All these details are themselves intricately intertwined to depict the collision between deadening uniformity and the transformative power of interest. Twain's double-edged illustration effectively depicts the mind's capacity to convert a chaotic sensory swarm (as William James might have put it) into cathartic outbreaks of restorative laughter that Twain and his friends at first elicit from a group of hard-working peasant girls and then experience for themselves. In the paragraphs that precede this side-trip, Twain complains about the "catchy ejaculations of rapture" with which tourists customarily greet the kind of artistic wonders that Titian's miraculous canvas exemplifies. He tabulates these expressions too in a series of notebook "dots":

"O, wonderful!"
"Such expression!"
"Such grace of attitude!"
"Such dignity!"
"Such faultless drawing!"
"Such matchless coloring!"
"Such feeling!"
"What delicacy of touch!"
"What sublimity of conception!"
"A vision! a vision!" (IA 136)

The painting that awakens this litany of trite admiration, da Vinci's "Last Supper," is so faded with age (to Twain's eye) that it takes the vision of a skilled artist to reconstruct a mental image of what it must have looked like when new: "But *I* can not work this miracle," Twain admits (IA 137; emphasis in the original). Only the copyists that ply their trade in every famous gallery have any hope of seeing through the ravages of time and transfiguring the ruin that remains—an achievement that amounts to the kind of painting in the dark that only a highly trained mind can achieve.[30]

During an extended stay in Paris while the *Quaker City* made its way slowly along the Italian coast, Twain anticipates both the ritualistic poverty of tourist routine and the imaginative vitality that enables a gifted copyist to revivify da Vinci's genius. A tour of the royal tombs at St. Denis, early in the Paris visit, proves unexpectedly stultifying. Only the "gray antiquity" of the crypt—another emblem of brute materiality—briefly stirs Twain's interest. The marble effigies of the nation's medieval kings were ultimately too remote to incite the imagination: "I touched their dust-covered faces with my finger," he wrote, "but Dagobert was deader than the sixteen centuries that have passed over him" (IA 98). The cemetery at Père la Chaise, however, provided an entirely different experience. There, Twain noted, the visitor's mind responded to the presence of "a nobler royalty," the artistic and intellectual heroes who had brought distinction to the nation through the work of "heart and brain." Actresses and soldiers, scientists and writers, inventors, physicians, lawyers, musicians—"Every faculty of mind, every noble trait of human nature"—was represented by a name on one of the famous cemetery's tombs. "Not every city is so well-peopled as this," Twain observed: "Few palaces exist in any city, that are so exquisite in design, so rich in art, so costly in material, so graceful, so beautiful" (IA 98).

In this distinguished company of the dead, the grave of Heloise and Abelard was the most famous tourist attraction: "more revered, more widely known, more written and sung about and wept over, for seven hundred years, than any other in Christendom, save only that of the Saviour" (IA 99). This uncritical flow of emotion quickly arouses Twain's indignation as he contemplates the celebrated monument. It is (he believes) an instance of fraudulent feeling, like the formulaic praise of the Old Masters that he soon overhears in Milan. Not one visitor in twenty thousand, he claims, has a clear grasp of this venerable legend, yet couples persist in making pilgrimages to the lovers' grave "to bail out when they are full of tears ... and to purchase the sympathies of the chastened spirits of that tomb with offerings of immortelles and budding flowers." Twain proposes to end this wasteful "snuffling" by retelling the story in such a way as to invert its transfiguring influence. Abelard, he insists, was simply "a cold-hearted villain" who abused the trust of his guileless victim. He was a rhetorician of the very worst kind, a verbal automaton, rather than a thinking and feeling intelligence. Eloquence and personal beauty had made him famous, Twain writes, but an untarnished "priestly reputation" was his sole interest in life, not the happiness of the girl he had seduced. To him Heloise was little more than a platitude, "a lamb in the power of a hungry wolf" (IA 101). When her outraged guardian ultimately hires some ruffians to castrate Abelard in revenge for his treachery, the physical mutilation is a suitable emblem for this inner sterility.

In time the separated lovers begin a correspondence that underscores Twain's distinction between dead aesthetic formulas and the vitality of living speech. After the violent end to the sexual phase of their relationship, both partners took holy orders out of penance:

> Heloise entered a convent and gave good-bye to the world and its pleasures for all time. For twelve years she never heard of Abelard—never even heard his name mentioned. She had become prioress of Argenteuil, and led a life of complete seclusion. She happened one day to see a letter written by him, in which he narrated his own history. She cried over it, and wrote him. He answered, addressing her as his "sister in Christ." They continued to correspond, she in the unweighed language of unwavering affection, he in the chilly phraseology of the polished rhetorician. She poured out her heart in passionate, disjointed sentences; he replied with finished essays, divided deliberately into heads and subheads, premises and argument. She showered upon him the tenderest epithets that love could devise, he addressed her from the North Pole of his frozen heart as the "Spouse of Christ!" The abandoned villain! (IA 102–103)

Ultimately Abelard's verbal "cunning" deserts him in a public debate with Saint Bernard, the final figurative castration that underscores the impotence of his rhetorical arts. But Twain too claims to have been seduced by the poignancy of the story before seeing through Abelard's manipulative nature. Like other, tearful Père la Chaise pilgrims he had left his own commemorative offerings at the lovers' grave. "I wish I had my immortelles back now," Twain complains, "and that bunch of radishes," a final reference to Abelard's physical mutilation that was sufficiently oblique to escape the notice of Twain's genteel censors (IA 104).

The melodramatic clichés that shape this long digression highlight Twain's own susceptibility to inherited verbal forms: the echo chamber of chilly phraseology to which Oliver Wendell Holmes would attribute the conventional dedication to *The Innocents Abroad*. All speech and all writing are an impure mixture of stale inheritance infused with a slight tincture of originality. However uncomfortable the discovery may make us, Twain implies, we are all parrots. This meticulous interplay between luxuriance and sterility threads its way throughout *The Innocents Abroad*, reframing the metamorphosis of Flores at every turn. Paris, as Twain's reader might expect, is an earthly aurora rather than a mud mountain: "a conflagration of gaslight" filled with music, life, and action, "so frisky, so affable, so fearfully and wonderfully Frenchy!" (IA 77). Twain and his companions had been well-prepared by illustrated guidebooks to recognize the city's famous landmarks—the Louvre, the Rue de Rivoli, the Place de la Bastille—but the illustrations offered no hint of the "wild chaos" filling the city streets, once the travelers leave the train station after their journey from Marseille, a spectacle that fills them with restless anticipation as they drift off to sleep in their hotel (IA 81).

The next morning, however, the French guide whom Twain and his friends hire to show them the sights turns out to be a deferential fraud, surreptitiously retained by various merchants to steer foreign customers to their shops. He speaks with the same meticulous "phraseology" that will mark Abelard's shallow character, and like Abelard the guide's polished manners barely conceal a calculated erotic license. The curved handle of his cane (Twain recalls) was shaped like "a female leg, of ivory" that he touched "meditatively" to his teeth before making any suggestions to his clients (IA 83). This telling gesture clearly implies the variety of intimate commercial needs that he is prepared to address, but Twain and his friends quickly lose interest in their "lackey" once they are swept up in the tide of the International Exposition. That event was among the many attractions that drew some of the *Quaker City* excursionists to make the side journey into France, but a fleeting visit of two hours convinces Twain and his friends that while the Exposition is indeed a "monstrous establishment," a "wonderful show," inanimate objects could not compete for attention with "the moving masses of people of all nations" circulating through the exhibits (IA 86).

A display of thirteenth-century tapestries briefly catches Twain's eye until he is enticed away by a passing party of "dusky" Arabs in their exotic dress. A mechanical swan holds his attention for a time, until "some tattooed South Sea Islanders approached and I yielded to their attractions." Hearing martial music in the distance, Twain and his companions hurriedly leave the Exhibition hall to catch a glimpse of the French emperor, Napoleon III, and his guest the sultan of Turkey as they review twenty-five thousand soldiers at the Arc de l'Etoile: "I had a greater anxiety to see these men than I could have had to see twenty Expositions" (IA 87). Napoleon III, as Twain perceives him, is a case study in the exhilarating allure of outlying interests: a buoyant survivor of poverty, exile, and imprisonment whose adventures echo the mental tenacity of Castle d'If's nameless victims. By contrast, the Turkish sultan Abdul Aziz impresses Twain as a vacuous puppet, the antithesis of Egypt's legendary modernizer, "the great Mehemet Ali," whose mental energy Twain associates with the transformative powers of the French emperor.[31]

The spectacle of the animate world exerts an irresistible grip on Twain's attention that neither the monuments of modernity nor antiquity can equal. The "fierce fascination" of a storm at sea (IA 39), the restless human "panorama" filling the streets of Gibraltar or Tangier (IA 44), the "flashing constellations" of light and life in Marseille and Paris captivate him, for better and for worse, as no celebrated object or famous place ever does (IA 65). Even the Great Pyramid of Cheops and its companion, the Sphinx, share in the stony uniformity from which the imagination strives to escape. Moving though they may be, they are less engrossing than the maniacal energy of the Arab guides who drag groups of tourists up the pyramid's steeply terraced sides, badger them for handouts, or eagerly offer to race from the top of one pyramid to the next in less than nine minutes for a single dollar. Twain briefly attempts a Shelleyan meditation as he looks out over the "mighty sea of yellow sand" from the Great Pyramid's summit, but like his effort on Mt. Tabor, the transfiguration doesn't take place. Romantic effusions are, in the end, just scripts: "One must bring his meditations cut and dried," Twain concludes, "or else cut and dry them afterward" (IA 475).

By contrast, the Egyptian donkeys that the *Quaker City* tourists ride on their side-trip from Cairo to Ghizeh reawaken the same lively explosion of interest that had marked Twain's frantic stampede in the Azores months earlier or his infatuation with the wonderful Frenchiness of Paris. "The donkeys were all good," he wrote as the touring party sets out from Cairo, "all handsome, all strong and in good condition, all fast and all willing to prove it":

> Some were of a soft mouse-color, and the others were white, black, and vari-colored. Some were close-shaven, all over, except

that a tuft like a paint-brush was left on the end of the tail. Others were so shaven in fanciful landscape garden patterns, as to mark their bodies with curving lines, which were bounded on one side by hair and on the other by the close plush left by the shears. They had all been newly barbered, and were exceedingly stylish. Several of the white ones were barred like zebras with rainbow stripes of blue and red and yellow paint. These were indescribably gorgeous. Dan and Jack selected from this lot because they brought back Italian reminiscences of the "old masters." (IA 471)

This gaudy spectacle too is a form of earthly aurora: an extraordinary conflation of the entire *Quaker City* excursion in an image as vivid as a children's book illustration. The "reminiscences" these donkeys evoke are, in effect, an antidote to Twain's disillusionment with the Old Masters, emblems of the resilient innocence of his book's title.

As a rule, the farther east and south Twain travels—the deeper he penetrates into the Islamic world—the more likely he is to recoil at the congested human communities in which he finds himself. Even with the assistance of moonlight, the Sea of Galilee cannot recover its ancient aura. The "freshets" of female loveliness that Twain admires in Genoa or Paris, the "soft-eyed Spanish girls" of Gibraltar or the "plump and pretty" Jewish women of Tangier, have no equivalents in Syria or Palestine. Constantinople is the nadir of these alienating worlds, an "eternal circus" (Twain calls it), a "wild masquerade" of outlandish costumes, crippled beggars, stray dogs, and peddlers "yelling like fiends" (IA 263). The great Mosque of St. Sophia seems nothing but "dirt, and dust, and dinginess, and gloom" (IA 265). Smyrna proves to be a similar urban "honeycomb," a noisy compound of dirt, fleas, and "broken-hearted dogs" that puts a decisive end to all Twain's childhood fantasies of Oriental splendor (IA 300). Though beautiful from a distance, Damascus is yet another dispiriting human "hive" (IA 341), and even Jerusalem is spoiled by the "wretchedness, poverty, and dirt" that Twain persistently associates with "Moslem" rule (IA 423).

But the Christian cities of Rome and Naples are equally notable for the mix of poverty, venality, and superstition that Twain finds in these nominally "western" places. Civita Vecchia, the port city of Rome, "is the finest nest of dirt, vermin, and ignorance" that Twain and his friends could recall encountering since their excursion to Tangier (IA 188). Like Damascus, Naples is "a picture of wonderful beauty" when viewed from the slopes of Vesuvius, "but do not go within the walls and look at it in detail," Twain cautions. The swarming streets and "filthy" habits of the people breed "disagreeable sights and smells": "Such masses, such throngs, such multitudes of hurrying, bustling, struggling humanity!" Twain exclaims, "We never saw the like of it, hardly even in New York, I think" (IA 232). Only when he and his companions can manage to control the "mad panorama" that surrounds them through a ridiculous charade of ignorance, a silly nickname applied to a guide, or a facetious relabeling of Syrian villages as obscure American towns is their mental buoyancy able to reassert itself (IA 142). That buoyancy, in turn, responds in a variety of ambivalent ways to the forms of imaginative control on display throughout the monstrous establishment of the Mediterranean world.

Among the highlights of the Paris excursion, for instance, was Twain's nighttime visit to a public pleasure garden in Asniéres, where he sees the scandalous can-can and marvels at the famous tightrope walker, Blondin, illuminated "far away above the sea of tossing hats and handkerchiefs" in a blaze of fireworks. The "great concourse of girls and young men" moving about the "fallen sun" of the garden's central "temple" constitutes one of several elaborate mechanisms in the book that seem engineered to appeal to the mind's kinetic appetites (IA 94–5). Before visiting Asniéres, Twain described two strikingly different social institutions that represent equally engineered forms of stillness: the Cathedral of Notre Dame and the city Morgue.

Notre Dame is immediately recognizable from the same illustrated guidebook entries that allow Twain to repeat some highlights from the building's history: the announcement of the third Crusade, the St. Bartholomew's Day Massacre, the Reign of Terror. The "stony, mutilated saints" on the church façade, however, are as mute as the royal effigies at St. Denis or the Egyptian Sphinx: emblems of the gray uniformity of the "real." Despite its decorative glory, Notre Dame is a mud mountain in disguise, its stained glass images of "crimson saints and martyrs," its "magnificent" papal robes and precious ceremonial "utensils" are good only for "an hour or two" of dutiful loitering (IA 92). One portion of the church's recent past, though, comes briefly to life when Twain describes the death of an archbishop of Paris who was shot on the city's barricades during the Revolution of 1848 as he tried, literally, to hold up an olive branch between the opposing factions. But even this courageous gesture is swiftly absorbed into the grotesque culture of relics. The cathedral's collection of venerated objects includes a death mask of the archbishop's face, the bullet that killed him, and two of the dead man's vertebrae where the bullet had lodged.

The Paris Morgue offers a remarkable complement to this visit with a gruesome exhibit of its own, but one that remains closely and vividly linked to the animate world. The anonymity of the dead who are on display in the Morgue, unlike the legendary publicity linked to the martyrs of the great cathedral, confers an emotional significance on the spectacle that Twain and his friends encounter there:

> We stood before a grating and looked through into a room which was hung all about with the clothing of dead men; coarse blouses, water-soaked; the delicate garments of women and children; patrician vestments, hacked and stabbed and stained with red; a hat that was crushed and bloody. On a slanting stone lay a drowned man, naked, swollen, purple; clasping the fragment of a broken bush with a grip which death had so petrified that human strength could not unloose it—mute witness of the last despairing effort to save the life that was doomed beyond all help. A stream of water trickled ceaselessly over the hideous face. We knew that the body and the clothing were there for identification by friends, but still we wondered if any body could love that repulsive object or grieve for its loss. We grew meditative and wondered if, some forty years ago, when the mother of that ghastly thing was dandling it upon her knee and kissing it and petting it and displaying it with satisfied pride to the passers-by, a prophetic vision of this dread ending ever flitted through her brain. (IA 93)

This nameless corpse, for all its inhuman rigidity, seems full of stories that are responsive to a mental touch. It is a repulsive object that does not immediately repel. Indeed, key details in the scene mirror those that had seemed so resistant to animation in Notre Dame: the drowning victim's broken bush and the archbishop's impotent olive branch; the contrasting death masks in plaster and in flesh; the crimson saints in the cathedral's windows and the vivid purple of the corpse. Twain has aligned these two pictures with considerable care in order to dramatize the capacity of selective interest to structure mental life. The tactile intimacy with which he presents these contrasting bodies gives the "accentuating finger of consciousness" a rich, imaginative immediacy.

* * *

The Innocents Abroad never tires of exploring the contrast between the banality of prescribed states of feeling and the intoxicating surprise of genuine ones. For the most part, the great artistic or religious monuments that Twain and his companions encounter during their tour amount to elaborate signaling mechanisms: cultural automata designed to prompt the viewer to deliver the appropriate outward response. The Church of the Holy Sepulchre in Jerusalem or St. Peter's in Rome are, in effect, religious exhibits analogous to the temporary displays of the Paris Exhibition. Milan Cathedral and the Athens Acropolis, however, prompt much richer forms of mental collaboration, generating an unstable blend of transfigurative potential with the fixed apparatus of spurious feeling that the culture of relics represents. At the outset of these two visits, guidebook formulas continue to play a role in shaping Twain's expectations. From the moment that Milan's "architectural autocrat" appears on the horizon, its outlines are familiar to him (IA 121). Invoking a barrage of Ruskinian clichés, he compares the Cathedral to a cloud mass rising "above the waste of waves, at sea," to a "forest of graceful needles, shimmering in amber sunlight," to "an anthem sung in stone." But the great church also exerts an irresistible measure of control over the senses. "When it is visible," Twain writes, "no other object can chain your whole attention": "Leave your eyes unfettered by your will but a single instant and they will surely turn to seek it" (IA 122).

The bas-relief sculpture "of birds and fruits and beasts and insects" decorating the Cathedral's central door is so intricately carved "that one might study it a week without exhausting its interest." The artistry of its stained glass windows anticipates the skill that Twain will soon discover in the mosaic studios of Florence. Two remarkable objects inside the building captivate the visitors as much by their horror as by their beauty, echoing the experiences of Notre Dame and the Paris morgue. The first is a "coffee-colored piece of sculpture" depicting a flayed man, a statue of St. Bartholomew by Marco d'Agrate, "with every vein, artery, muscle, every fibre and tendon and tissue of the human frame, represented in minute detail." This object rivets Twain's attention and elicits his praise for its "faultless accuracy," at the same time that it takes unwelcome possession of his memory, imposing fetters on the mind much as the massive spectacle of the church itself fetters the eye (IA 123). "It is hard to forget repulsive things," Twain writes, acknowledging the extent to which the brain can fall victim to its own conceptions.

The Cathedral crypt contains another of Catholicism's formal veneration machines: an elaborate exhibit, not unlike the mechanized silver swan in Paris, aimed at inciting the same blend of wonder and horror that Twain associates with the fetish of religious relics or the flayed man. The desiccated corpse of Charles Borroméo, a bishop of Milan famous for ministering to the sick during an outbreak of plague, is laid out in full priestly vestments, sealed in a rock crystal coffin that can be exposed for viewing by a windlass that opens the bishop's tomb. The gems and gold embroidery that encase the "decaying head" seem to Twain little more than crude material emblems of Borroméo's compassionate "hand and brain and purse," substituting the "ghastly smile" of a skull for the complex intelligence it had once contained: "Over this dreadful face, its dust and decay, and its mocking grin, hung a crown sown thick with flashing brilliants; and upon the breast lay crosses and croziers of solid gold that were splendid with emeralds and diamonds" (IA 125). This glittering encrustation Twain bitterly compares to "the glass beads, the brass ear-rings, and tin trumpery of the savages of the plains!"—a raw outburst amplifying the onslaught of repulsive things that the flayed man had introduced.

From the moment the travelers pass through the Cathedral's emblematic central door, with its intricately carved bas-relief of plants and animals, they leave behind the naturalistic order of the outer world to confront a series of troubling mental exhibits, crossing a psychic threshold that Twain unexpectedly ties to a vivid recollection from his boyhood. This memory too is an inside excursion in several phases, inscribed across the dark background of Twain's past by the shifting outline of a window frame. The sculpture of the flayed man triggers his recollection:

> I remember yet how I ran off from school once, when I was a boy, and then, pretty late at night, concluded to climb into the

window of my father's office and sleep on a lounge, because I had a delicacy about going home and getting thrashed. As I lay on the lounge and my eyes grew accustomed to the darkness, I fancied I could see a long, dusky, shapeless thing stretched upon the floor. A cold shiver went through me. I turned my face to the wall. That did not answer. I was afraid that that thing would creep over and seize me in the dark. I turned back and stared at it for minutes and minutes—they seemed hours. It appeared to me that the lagging moonlight never, never would get to it. I turned to the wall and counted twenty, to pass the feverish time away. I looked—the pale square was nearer. I turned again and counted fifty—it was almost touching it. With desperate will I turned again and counted one hundred, and faced about, all in a tremble. A white human hand lay in the moonlight! Such an awful sinking at the heart—such a sudden gasp for breath! I felt—I can not tell *what* I felt.... I put my hands over my eyes and counted till I could stand it no longer, and then—the pallid face of a man was there, with the corners of the mouth drawn down, and the eyes fixed and glassy in death! (IA 124; emphasis in the original)

The pale square of light moved "line by line—inch by inch" down the dead man's breast until it finally reached a fatal stab wound, when (Twain remembers) he fled in a panic, went home, and took his whipping. But the memory of the experience is ineradicable: "I have slept in the same room with him often, since then—in my dreams." Bishop Borroméo's corpse in its rock crystal coffin, for all its gems and ceremonial robes, cannot match this indelible impression, just as the death mask of Notre Dame's peace-loving bishop cannot match the impact of an anonymous drowning victim in the Paris morgue.

Twain's nighttime vision of Athens, from the edge of the Acropolis, underscores the mind's unpredictable selective energy, linking it once more to a haunting confrontation with lifeless faces. The *Quaker City*'s visit to the Mediterranean coincided with the nineteenth century's third cholera pandemic, a fact that results in an unpleasant experience with preventive fumigation in Italy and that ultimately forces the passengers to skip visiting Greece altogether rather than wait out an eleven-day quarantine. Twain and a group of companions, however, are determined not to be disappointed. They decide to risk capture by the quarantine patrols in order to pay a furtive, nighttime visit to the Acropolis, just visible from the ship's anchorage in Piraeus. Eager "to see the great Parthenon face to face" before the ship passes on to Constantinople, Sebastopol, and the Holy Land, they slip away after dark and wander across the Attic plain, raiding nearby vineyards for fresh grapes as they go, and after bribing four Greek guards at the gates, they get access to the citadel:

> What a world of ruined sculpture was about us! Set up in rows—stacked up in piles—scattered broadcast over the wide area of the Acropolis—were hundreds of crippled statues of all sizes and of the most exquisite workmanship; and vast fragments of marble that once belonged to the entablatures, covered with bas-reliefs representing battles and sieges, ships of war with three and four tiers of oars, pageants and processions—everything one could think of. History says that the temples of the Acropolis were filled with the noblest works of Praxiteles and Phidias, and of many a great master in sculpture besides—and surely these elegant fragments attest it. (IA 254)

Artistic elegance, however, is only part of the experience. Everywhere Twain and his friends turn in the ancient temple, they encounter the mutilated images of men and women, gleaming in the moonlight like the body that lay on his father's office floor, "some of them armless, some without legs, others headless," propped against marble blocks or peering out of the shadows with stony eyes. Over the centuries, the outer surface of the marble had acquired a "pinkish stain," but it is as white as loaf sugar where the pieces have broken, aping flesh and bone like the grotesque anatomy of the flayed man. "The place seemed alive with ghosts," Twain wrote.

Like Charles Borroméo's tomb, the Parthenon too is a veneration machine, but one that had been shattered by a Turkish artillery shell, leaving only ruins to attest to its beauty. An unexpected view of Athens itself, however, almost compensates for the loss. Twain and his friends are strolling "carelessly and unthinkingly" near the edge of the Acropolis when they are suddenly struck by the beauty and silence of the scene below:

> Athens by moonlight! The prophet that thought the splendors of the New Jerusalem were revealed to him, surely saw this instead!

It lay in the level plain right under our feet—all spread abroad like a picture—and we looked down upon it as we might have looked from a balloon. We saw no semblance of a street, but every house, every window, every clinging vine, every projection, was as distinct and sharply marked as if the time were noonday; and yet there was no glare, no glitter, nothing harsh or repulsive—the noiseless city was flooded with the mellowest light that ever streamed from the moon, and seemed like some living creature wrapped in peaceful slumber. On its further side was a little temple, whose delicate pillars and ornate front glowed with a rich lustre that chained the eye like a spell; and nearer by, the palace of the king reared its creamy walls out of the midst of a great garden of shrubbery that was flecked all over with a random shower of amber lights—a spray of golden sparks that lost their brightness in the glory of the moon, and glinted softly upon the sea of dark foliage like the pallid stars of the milky-way. Overhead the stately columns, majestic still in their ruin—under foot the dreaming city—in the distance the silvery sea—not on the broad earth is there another picture half so beautiful. (IA 254–5)

This unscripted vision presents itself without interference from gates, guides, or guards and without the kind of stately frame designed to structure the mind's response to famous places or famous paintings. Its materials are largely ephemeral—mellow light, a spray of sparks, a glimpse of silvery sea—but even so they chain the attention as irresistibly as the Parthenon's majestic ruins. The sleeping city appears virtually empty of its inhabitants, as if a visionary quarantine had been imposed on all the mundane business of human life, leaving intact only the vivid illusion that Twain's words create, forged by acts of conscious choice out of a random shower of introspective events.

 Near the end of *The Innocents Abroad*, Twain belatedly describes a visit to the Pallavicini Gardens near Genoa not when it actually occurs along the *Quaker City*'s Mediterranean route but in the middle of the Holy Land tour, as he and his friends are standing on the top of Mt. Tabor, gazing though a stone window arch at the empty plain below (IA 391). After a climb through "breezy glades of thorn and oak" to reach the setting of Raphael's biblical painting, Twain studies the "chess-board" of fields and villages below and recalls his visit to Count Pallavicini's "mimic land of enchantment" near Genoa, where he claims to have learned the importance of a "strong framework" to bring out natural beauty. This elaborate park is a labyrinth of paths, streams, bridges, and lakes sprinkled with modern replicas of ruined tombs, toy palaces, and rude huts aimed at creating a meditative mood in the visitor. Imitation Roman roads and arches, a subterranean lake, and bowers of exotic plants highlight "the chiefest wonder" of the garden: an "unpretending pane of glass, stained yellow," set in a temple door and framing a glimpse of Genoa in the distance.

This simple apparatus introduces "the faintest, softest, richest picture" that any human being had seen, Twain declares, "since John saw the new Jerusalem glimmering above the clouds of heaven." As his eye drifts over the details that this frame encloses, the distinction between outer and inner vision melts away:

> A broad sweep of sea, flecked with careening sails; a sharp, jutting cape, and a lofty lighthouse on it; a sloping lawn behind it; beyond, a portion of the old "city of palaces," with its parks and hills and stately mansions; beyond these, a prodigious mountain, with its strong outlines sharply cut against ocean and sky; and over all, vagrant shreds and flakes of cloud, floating in a sea of gold. The ocean is gold, the city is gold, the meadow, the mountain, the sky—every thing is golden—rich, and mellow, and dreamy as a vision of Paradise. (IA 393)

This is one of the last in the series of rich pictures that fill the mental gallery of *The Innocents Abroad*, a successor to the shimmering tints of Flores, at the outset of the voyage, or the exquisite shadings of a Florentine mosaic. But unlike the memorable vision of Athens by moonlight, Pallavicini's enchanted vista is a contrivance of yellow glass as artificial as Bishop Borroméo's crystal tomb. It is both a sensory surfeit and an illustration of the mind's propensity to impose its inner wealth on the equivocal experience of outer life. Twain both succumbs to the enchantment and dismisses it as a pretentious illusion: "Such is life," he writes, as his thoughts return to the slopes of Mt. Tabor and the empty plain of Esdraelon below: "the trail of the serpent is over us all" (IA 393). Pallavicini's "deep human design" both embodies and parodies the slow accumulation of choices that the mind must make as it extricates a meaningful world from the jointless continuity of space.[32]

* * *

Roughing It and *The Innocents Abroad* overlap one another in an intimate imaginative partnership that reflects their common origin in Twain's experience as a traveling correspondent for several California and Nevada newspapers. Vivid memories of western life mix with Twain's account of his Mediterranean excursion, even before his struggle with the editors of the *Alta California* over publishing rights to his *Quaker City* letters. The tedium of French train travel, he complains, cannot match the exhilaration of a stagecoach ride across the Rocky Mountains (IA 73). The view of Lake Como from Twain's Bellagio hotel prompts a tribute to the beauty of "that noble sea," Lake Tahoe, along with a startling diatribe on what he considers the degradation of the Digger Indians, both topics to which *Roughing It* returns (IA 144–5). He mimics the language of a Nevada claim notice when he takes mock possession of the oyster shell deposits above Smyrna and retells the story of Joseph during his ride across Palestine, anticipating a Sunday school lesson that Scotty Briggs will teach to the children of Virginia City. The early chapters of *Roughing It* borrow material directly from Twain's Holy Land journals, and near the end of his Sandwich Islands tour he notes that the crater of Vesuvius was "a mere toy" in comparison to the vast cauldron of Kilauea. The two books clearly coexisted with one another in Twain's mind long before *Roughing It* began to take shape.

The direction in which their confluence steers Twain's work, however, is largely inward.[33] The vast spaces of *Roughing It* provide him with an extraordinary mental terrain in which to exercise an inexhaustible imagination: to explore the feeling of repletion that nearly every page of the book dramatizes, beginning with its unusual "Prefatory" address to the reader. For the second time Twain introduces a long volume of travel adventures by disavowing any serious motives that might lie behind it. *The Innocents Abroad* (he insists) is a literary picnic; *Roughing It* is an account of its author's "variegated vagabondizing" aimed at the idle reader who hopes to avoid the weighty subjects of history, philosophy, metaphysics, or science. Like large portions of the west itself, then, this book promises to be barren, despite Twain's facetious "Prefatory" observation that it is also peculiarly full: overflowing with information about the Nevada mining boom that Twain feels a kind of mania to describe. "I would give worlds if I could retain my facts," he laments in a boozy joke, "but it cannot be. The more I calk up the sources, and the tighter I get, the more I leak wisdom" (RI 33). This mild outburst of bathroom humor is in itself a kind of leakage, a completely unexpected mental overflow of excruciating puns that anticipates *Roughing It*'s many formidable floods: the stunning overnight transformation of the Carson River from a trickle to a menacing ocean, the thrilling surges of money and mining stock that inundate Virginia City, the human deluge that swarms into the Nevada mountains whenever news of a fresh silver strike overspreads the territory, the cascades of lava that pour out of Hawaii's volcanoes and rush down their sides to the Pacific.

Unlike the old prospector Jim Blaine, later in the book, who has to be properly stewed in order to begin the endless tale of his grandfather's ram, the narrator of *Roughing It* is naturally intoxicated by the feverish interest that he takes in every curious episode, startling sight, or remarkable character that he encounters during his western years. The book as a whole is a kind of inundation narrative, a product of the luxuriant mental experience that begins to take hold the instant that Orion Clemens offers his brother "the sublime position of private secretary" to the secretary of the Nevada Territory: "My contentment," Twain declares, "was complete" (RI 50). Even the first leg of their journey, the tedious riverboat trip to St. Joseph, doesn't mar the mood. The Missouri is obstructed by snags and sand-bars that tax the traveler's patience, but Twain shows an uncharacteristic measure of "deep sagacity" in restraining his impulse to mock the performance of the Missouri captain's "bully" boat. Shallows and depths, emptiness and fullness, in a variety of remarkable forms pervade the journey that follows.[34]

A "Sphynx-like" passenger at the beginning of their overland stage route through Kansas breaks her silence when Twain politely commiserates with her over the mosquitos that she has been methodically swatting as they feed on her arm. The result of his cordial overture is an apocalyptic flood of local gossip and unsolicited advice that leaves her fellow passengers dazed beneath the "tossing waste" of her words. The stage driver is an equally replete human vessel who has to struggle to repress the convulsive pleasure that he takes in his own jokes (RI 55). At the crack of a twig or the discharge of a pistol, the seemingly quiescent "jackass rabbit" of the plains unleashes an "enchanting" display of pent-up speed: "Long after he was out of sight," Twain admiringly writes, "we could hear him whiz" (RI 61). The ubiquitous western sage brush is at first deceptively unprepossessing, a meager index to the barrenness of the landscape, growing "where nothing else in the vegetable world would try to grow." Once Twain sets out to describe it, however, he finds it to be surprisingly fertile fuel for the imagination, a "venerable live oak-tree" in miniature that becomes an incitement to reverie. "Often on lazy afternoons in the mountains," he remembers, "I have lain on the ground with my face under a sage-bush, and entertained myself with fancying that the gnats among its foliage were liliputian birds ... and myself some vast loafer from Brobdingnag waiting to catch a little citizen and eat him" (RI 61). Without the limitless source of firewood that the sage provides on the treeless prairie, there would be no "hot suppers" and no entertaining campfire exchanges, no circulating of "impossible reminiscences" among prospectors and travelers over a fire pit "full to the brim with glowing coals," a smokeless domestic convenience that seldom needs replenishing.[35]

The long trip to Carson City, where Orion is to begin his territorial duties, forms a running record of the incitement and satisfaction of one "consuming desire" after another, as Twain and his brother keep an eye out for novelties: the first prairie dog village, the first coyote, the Pony Express rider, or a buffalo hunt, all of which ignite Twain's verbal energies. Even the legendary desperado Slade, a stage company agent who oversaw a particularly violent stretch of the route across the Rocky Mountains, shares some of the comforting domestic attributes and narrative enticements of the sagebrush. After days of listening to tantalizing gossip concerning Slade's exploits, the Clemens brothers were bursting with curiosity:

> We had gradually come to have a realizing sense of the fact that Slade was a man whose heart and hands and soul were steeped in the blood of offenders against his dignity; a man who awfully avenged all injuries, affronts, insults, or slights, of whatever kind—on the spot if he could, years afterward if lack of earlier opportunity compelled it; a man whose hate tortured him day

and night till vengeance appeased it—and not an ordinary vengeance either, but his enemy's absolute death—nothing less; a man whose face would light up with a terrible joy when he surprised a foe and had him at a disadvantage. A high and efficient servant of the Overland, an outlaw among outlaws and yet their relentless scourge, Slade was at once the most bloody, the most dangerous and the most valuable citizen that inhabited the savage fastnesses of the mountains. (RI 103)

The inaccessible enclosure of mountain "fastnesses" is the only sign of mental containment in this passage. Twain's "realizing" sense of Slade's homicidal nature overflows the ordinary categories of understanding, just as Slade's barely appeasable appetite for "absolute death" seems to overflow the limits of mortality.

Despite the Wild West caricature that Slade's homonymic name evokes, he is (Twain suggests) more a "conundrum" than a stereotype (RI 119). He is among the first of the extraordinary array of unusual minds that *Roughing It* meticulously explores. With a few brief exceptions, Twain's companions on the *Quaker City* excursion remain anonymous, part of an implicit but seldom prominent social background to the performance of a single consciousness that seems, at times, as isolated as the prisoner in Castle d'If, carving his dungeon walls. But the vivid figure of George Bemis in the opening pages of *Roughing It* makes clear that Twain intends to savor the mental variety that filled his Nevada and California years, even when that variety first displays itself in the capacity to construct fantastic lies, as Bemis does, after he disgraces himself in a buffalo hunt. Slade is a much more formidable figure with a firearm than Bemis or either of the Clemens brothers proves to be, but once Twain sifts through the "mass" of gossip surrounding him, the figure that emerges has an unexpected mental complexity.

Twain rebuilds Slade's story in *Roughing It*, much as he does the legend of Heloise and Abelard in *The Innocents Abroad*, by drawing on various printed sources and fitting them into the contours of his own narrative. Like Abelard, Slade too has a selfless wife whose loyalty is completely unaffected by her husband's moral flaws, though in Slade's case those flaws are mixed with a surprising variety of admirable inner resources. A pair of violent quarrels early in Slade's life result in two murders that send him into hiding, fighting Indians in the far west while scrupulously "avoiding an Illinois sheriff" who was trying to bring him back east for trial—a curious blend of license and restraint that contributes to the enigma of Slade's character. Initially at least, he was not a particularly gifted "artist" with his pistol, Twain notes, having been beaten to the draw in a dispute with a wagon driver that Slade only survives because of the wagon driver's fatal gullibility (RI 104). But even after fleeing Illinois to escape arrest, Slade managed to earn the prestigious post of "train-master" for an expedition of California emigrants, a biographical anomaly that points toward qualities in Slade's nature that quickly lead to his influential, executive role in helping to manage the Overland Stage Company. In the course of administering the first stage division that he oversees, Slade imposes such a degree of "peace and order" on the region that his employers decide to transfer him to an even more dangerous stretch of the Rocky Mountain route, "the very paradise of outlaws and desperadoes," where "violence was the rule":

> Slade took up his residence sweetly and peacefully in the midst of this hive of horse-thieves and assassins, and the very first time one of them aired his insolent swaggerings in his presence he shot him dead! He began a raid on the outlaws, and in a singularly short space of time he had completely stopped their depredations on the stage stock, recovered a large number of stolen horses, killed several of the worst desperadoes of the district, and gained such a dread ascendancy over the rest that they respected him, admired him, feared, him, obeyed him! He wrought the same marvelous change in the ways of the community that had marked his administration at Overland City. He captured two men who had stolen overland stock, and with his own hands he hanged them. He was supreme judge in his district, and he was jury and executioner likewise—and not only in the case of offences against his employers, but against passing emigrants as well. (RI 107)

The melodramatic aggregation of potent social roles in this passage is strikingly varied. Slade seems, at first, a superficially peaceful newcomer, but his explosive response to a hapless outlaw's swaggering "airs" initiates a flood of marvelous changes. The worst desperadoes Slade promptly kills, but the bulk of the horse thieves and assassins in the region respond to his "dread ascendancy" with a cascade of psychological adjustments, prompted by the example of the incorruptible disciplinarian who has come to live among them. Slade secures their obedience, rather than their extermination, and extends his commercial jurisdiction to the protection of emigrants passing through his district. When "in the fullness of time" Slade captures and kills his outlaw nemesis, a renegade stage company official named Jules, it is the culmination of many kinds of fullness that he evokes (RI 110).

Ultimately Slade makes an unexpected personal appearance in Twain's narrative, presiding over the breakfast table at an Overland station where the Clemens brothers' stage has stopped for a change of mules and a meal. Much to Twain's surprise, Slade seems "the most gentlemanly-appearing, quiet and affable officer" of the Overland Company that they have met along their route:

> It was hardly possible to realize that this pleasant person was the pitiless scourge of the outlaws, the raw-head-and-bloody-bones the nursing mothers of the mountains terrified their children with. And to this day I can remember nothing remarkable about Slade except that his face was rather broad across the cheek bones, and that the cheek bones were low and the lips peculiarly thin and straight. But that was enough to leave something of an effect upon me, for since then I seldom see a face possessing those characteristics without fancying that the owner of it is a dangerous man. (RI 110)

Not unlike one of the nursing mothers of the mountains, Slade politely insists on refilling Twain's coffee cup, rather than feeding his irrational fancies, and rearranges the mailbags in the stagecoach so that the passengers would be more comfortable. Fullness and emptiness repeatedly change places in this passage, as Twain grapples with the riddle of Slade's menacing appearance and seemingly solicitous behavior. "Here was romance," he had initially exulted when he sat down to breakfast with this "actual ogre": "I suppose I was the proudest stripling that ever traveled to see strange lands and wonderful people." But in the space of a paragraph, Twain dramatizes a marvelous change in his own response to Slade's presence that carries him from the shallow enthusiasms of pulp fiction to a more probing assessment of the inexplicable depths of Slade's nature (RI 111).

Slade's portrait is one of the most elaborate depictions of human repletion that *Roughing It* contains, but it is by no means unusual in its focus on the inner rather than the outer attributes of the remarkable individuals that populate Twain's chapters. In Salt Lake City, Twain and his brother "flitted hither and thither and enjoyed every hour" of their visit, much as the *Quaker City* travelers did through the wonders of Paris. "This was fairy-land to us," Twain confessed, "a land of enchantment, and goblins, and awful mystery" prompted by the exotic tales of Mormon polygamy that they longed to confirm through one "good satisfying look" at the "comprehensive ampleness" of a representative Mormon family at home (RI 130). This particular glimpse of sensational repletion never takes place. Instead, they find themselves so drawn to the spectacle of the city's beautifully irrigated streets and gardens, its "hum" of urban activity, and the people they meet that they completely neglect to visit the Great Salt Lake that they had spent much of the first part of their trip yearning to see. "Now when it was only arm's length away," Twain noted, "it had suddenly lost nearly every bit of its interest" (RI 133).

Mr. Street, a U.S. government official charged with running a telegraph line across Utah, tells the brothers a story of a meeting with Brigham Young that opens Street's eyes to the absolute authority that the Mormon patriarch exercises over his remote domain. "I am a business man," Mr. Street proudly declares, "have always been a business man—do not know anything *but* business," so he is doubly struck by the businesslike way in which Brigham Young scrutinizes contracts and "showed a strong interest" in their wording when Street cannot get his Mormon subcontractors to fulfill their obligations. Twain weaves the characters of both men into his story, through the vehicle of Street's narrative, allowing this superabundant business man to draw a resounding conclusion about the actual sources of power in the Salt Lake Valley: "There is a batch of governors, and judges, and other officials here, shipped from Washington, and they maintain the semblance of a republican form of government—but the petrified truth is that Utah is an absolute monarchy and Brigham Young is king!" (RI 137).

When Twain himself purports to have finally met "the king" during a courtesy call that Orion's new territorial position obliges him to make, the monarch proves to be anything but petrified:

He seemed a quiet, kindly, easy-mannered, dignified, self-possessed old gentleman of fifty-five or sixty, and had a gentle craft in his eye that probably belonged there. He was very simply dressed and was just taking off a straw hat as we entered. He talked about Utah, and the Indians, and Nevada, and general American matters and questions, with our secretary and certain government officials who came with us. But he never paid any attention to me, notwithstanding I made several attempts to "draw him out" on federal politics and his high handed attitude toward Congress. I thought some of the things I said were rather fine. But he merely looked around at me, at distant intervals, something as I have seen a benignant old cat look around to see which kitten was meddling with her tail. (RI 133)

By the end of the meeting, while the official conversation "flowed on as sweetly and peacefully and musically as any summer brook," Young finally appears to have sensed Twain's simmering resentment (RI 134). As the visitors prepare to depart, their host retaliates for the unspoken comparison to an old mother cat by placing a hand on Twain's head and inquiring of Orion whether his child was a boy or a girl.[36] This improbable scene never took place, of course, but Twain exploits his intriguing picture of Brigham Young's mental gifts as a sharp contrast to the "insipid mess" that he finds the Book of Mormon to be. "It is chloroform in print," Twain declares: "If Joseph Smith composed this book, the act was a miracle—keeping awake while he did it was, at any rate. If he, according to tradition, merely translated it from certain ancient and mysteriously-engraved plates of copper, which he declares he found under a stone, in an out-of-the-way locality, the work of translating was equally a miracle, for the same reason" (RI 146). Unlike Twain's make-believe indignation at Brigham Young's behavior, these resentments are genuine, an assault based less on the religious deficiencies of the Book of Mormon than on its failure to be interesting.

An anonymous Salt Lake City bootblack displays infinitely more mental life than the Book of Mormon, when Twain tries to pay for his services before learning to appreciate the inflationary effect of long-distance freight charges on local prices:

A young half-breed with a complexion like a yellow-jacket asked me if I would have my boots blacked. It was at the Salt Lake House the morning after we arrived. I said yes, and he blacked them. Then I handed him a silver five-cent piece, with the benevolent air of a person who is conferring wealth and blessedness upon poverty and suffering. The yellow-jacket took it with what I judged to be suppressed emotion, and laid it reverently down in the middle of his broad hand. Then he began to contemplate it, much as a philosopher contemplates a gnat's ear in the ample field of his microscope. Several mountaineers, teamsters, stage-drivers, etc., drew near and dropped into the tableau and fell to surveying the money with that attractive indifference to formality which is noticeable in the hardy pioneer. Presently the yellow-jacket handed the half dime back to me and told me I ought to keep my money in my pocket-book instead of in my soul, and then I wouldn't get it cramped and shriveled up so! (RI 159)

A roar of appreciative laughter from the crowd of bystanders greets the bootblack's performance. These knowing mountaineers and teamsters had gathered about the transaction fully aware of how the "tableau" would unfold, making the same use of Twain's inexperience and his smug demeanor that the entire population of Carson City will later conspire to make of the self-important new U.S. attorney, General Buncombe, in the mock trial that they stage for the great landslide case of *Hyde vs. Morgan*.

This practical joke is another elaborate mental tableau that requires the collusion of the two parties to the bogus suit, a local lawyer, the Carson City sheriff's deputies and an ex-governor of the Nevada Territory, along with a parade of carefully coached witnesses. Their nominal goal is to convince Buncombe, a new appointee from the east, that the citizens of the Territory were fools and their ex-governor an "inspired idiot" for ruling against a distraught rancher whose property had been completely buried when a landslide deposited another man's perfectly intact ranch—"fences, cabins, cattle, barns, and everything"—precisely on top of it (RI 253). The prudential intelligence of the U.S. attorney is outraged by this abuse of common sense, but the citizens themselves luxuriate in the success of their charade. It took two months for General Buncombe to realize that he had been the victim of a hoax, and even then (Twain implies) his sense of humor had none of the explosive capacity for pleasure that the Salt Lake City locals displayed at the bootblack's withering sarcasm. A recognition that he has been fooled has to "bore" its way "like another Hoosac Tunnel, through the solid adamant of his understanding"—a sly conclusion to the anecdote that manages to mix an insulting pun with a surprising acknowledgment of the stubborn (if unimaginative) integrity that makes Buncombe's character indispensable to the success of the joke.

The mental resources brought into play during the Nevada silver boom are at least as conspicuous a part of Twain's subject as the "interesting episode" of the mining boom itself: the psychological "fever" that underlies the territory's volatile economic life. In the course of Twain's newspaper work for the Virginia City *Enterprise*, he is invited to descend into the vast, subterranean labyrinth of shafts and tunnels, all shored up with a "forest" of timber beams, that cross-crosses the rich metallic veins of the Comstock Lode. The mine owners loved to encourage local reporters to write up their fabulous discoveries and document the scope of their work as a means of promoting investment in the frenzy of stock speculation going on above ground. But once you have observed this extraordinary underworld in action, Twain writes, "You need never go down again, for you have seen it all" (RI 382). Even extraordinary feats of engineering have, at best, a limited interest. By contrast the hidden world of Jim Blaine's memory as he attempts to tell "The Story of the Old Ram," repays endless visits by his reverential friends, who keep a close eye on Blaine's state of intoxication until they are satisfied that he is "symmetrically drunk" and ready to begin (RI 385–6). Then they gather around him in complete silence, preparing to savor the comic extravagance of the mental "lode" through which Blaine's narrative will wander until he drifts off to sleep.[37]

"I perceived that I was 'sold,'" Twain complains after he is enticed to one of Blaine's performances on the pretext of hearing the "stirring story" of the ram. In fact this anecdote is a definitive example of the human abundance of the flush times: a species of bankruptcy that is actually a surfeit in disguise. The pure lucidity of Jim Blaine's mind as he begins his story without "a cloud upon his brain thick enough to obscure his memory" precedes his slow descent into the "dark mystery" of sleep without ever getting to his subject, like a miner who spends years underground and never strikes it rich. The tears that Twain's friends shed as they struggle to suppress their laughter pay tribute to the indiscriminate tenacity of a mind for which all the ludicrous minutiae of life exert an equal and irresistible claim on its attention. The "boys" themselves who relish Blaine's monologue remain as anonymous as most of Twain's companions on the Quaker City voyage, but their anonymity is the exception rather than the rule in *Roughing It*.

Some of the individualized portraits that Twain supplies are no more than vivid sketches that capture the presence of an active mind, often without a name attached, like the convulsive stage driver at the beginning of the westward journey or the sharp-witted bootblack in Salt Lake City. Others, like Old Abe Curry in Carson City announce their names with an emphatic flair and offer a glimpse of mental energy that is as enticing as the assay specimens of silver-bearing quartz that prospectors chip away from their mining claims. Curry introduces himself in just this fashion as Twain is nursing his injuries after attempting to ride the Genuine Mexican Plug:

> One elderly-looking comforter said:
> "Stranger, you've been taken in. Everybody in this camp knows that horse. Any child, any Injun, could have told you that he'd buck; he is the very worst devil to buck on the continent of America. You hear *me*. I'm Curry. *Old* Curry. Old *Abe* Curry. And moreover, he is a simon-pure, out-and-out, genuine d-------d Mexican plug, and an uncommon mean one at that, too. Why, you turnip, if you had laid low and kept dark, there's chances to buy an *American* horse for mighty little more than you paid for that bloody foreign relic." (RI 199–200; emphases in the original)

This brief speech mixes its egocentric *me* with a blend of jingoism and tenderness that eases the painful transition from "stranger" to "you turnip," the kind of companionable insult that signals a more reassuring form of being taken in. A few pages later Curry makes a final appearance in the book to offer a rent-free building for the use of the new Territorial legislature that Orion is responsible for establishing. "But for Curry," Twain gratefully writes, "the government would have died in its tender infancy" (RI 205).

The head of that infant government, a former New York City police commander who plans to use the post of territorial governor as a stepping-stone to the U.S. Senate, is an equally memorable figure. Like Twain himself, he is drawn to Nevada for private motives, bringing in his wake a retinue of followers who hope to make their fortunes off of a meager territorial budget. But Governor Nye also comes equipped with a sense of humor. He gets an "old time pleasant twinkle" in his eye, Twain writes, as he explains a ruse for disposing of his band of self-appointed "henchmen," the Irish Brigade, by assigning them the "lucrative and useful service" of surveying a railroad route across the Nevada desert until they enter Utah, when he plans to encourage Brigham Young "to hang them for trespass!" (RI 183). The members of the Brigade play along with the Governor's scheme up to a point, surveying "very slowly, very deliberately, very carefully" at first, making sure not to get too far east of Carson City so that they can return each night to their boarding house, in a "very jolly" frame of mind, with an extensive collection of desert tarantulas as souvenirs—hairy, muscular, sensitive creatures (Twain insists) that have a certain physical and temperamental resemblance to the Brigade members themselves. "Indeed," he writes, these formidable spiders "would take up a straw and pick their teeth like a member of Congress" (RI 183). Like the great landslide case later in the book, this episode too is an improvised "entertainment" on the part of all of its participants, a strategy for making life tolerable amid the alien, external world in which they find themselves.

Governor Nye's brother accompanied him to the new territory, much like Sam Clemens had accompanied Orion, bringing with him a unique array of mental attributes similar, in some respects, to those of the voluble woman on the Kansas stage coach or to Jim Blaine's tenacious memory. But unlike these spectacularly replete speakers, or the compulsive practical jokers of Carson City, Captain John Nye is an unqualified social asset, with endlessly adaptable verbal gifts rather than indiscriminate ones. He joins Twain and his mining partners, Mr. Ballou and a Prussian named Ollendorff, on the second of their fruitless prospecting expeditions and quickly establishes his incomparable value as a traveling companion. In addition to extraordinary "conversational powers" and great practical ingenuity, Captain Nye possesses a miraculous "spirit of accommodation" that allows him to befriend virtually everyone he meets, never failing "to find vacant beds in crowded inns, and plenty to eat in the emptiest larders" (RI 258). His cordial nature later prompts Twain to postpone work on the Blind Lead, a fabulously rich vein of ore to which he and his partner Cal Higbie had staked a claim, in order to nurse Captain Nye through a painful bout of rheumatism (RI 293). Amid the barrage of profanity that his patient emits—another of Nye's inexhaustible verbal resources—Twain consoles himself with detailed fantasies about how he and Higbie will spend their newfound riches.

A skilled miner, Twain observes, can distinguish one pile of rock from another as easily as a confectioner can classify candy. The Bind Lead vein was composed "not of hard rock," he explains, but of "black, decomposed stuff which could be crumbled in the hand like a baked potato, and when spread out on a paper exhibited a thick sprinkling of gold and particles of 'native' silver" (RI 286). Silver ores (as Twain had ruefully discovered) usually required an industrial stamping mill, a series of washing tubs and retorts, a number of chemical additives, and a great deal of hard labor to "digest" the excavated contents of a mine into a "frosty looking" brick of precious metal. But Higbie mashes up the soft ore from the Blind Lead in a hand mortar and washes out its rich contents in a horn spoon, puzzling over its geological peculiarities until his experiments yield an exhilarating conclusion: the Blind Lead is a unique mineral vein running across the strata of rock owned by another mine and hence available to any savvy prospector who chooses to claim it.

Higbie is the second such savvy mind to school Twain in the skills of his complex trade. The first, Mr. Ballou, resembles Higbie in possessing a deep, sensory appreciation for the qualities of rock. When he and his inexperienced partners first decide to stake a claim to a mine they call the Monarch of the Mountains, Ballou repeatedly licks a sample of the ore and studies it with a magnifying glass to determine its mineral potential (RI 226). Twain can detect little more than a "ragged thread of blue" deposits running through a block of white quartz, much like the slender track of ink across a sheet of paper. And like the countless individual sentences necessary to make a book, Twain estimates that it would take a "couple of tons" of Monarch rock to yield anything of value. But there are worse mineral ledges than this one, Mr. Ballou insists, before offering his feckless comrades another homely analogy for their discovery that mixes fact and fantasy much like the ore mixes gold and quartz. The Monarch, he explains, is like a curbstone that runs deep underground, framed by bands of "casing rock" as it descends and preserving "its distinctive character always, no matter how deep it extended into the earth or how far it stretched itself through and across the hills and valleys" (RI 227). The deeper it went, the richer it grew, Mr. Ballou believed, superimposing the mythic allure of buried treasure on his practical, curbstone geology in order to persuade himself and his companions that the "Monarch" is more than an empty name.

As a rule, verbal dexterity is not Mr. Ballou's natural idiom. His ordinary conversation is an indecipherable collection of malapropisms that he produces, on every occasion, out of an indiscriminate love of the big words he utters, rattling them off with an "air" that is "so natural and so simple that one was always catching himself accepting his stately sentences as meaning something, when they really meant nothing in the world" (RI 217). Even so, Mr. Ballou is enough of a verbal adept to modify Twain's trite announcement that "all that glitters is not gold," after learning about the deceptive appearance of mica. Ballou immediately explains "that *nothing* that glitters is gold" (emphasis in the original):

> So I learned then, once for all, that gold in its native state is but dull, unornamental stuff, and that only low-born metals excite the admiration of the ignorant with an ostentatious glitter. However, like the rest of the world, I still go on underrating men of gold and glorifying men of mica. Commonplace human nature cannot rise above that. (RI 224)

This refinement of the old adage is itself a commonplace, but its presence in the story has the effect of underscoring the rich array of underrated men that fills the pages of *Roughing It*, many of whom mix the unrefined attributes elicited by the rough environment that they inhabit with remarkable mental reserves.

After the crushing disappointment of losing the Blind Lead, Twain abandons his dreams of striking it rich in the silver fields and begins working for Joe Goodman on the staff of the Virginia City *Territorial Enterprise*. "What to do next?" he had asked himself at this momentous turning point in his life, not (as one might expect) "What to do now?" The first question suggests an inexhaustible degree of openness to fresh interests rather than a frantic scramble for expedients.[38] Journalism soon introduces Twain to another generous selection of intriguing minds, among them Jim Blaine, Scotty Briggs, and the anonymous minister who learns to mock his own eastern formality and to relish Briggs's western slang in the course of their pastoral conversations. Observing the behavior of local juries, in order to fill his newspaper column, triggers Twain's assault on the weaknesses of the judicial system and leads to a digression on the exploits of Captain Ned Blakely, commander of a guano ship, who "had all a sailor's vindictiveness against the quips and quirks of the law," as well as a rich mix of racism, piety, and tenderness in his nature, all of which come into play when he avenges the murder of his negro mate, a narrative side excursion that Twain cannot resist including in his pages (RI 359–65).

Another wily professional reporter named Boggs helps Goodman tutor Twain in the nuances of the newspaper business. Eventually he decides to join a group of ambitious collaborators who hope to establish Virginia City's first literary magazine, the *Weekly Occidental*, an indisputable sign (Twain notes) that the flush times were "at the flood" (RI 366). These collaborators soon include a "dissolute stranger with a literary turn of mind" whose gentle demeanor and skillful pen win their confidence, along with an invitation to contribute a chapter to the magazine's serialized novel. After drinking his imagination "into a state of chaos" and reviewing the preceding chapters that Twain and his coauthors had written, the stranger set to work generating surreal plot twists and improbable disasters that enraged his colleagues and contributed to the magazine's peaceful death. Twain is able to salvage for the pages of *Roughing It* the text of a poem he had written for the *Weekly Occidental*'s final issue, a burlesque of Coleridge titled "The Aged Pilot Man" that hints at the comic gusto of Nevada's verbal community (RI 374). The magazine's founding editor once disposed of a newspaper attack on his character by observing that "the logic of our adversary resembles the peace of God," confident that his readership would appreciate the incomplete biblical rejoinder (RI 366).

Virginia City's lofty perch on the slopes of Mount Davidson contributes to the reinvigorated breadth of view that Twain displays once he turns his attention to a journalistic survey of the flush times, documenting the speculative excess, intoxicating mineral wealth, and endemic violence that had taken hold of "the mining brain of the community" (RI 317). In time Twain's brain, too, succumbs to its own feverish energies when (out of boredom, he implies) he publishes a defamatory article in the pages of the *Enterprise* that seems likely to involve him in a duel.[39] Advised by friends to leave the territory, he departs for San Francisco to await the fortune that he expects to collect, one way or another, from the eagerness of eastern investors in search of profitable mines to buy or from his trunk full of wildly inflated stock (RI 400). This dream of riches too evaporates, casting Twain into a suicidal depression and ultimately prompting an extraordinary meditation on the human cost of the gold and silver booms that unfolded in California and Nevada during the two decades between the first gold strikes in the Sacramento Valley and the end of the Civil War.

Dozens of "fiercely flourishing" little towns had once filled these mountain canyons, Twain observed, but no sign of their energetic presence remains. Only the disfigured landscape, scarred by crude mining operations, indicated that "a driving, vigorous, restless population" had abruptly flooded this inhospitable region in search of fortune and receded just as swiftly as it rose. Once as large as the Army of the Potomac, this "gallant host" of prospectors and other opportunists had wasted its youthful promise and disappeared:

> It was a driving, vigorous, restless population in those days. It was a *curious* population. It was the *only* population of the kind that the world has ever seen gathered together, and it is not likely that the world will ever see its like again. For, observe, it was an assemblage of two hundred thousand *young* men—not simpering, dainty, kid-gloved weaklings, but stalwart muscular, dauntless young braves, brim full of push and energy, and royally endowed with every attribute that goes to make up a peerless and magnificent manhood... .And where are they now? Scattered to the ends of the earth—or prematurely aged and decrepit—or shot or stabbed in street affrays—or dead of disappointed hopes and broken hearts—all gone, or nearly all—victims devoted upon the altar of the golden calf—the noblest holocaust that ever wafted its sacrificial incense heavenward. It is pitiful to think upon. (RI 414; emphases in the original)

The loss that this passage laments is as much mental as physical. Though Twain celebrates the manly vigor of this human flood, and takes note of the devastation that the prospectors left behind in their furious hunt for gold, their intelligence is the most conspicuous sacrifice they made, "for all the slow, sleepy, sluggish-brained sloths staid at home," Twain wrote, "you never find that sort of people among pioneers." It was in at least two senses a curious population—a fusion of the outward and inward vitality that sustained their ephemeral world.

Afflictions of the brain play a prominent role in the final episodes of *Roughing It*. Dick Baker, a California pocket-miner, manages to avoid the lunatic asylum that Twain associates with that form of prospecting by nursing memories of his pet cat, Tom Quartz. Kindly men like Baker, Twain writes, in the absence of women and children "take up with pets, for they must love something" (RI 437). In his owner's eyes Tom Quartz "had more hard, natchral sense" than any of Baker's human companions, along with "a power of dignity," and a measure of curiosity about mining techniques that nearly gets him killed by an unexpected dynamite blast. The "affection and pride" with which Baker embellished the tale of this last adventure suggests the extent to which Tom Quartz had kept alive his owner's imagination as well as his powers of feeling. Other marginal figures whom Twain meets late in the book are less successful instances of mental resilience: the delusional, alcoholic "Admiral" Twain encounters en route to the Sandwich Islands who is enraged to the point of psychosis over the defeat of the Confederacy; the compulsive liar Markiss who cannot even write a credible suicide note; a gentle island exile from Michigan who is driven insane by an illegible letter from Horace Greeley.

But crippled imaginations are much less conspicuous in the pages of *Roughing It* than overflowing ones: the stage-traveler Bemis with his flair for lies, Slade's administrative zeal and unappeasable passions, Mr. Ballou's deep love for his incomprehensible verbiage, John Nye's inexhaustible gregarious gifts. Among the most vivid of the many images of repletion in the book is the double inundation prompted by Twain's visit to the crater of Kilauea during his horseback tour of Hawaii. He had returned to San Francisco from his excursion among the Sierra pocket-miners, taken a job as California correspondent for the *Enterprise*, and escaped from debt, "but my interest in my work was gone.... I wanted another change" (RI 442) The opportunity to contribute letters about the Sandwich Islands to a Sacramento newspaper rescues him from this latest temperamental dilemma. Twain delights in the exotic spectacle of the Hawaiian people, complains about the equally exotic insects that he encounters, ransacks his notebooks for material, and reprints the program of a royal funeral procession as he feeds the curiosity of his mainland readers, but his visits to two great volcanoes are the heart of these closing chapters. Each offers a figurative answer to the ubiquitous dilemma of what to do next. Kilauea's crater in particular, Twain notes, proved to be "a vast, perpendicular, walled cellar, nine hundred feet deep in some places, thirteen hundred in others, level-floored, and *ten miles in circumference*! Here was a yawning pit upon whose floor the armies of Russia could camp, and have room to spare" (RI 528; emphasis in the original).

Visiting the rim at night confirms this first hint of the verbal exhilaration that the mountain will ultimately awaken:

> I turned my eyes upon the volcano again. The "cellar" was tolerably well lighted up. For a mile and a half in front of us and half a mile on either side, the floor of the abyss was magnificently illuminated; beyond these limits the mists hung down their gauzy curtains and cast a deceptive gloom over all that made the twinkling fires in the remote corners of the crater seem countless leagues removed—made them seem like the camp-fires of a great army far away. Here was room for the imagination to work! You could imagine those lights the width of a continent away— and that hidden under the intervening darkness were hills, and winding rivers, and weary wastes of plain and desert—and even then the tremendous vista stretched on, and on, and on!—to the fires and far beyond! You could not compass it—it was the idea of eternity made tangible—and the longest end of it made visible to the naked eye! (RI 530)

This eruption of metaphor continues over the next several pages as Twain depicts the "thousand branching streams of liquid fire" that etch the lava crust beneath them, radiating in all directions like the spokes of a wheel, or like "huge rainbow curves," or like jagged "worm-fence angles," or like bolts of lightning that "crossed and re-crossed each other" like the tracks of ice skaters "on a popular skating ground." Occasionally bits of the darkened crust would float off on the lava streams "like rafts down a river" (RI 531). The spectrum of colors on display formed "aurora borealis rays" as the white-hot rock shaded into "flaming yellow," then tapered to crimson or "pale carmine" before congealing into the brittle surface that Twain set out to explore on foot on a second nighttime visit.

This close encounter with the seething energy of a molten lake prompts another verbal cascade, as Twain's language attempts to compete with the tremendous geological spectacle. "Kilauea never overflows its vast crater," he reports, "but bursts a passage for its lava through the mountain side when relief is necessary, and then the destruction is fearful" (RI 537). Until such moments of catastrophic release, however, the mountain grips the eye "with its unapproachable splendor," satisfying the same appetite for transfiguration that had marked every stage of the *Quaker City* excursion in *The Innocents Abroad*. Both of the great craters that Twain visits in the Sandwich Islands, Kilauea and Haleakala, engage all of his figurative resources, but his most lasting impression of each is of a great fullness, a great belly or a great womb, rather than a reservoir of hellish fire. Haleakala in fact might have swallowed all of London (Twain thought) so vast is its "vacant stomach": a crater nearly three times the circumference of Kilauea's and over twice as deep.[40]

Even this great vacancy, however, is a form of repletion: a dress rehearsal for the next stage in Twain's personal transfiguration from vagabond miner and journalist into a member of the artistic establishment. As he takes in the expansive horizon of ocean and mountains from Haleakala's rim, puzzling over the optical confusion of height and depth that the great distances create, white clouds begin to drift by, first singly, then in "couples and groups," until at last "imposing squadrons" form a solid bank of vapor completely filling the crater and blotting out the view. Only the edge of the rim itself appears above the blanket of "fleecy fog":

> Thus banked, motion ceased, and silence reigned. Clear to the horizon, league on league, the snowy floor stretches without a break—not level, but in rounded folds, with shallow creases between, and with here and there stately piles of vapory architecture lifting themselves aloft out of the common plain—some near at hand, some in the middle distances, and others relieving the monotony of the remote solitudes. There was little conversation, for the impressive scene overawed speech. I felt like the Last Man, neglected of the judgment, and left pinnacled in mid-heaven, a forgotten relic of a vanished world. (RI 543–4)

This sense of abandonment is fleeting. Sunrise soon transfigures the surrounding "cloud-waste," flooding it with a brilliant array of colors, "glorifying the massy vapor-palaces and cathedrals with a wasteful splendor," much as shafts of sunlight had converted the mud mountain of Flores into an earthly aurora. The description is not only perfectly adapted to the lecture platforms where Twain will soon deliver it, it perfectly depicts the anxieties and the triumphs of the lecture experience itself.

Two chapters later, as *Roughing It* draws to a close, the audience for Twain's first stage appearance in San Francisco signals its presence in much the same way that the fog accumulates in Haleakala's vast crater: gradually filling the depressing silence and emptiness of the theater by couples and by groups until a "crash, mingled with cheers ... made my hair raise, it was so close to me, and so loud." Waiting in the dark backstage, hours before the performance was to begin, Twain had felt once more like the last inhabitant of a vanished world. But as the murmur of the arriving audience swells, and he finds himself thrust before the "sea of faces" under the glare of the lights, he becomes acutely aware that he is the only man on stage, not the last one on earth, "quaking in every limb" at the task he has set himself. Even the theater aisles were full. During the suspenseful days leading up to his debut, Twain had lost confidence in his lecture and had asked several friends to help prompt the audience to laughter if his jokes fell flat. The result of this scheme is another gratifying flood. "Inferior jokes never fared so royally before," Twain remembered, and even a "little morsel of pathos" that he had inserted among his comic vignettes triggers a raucous explosion when one of his audience accomplices misreads his signal and delivers "a mellow laugh" that destroys the "absorbed hush" Twain's words had invoked (RI 555). The reigning silence and wasteful splendor of Haleakala had forecast this moment. They are an outward index to the challenges of introspective representation and control that would preoccupy Twain for the remainder of his writing life.

3

Attention

The great volcanoes of the Sandwich Islands that Twain visits in the closing chapters of *Roughing It* seize his attention in a way that Vesuvius never quite achieves in *The Innocents Abroad*. When the *Quaker City* excursion reaches Naples, Twain treats his ascent of that celebrated mountain as a whimsical study in the mind's love of side-excursions, breaking up the climb into nine labeled segments spread across two chapters that mix his account of the trail, the mules, and the guides with a profusion of largely irritating distractions: his disgust with aggressive Italian beggars and the bad manners of a Neapolitan theater audience; his vivid impressions of the city's claustrophobic streets; his scorn for Catholic religious processions, bogus miracles, and the inflated prices the travelers repeatedly encounter. Only the Blue Grotto at Capri lives up to Twain's expectations. Near the volcano's summit portions of an old lava flow suggest a "turbulent panorama" petrified into an emblem of the "impotent rage" that Twain experiences as he contemplates the grotesque wealth of the Catholic Church, the degradation of the Italian people, or the government's intrusive quarantine measures aimed at controlling the spread of cholera (IA 236).

Once he reaches the mountain's summit, the crater itself proves to be little more than a "circular ditch," a few hundred feet wide and two hundred feet deep, surrounding a heap of volcanic debris in its center (IA 237). The sulfur fumes that condense on the debris have turned it into a gorgeous encrustation of color, Twain admits, "and when the sun burst through the morning mists and fired this tinted magnificence, it topped imperial Vesuvius like a jeweled crown!" But this outbreak of enthusiasm is quickly cut short by recurrent mists, noxious fumes, and the resistant temperaments of the travelers themselves. Vesuvius, Twain ultimately concludes, is a poor affair. By contrast, when the sun finally illuminates the vast fog-filled crater of Haleakala, the motionless silence that had briefly overwhelmed Twain with a sense of supreme isolation becomes an eruption of shape and color: a "wasteful splendor" far more impressive than the tinted magnificence of Vesuvius. "It was the sublimest spectacle I ever witnessed," Twain wrote, "and I think the memory of it will remain with me always" (RI 544).

This equivocal assertion of memory's stability is a mental construct in its own right: a mix of Twain's personal experience with a cluster of allusions that he cribbed from an 1854 book entitled *Sandwich Island Notes* by George Washington Bates, one of several sources that Twain ransacked for information and ideas much as he did with the various guidebooks that he consulted as he wrote *The Innocents Abroad*. The view from Haleakala's rim is a hybrid of recollection and reading, like the sentimental dedication that Twain would inadvertently absorb from Oliver Wendell Holmes's poems and later claim as his own. Unlike that instance of unconscious assimilation, however, Haleakala's wasteful splendor is carefully positioned in Twain's Hawaiian narrative in order to temper the potent energies unleashed by his visit to Kilauea.[1]

In contrast to the reflective silence imposed by Haleakala, Kilauea's explosive impact requires several pages and parts of two chapters to record. Vesuvius, Twain declares, is "a soup bowl" by comparison. From a crude lookout house on Kilauea's rim, Twain and his companions spend the better part of one night studying through opera glasses the lava cascades and fiery streams that form an intricate map on the crater floor. This incandescent "inside" view is so tempting that Twain and a companion named Marlette soon cast aside all prudential concerns and decide to venture out across the slowly cooling crust of the crater floor to inspect the North Lake of liquid magma that is visible two miles away.[2] As the two are slowly "threading" their way toward the molten lake, Marlette suddenly notices that the sounds their feet are making as they crush the fine needles of hardened lava indicate that they have wandered from the smooth path worn by earlier explorers. Searching patiently "with his boots instead of his eyes," Marlette is able to find the smooth pathway once again. Walking thereafter as much by ear as by eye, they gradually arrive at their goal:

The spectacle presented was worth coming double the distance to see. Under us, and stretching away before us, was a heaving sea of molten fire of seemingly limitless extent. The glare from it was so blinding that it was some time before we could bear to look upon it steadily. It was like gazing at the sun at noonday, except that the glare was not quite so white. At unequal distances all around the shores of the lake were nearly white-hot chimneys or hollow drums of lava, four or five feet high, and up through them were bursting gorgeous sprays of lava-gouts and gem spangles, some white, some red and some golden—a ceaseless bombardment, and one that fascinated the eye with its unapproachable splendor. The more distant jets, sparkling up through an intervening gossamer veil of vapor, seemed miles away; and the further the curving ranks of fiery fountains receded, the more fairy-like and beautiful they appeared. (RI 532)

Rising bubbles of gas occasionally release "a pale green film of vapor" as they burst, agitating the molten billows and shaking the ledge on which the two observers are sitting. Eventually part of the ledge breaks off and tumbles into the lake, awakening the two to their danger and prompting them to make their way back to the crater wall, but not before once more losing the path and confusing the beacon lantern that their friends had left behind at the lookout house with a star.

Thirty-two years earlier, Twain reported, a powerful eruption broke through Kilauea's crater wall in a fiery river of molten rock, five miles wide in places, capable of carrying acres of farmland to the sea on "bosom-like rafts." The mountain's repeated explosions filled the night sky with "rocket sprays" of lava that made it possible for witnesses forty miles at sea to read fine print at midnight (RI 537). Like the splendid vision from Haleakala's rim, the record of this old cataclysm, too, fuses with Twain's present experience to form a rich imaginative amalgamation, hinting at the dramatic shift in artistic focus that his career was about to take. The glowing river systems of lava weaving through Kilauea's crater floor produce hissing and coughing sounds that remind him of "a large low-pressure" riverboat releasing excess steam through its escape valves. At the height of a full eruption, Twain's sources report, the entire "laboring mountain" seemed on the point of giving birth, as it "voiced its distress in moanings" and emitted "a tumbled canopy" of smoke, much as approaching steamboats did to announce their arrival at the sleepy river towns of Twain's boyhood. Kilauea, he concludes, represents "Nature's great palsy" of creative splendor and destructive power, but without a Pompeii or Herculaneum at the mountain's base, its impact on history is lost (RI 538).

Its impact on Mark Twain's mind, however, is unexpectedly fertile. As he was bringing *Roughing It* to a conclusion, his own attention was beginning to turn toward a new set of commanding interests. In part these grew out of the transformation of his domestic life. Samuel Clemens and Olivia Langdon were married on February 2, 1870. Two days after the wedding, Twain wrote an extraordinary letter to his childhood friend, Will Bowen, describing the flood of memories that his marriage seemed to trigger. "The fountains of my great deep are broken up & I have rained reminiscences for four & twenty hours," he wrote, employing the same biblical hyperbole that he would use a few months later to describe the verbal floods of *Roughing It*. "The old life has swept before me like a panorama," he continued: "the old days have trooped by in their old glory again; the old faces have looked out of the mists of the past; old footsteps have sounded in my listening ears; old hands have clasped mine; old voices have greeted me & songs I loved ages & ages ago have come wailing down the centuries!"[3]

Within a few months Livy was pregnant, but later in the summer of 1870, the death of her father and that of a childhood friend who had fallen ill while visiting the new couple may have played some role in the premature birth of Langdon Clemens in November 1870, followed by Livy's postpartum collapse and a near-fatal bout with typhoid late in the winter of 1871.[4] This great palsy of creation and destruction within Twain's own household was almost certainly present at some level in his mind as he worked through the final chapters of *Roughing It*, where the fantastic laws of clinging to which William James would soon trace the operations of consciousness produced a compound description of Kilauea's crater that blended almost seamlessly with the flood of reminiscences released by Twain's marriage. The collective result of this psychic entanglement would make its way, almost immediately, into his fiction.

The first indication of this form of imaginative overflow appears in the early pages of *The Gilded Age*, the collaborative novel that Twain and Charles Dudley Warner began within a few months of the publication of *Roughing It*. The spectacle of a Mississippi River steamboat churning upriver at night resituates the vision of Kilauea's crater at the heart of Twain's boyhood world:

> A deep coughing sound troubled the stillness, way toward a wooded cape that jutted into the stream a mile distant. All in an instant a fierce eye of fire shot out from behind the cape and sent a long brilliant pathway quivering athwart the dusky water. The coughing grew louder and louder, the glaring eye grew larger and still larger, glared wilder and still wilder. A huge shape developed itself out of the gloom, and from its tall duplicate horns dense volumes of smoke, starred and spangled with sparks, poured out and went tumbling away into the farther darkness. Nearer and nearer the thing came, till its long sides began to glow with spots of light which mirrored themselves in the river and attended the monster like a torchlight procession.[5]

The next several pages of the book describe in considerable detail a fatal steamboat race. Twain fills this account with the indecipherable slang, the casual racism, and the urgent skill of the pilots as each straining vessel becomes "a moving earthquake," while the passengers cheer wildly from their decks. In the terrible explosion that results, one boat is reduced to a burning wreck in which her trapped crewmen scream for rescue from the advancing flames while the survivors listen helplessly to their pleas.

Less than a year after the publication of *The Gilded Age*, Twain began to write "Old Times on the Mississippi," followed in quick succession by *The Adventures of Tom Sawyer* and by almost half of what would eventually become the *Adventures of Huckleberry Finn*. Each of the three is fueled by an imagistic amalgamation that first emerges during Twain's description of the Kilauea descent. As he and Marlette instinctively follow an invisible channel across Kilauea's lava crust, they anticipate the remarkable mental gifts that Twain will celebrate in the account of steamboat piloting that initiates his imaginative return to the river.

* * *

The creative outpouring of these years does not emerge in a smooth and steady productive stream. It anticipates, in some respects, the erratic narrative of the duplicate, Emil Schwarz, in "No. 44, The Mysterious Stranger": an uneven emotional performance "scatteringly seasoned with strange words and phrases, picked up in a thousand worlds, for he had been everywhere" (MS 376). At moments the brilliantly lit stretches of the universe that Schwarz describes resemble the richness of Kilauea's fiery volcanic display, before abruptly giving way to the shoreless vacancy of *"general space,"* a variation on the infinite fog that buries the vast rim of Haleakala. Even the miraculous experiences of a dream-sprite are subject to states of dormancy and eruptive amplitude that are parts of the same regenerative mental system. When Twain takes up the story of his river piloting days, in seven sketches that he wrote for the *Atlantic Monthly* in 1875, he employs just such a regenerative system to describe the steamboat pilot's extraordinary adaptation to the interior and exterior currents that shape his world.

These pages too are scatteringly seasoned with strange words and phrases, but "Old Times on the Mississippi" gradually offers an interpretive guide to the specialized languages that Twain sets out to explore. The challenge is more complicated than simply compiling a glossary or filling in the pages of a cub pilot's notebook with the thousands of navigational details one must master in order to keep a steamboat moving safely through a channel of "easy" water. A particular form of attention needs to take root in the pilot's mind, a constantly shifting equilibrium of inner and outer worlds, sustained by the multifaceted state of consciousness that river navigation requires. A pilot's memory, Twain will write late in the *Atlantic* series, "is about the most wonderful thing in the world," but even the strongest memory provides only a fraction of the elaborate mental equipment that a pilot needs: the animating energies and specialized forms of awareness that bring a pilot's array of arcane knowledge into play (OM 5.571).

Piloting a steamboat, Twain repeatedly insists, is a "science" rather than a skill. It combines the observational acuity of a physician with the lexical aptitudes of a sophisticated reader who can interpret the signs on the river's surface—both comparisons that Twain makes in an effort to explain a pilot's unique makeup. Neither analogy, though, accounts for the complex of mental engagements that fuses a pilot's consciousness with the fluid nuances of the world through which a steamboat moves. Even the term "science" is misleadingly narrow, since the physical laws that govern the river's behavior are not of much interest to a pilot. Near the end of "Old Times on the Mississippi" Twain goes out of his way to mock the "wholesale returns of conjecture" that science seems able to derive from "a trifling investment of fact" (OM 7.193). Nor, despite one instance of experimental stubbornness that Twain records, does a working pilot have the luxury of testing hypotheses when he is feeling his way through an intricate and invisible channel.

Ceaseless acts of measurement occupy part of a pilot's mind: How full is the river at any given point in a trip? Is the level rising or falling? Which island chutes are navigable now and will they be navigable in a day or two, when the steamboat finally reaches them? What do the leadsman's cries reveal about the unpredictable changes taking place beneath the river's turbid surface? But even these calibrations are subsidiary to a level of mental attentiveness that can only be described as a kind of comprehensive "knowing," a science in the root sense of the word, that constantly integrates the observer's inner and outer environments, often without the observer's direct participation in the process.[6] "Take an instance," Twain writes in the fifth installment of the "Old Times" series, as he describes a pair of perceptual experiments quite similar to those that William James often summarizes in *The Principles of Psychology*:

> Let a leadsman cry, "Half twain! half twain! half twain! half twain! half twain!" until it becomes as monotonous as the ticking of a clock; let conversation be going on all the time, and the pilot be doing his share of the talking, and no longer listening to the leadsman; and in midst of this endless string of half twains let a single "quarter twain!" be interjected, without emphasis, and then the half twain cry go on again, just as before: two or three weeks later that pilot can describe with precision the boat's position in the river when that quarter twain was uttered, and give you such a lot of head-marks, stern-marks, and side-marks to guide you, that you ought to be able to take the boat there and put her in that same spot again yourself! The cry of quarter twain did not really take his mind from his talk, but his trained faculties instantly photographed the bearings, noted the change of depth, and laid up the important details for future reference without requiring any assistance from him in the matter. (OM 5.571)

The city-bound reader (Twain suggests) can repeat the same experiment, walking and talking with two friends, one of whom takes part in the conversation while the other quietly and monotonously repeats a string of identical vowels with a single consonant interjected in the series. Most people would be unable to recall the interjection at all, three weeks later, let alone reconstruct where they were walking when the incident took place: "But you could if your memory had been patiently and laboriously trained to do that sort of thing mechanically." In this pair of experiments Twain appears to treat the pilot's mind as a kind of automaton. In fact a much richer form of awareness is at work beneath the surface noise: a comprehensive attentiveness to the location of a moving steamboat in three dimensions, all synchronized with a single, slight variation in a string of barely noticeable background sounds. The mechanistic linkage between listening and memory is far too crude to account for the performance that this scenario displays. A pilot's consciousness (as Twain depicts it) is uniquely alert as well as replete. For this reason, too, like the seasonal rhythms of the Mississippi, it is a consciousness prone to overflow.

Dormancy and eruptive vitality are the definitive features of river life that dominate the opening and closing sections of "Old Times on the Mississippi." The collective mental "picture" composed by the seven sketches recasts the deceptive sleep and explosive extremes of Hawaii's volcanoes as ingredients of Twain's Missouri past. These forces take their most spectacular form in his vivid recollection of the New Orleans wharf as two or three miles of docked steamboats prepared for departure. For two hours every vessel would burn rosin and pitch pine to signal the last stages of preparation, covering the city with a "sable roof" of black smoke from the long "colonnade" of their chimneys:

> Two or three miles of mates were commanding and swearing with more than usual emphasis; countless processions of freight barrels and boxes were spinning down the slant of the levee and flying aboard the stage-planks; belated passengers were dodging and skipping among these frantic things, hoping to reach the forecastle companion way alive, but having their doubts about it; women with reticules and bandboxes were trying to keep up with husbands freighted with carpet-sacks and crying babies, and making a failure of it by losing their heads in the whirl and roar

and general distraction; drays and baggage-vans were clattering hither and thither in a wild hurry, every now and then getting blocked and jammed together, and then during ten seconds one could not see them for the profanity, except vaguely and dimly; every windlass connected with every fire-hatch, from one end of that long array of steamboats to the other, was keeping up a deafening whiz and whir, lowering freight into the hold, and the half-naked crews of perspiring negroes that worked them were roaring such songs as De Las' Sack! De Las' Sack!—inspired to unimaginable exaltation by the chaos of turmoil and racket that was driving everybody else mad. (OM 7.190)

The desperate dodging and skipping that carry Twain and Marlette across the floor of Kilauea's boiling crater help shape this account, no single detail of which can really be "seen" except "vaguely and dimly" through the screen of Twain's verbal exaltation. His language captures a constellation of thought, feeling, and movement that had first announced its presence in the opening paragraphs of the *Atlantic* series.[7]

That initial installment presents two versions of the pervasive contrast between the mind's languid intervals and its outbreaks of acute interest. In the first, Twain's boyhood friends experience an alternation of "burning" and fading fantasies that prefigures the psychic flux of the Mysterious Stranger tales. Piracy, minstrel shows, and circuses are all capable of inflaming their imaginations with dreams of adventurous escape from small-town tedium, but beneath these attractions the lure of the steamboat man exercises a durable mental influence: an enticement that blends the seemingly opposed possibilities of escape from, and mastery of, their highly constricted world. Twice each day the seemingly lifeless and lonely "river-glimpse" that formed the mental boundary of their town gives way to an explosion of formerly latent activity when a steamboat signals its approach:

> Presently a film of dark smoke appears above one of those remote "points"; instantly a negro drayman, famous for his quick eye and prodigious voice, lifts up the cry, "S-t-e-a-m-boat a-comin'!" and the scene changes! The town drunkard stirs, the clerks wake up, a furious clatter of drays follows, every house and store pours out a human contribution, and all in a twinkling the dead town

is alive and moving. Drays, carts, men, boys, all go hurrying from many quarters to a common centre, the wharf. Assembled there, the people fasten their eyes upon the coming boat as upon a wonder they are seeing for the first time. (OM 1.70)

The boat itself dominates the scene: "long and sharp and trim and pretty," with painted paddle boxes and gilded ornaments, a "fanciful" pilot house, "clean white railings," decks "black with passengers" and glaring furnaces left open for dramatic effect. The passage reads like a set of stage directions in part because Twain had just completed a five-act dramatization of *The Gilded Age* that opened in New York in September 1874, a month or two before he began writing the first installment of "Old Times on the Mississippi." This boat, in turn, resembles a spectacular backdrop for an elaborate theatrical production.[8]

Ten minutes after the steamboat backs away from the landing, Twain continues, "the town is dead again," but not the latent desire that it represents: the urge to get on the river that keeps "intruding" into the waking and sleeping fantasies of nearly every boy in the village. Dreams in fact are highly permeable mental zones in "Old Times on the Mississippi." They are rarely the kind of insular and distinct spheres of experience represented by the mysterious Emil Schwarz and his fellow dream sprites, utterly cut off from their work-a-day hosts. Nor are they simply blank gaps in consciousness. Once Twain begins to focus his own mind on mastering the navigational contours of the river's channel, filling his notebook with a pilot's elaborate blend of informative "marks" and steering shorthand, this profusion of information begins to invade his sleep with a "frantic and tireless nightmare" of names, observations, and experiences that "reveled all through my head till sunrise," blending his conscious and unconscious states.[9]

Late in the *Atlantic* series he describes a legendary feat of steering that is actually executed by an accomplished pilot and notorious somnambulist, Mr. X, who is known for doing "strange things" in his sleep when his mind is troubled by a bad stretch in the river. Quite unexpectedly one "drizzly, sullen, and dark" night, X appeared in the pilot house of a great New Orleans packet to relieve his partner as the boat approached a particularly treacherous stretch of water. Mr. E, the pilot on duty, was grateful for the assistance, frankly admitting to a degree of panic as he had found himself spinning the boat around like a whirligig in his efforts to avoid danger. "Let me take her," his partner said, "I've seen this place since you have, and it is so crooked that I reckon I can run it myself easier than I could tell you how to do it." In the darkened pilot house, E can just make out the shape from which X's reassuring voice appears to emerge:

> The black phantom assumed the wheel without saying anything, steadied the waltzing steamer with a turn or two, and then stood at ease, coaxing her a little to this side and then to that, as gently and as sweetly as if the time had been noonday.... He rang for the leads; he rang to slow down the steam; he worked the boat carefully and neatly into invisible marks, then stood at the centre of the wheel and peered blandly out into the blackness, fore and aft, to verify his position; as the leads shoaled more and more, he stopped the engine entirely, and the dead silence and suspense of "drifting" followed; when the shoalest water was struck, he cracked on the steam, carried her handsomely over, and then began to work her warily into the next system of shoal marks; the same patient, heedful use of leads and engines followed, the boat slipped through without touching bottom, and entered upon the third and last intricacy of the crossing; imperceptibly she moved through the gloom, crept by inches into her marks, drifted tediously till the shoalest water was cried, and then, under a tremendous head of steam, went swinging over the reef and away into deep water and safety!
>
> E------ let his long-pent breath pour out in a great, relieving sigh, and said:
>
> "That's the sweetest piece of piloting that was ever done on the Mississippi River! I wouldn't believed it could be done if I hadn't seen it." (OM 4.451)

As it happens, Mr. X himself hadn't seen it. He was asleep throughout the entire series of exquisitely choreographed steps that the passage describes. Pent-up anxiety drove him from his bed to run a difficult stretch of the channel that his partner was ill-equipped to manage. Pent-up suspense escapes from Mr. E in the form of a great sigh of relief, much as the carefully marshaled reserves of steam in the boat's boilers respond to X's heedful signals. Twain carefully orchestrates this blend of inner and outer energies to dramatize the stored mental reserves behind them.

Other instances of mental abundance are less dramatic than this one but no less central to the cumulative impression that Twain gradually creates, over the course of the "Old Times" sketches. Pilots are not only extraordinary mental storage vessels, as Twain depicts them, but "tireless talkers" and avid listeners, as they gather in a pilot house to exchange stories and refresh their knowledge about the changing state of the channel by taking a short trip to "look at the river." In that setting they are "always understood," Twain notes, and "always interesting," though their presence reduces a cub pilot-in-training like Sam Clemens to a nonentity, below the notice of even the poorest of the licensed pilots in the group who are trying to keep their river knowledge current (OM 2.221). "Your true pilot cares nothing about anything on earth but the river," Twain observes, a mixture of inner wealth and inner impoverishment that mimics the sharp distinction in class between "gorgeous" diamond-studded pilots who are legendary for their skills and "poor fellows" struggling for work. It echoes as well Twain's comic account of the spendthrift pilot he calls "Stephen" who is perpetually borrowing from his colleagues, never repaying his debts, but overflowing with ingratiating words and "gushing with apologies" whenever he encounters an especially gullible creditor.

The Pilot's Benevolent Association of which Stephen is a celebrated member plays a critical role in the brief evolution of the profession. It is an institutional bank in several senses of the word: a joint economic corporation and an aggregation of mental resources that Twain compares to the collective acuity of "a hundred sharp eyes" and "bushels of intelligent brains," pooling their piloting experience into secure deposits of river reports that only Association members, equipped with special keys and a system of secret signals, can access. The perpetually needy Stephen is a lavish contributor to this mental conglomerate. Indeed he brings an excess of mental energy to bear on even the most hazardous stretches of a journey, conferring "a sort of splendor around a bit of harum-scarum, devil-may-care piloting, that made it almost fascinating—but not to everybody" (OM 7.723). One "good old gentle spirited" steamboat captain was unable to cope with Stephen's wild displays:

> Why, bless me! I wouldn't have such a wild creature on my boat for the world—not for the whole world! He swears, he sings, he whistles, he yells—I never saw such an Injun to yell. All times of

the night—it never made any difference to him. He would just yell that way, not for anything in particular, but merely on account of a kind of devilish comfort he got out of it.... And he kept a fiddle and a cat. He played execrably. This seemed to distress the cat, and so the cat would howl. Nobody could sleep where that man—and his family—was. And reckless? There never was anything like it. Now you may believe it or not, but as sure as I am sitting here, he brought my boat a-tilting down through those awful snags at Chicot under a rattling head of steam, and the wind a-blowing like the very nation, at that! My officers will tell you so. They saw it. And, sir, while he was a-tearing right down through those snags, and I a-shaking in my shoes and praying, I wish I may never speak again if he didn't pucker up his mouth and go to whistling! Yes, sir; whistling "Buffalo gals, can't you come out to-night, can't you come out to-night, can't you come out tonight;" and doing it as calmly as if we were attending a funeral and weren't related to the corpse. (OM 7.722)

As Twain's gentle-spirited captain repeats "Buffalo Gal's" familiar chorus, he inadvertently suggests one reason for the "devilish comfort" that Stephen extracts from his vocal energy. It is a kind of choral tool for occupying some aspects of the mind while focusing intently on others, like the monotonous series of leadsman's cries that bracket the single flicker of variation a pilot needs to heed. Even the cat and the fiddle seem calculated to evoke the thoughtless sing-song of an old nursery rhyme and to serve, at the same time, as figures for acute attention. "Now watch her; watch her like a cat," Twain's mentor, Mr. B, exhorts, as he coaches his inept cub through the challenge of navigating a tricky stretch of river (OM 3.287).

Stephen's crazed animation is unusual even among the pilot's fraternity, but animation itself is a key ingredient in the make-up of a pilot's intelligence. As Twain's training proceeds and his sophistication grows, he soon realizes that the simple acquisition of river knowledge is like stockpiling an "inanimate mass of lumber" in one's head, without the constant application of subtle kinetic energy that takes such an alarming external form in Stephen's whistling and war whoops. Exacting attention and apparent distraction are not, in fact, incompatible with one another in the complex science of piloting.[10]

Twain's paragon of piloting excellence, Mr. B, shares some of Stephen's fondness for making noise during tense moments of river work, casually singing a hymn at the wheel of his steamboat as he calmly proposes to deposit a passenger at a particular plantation landing on a night "when all plantations were exactly alike and all the same color." To his cub's amazement, Mr. B is more than equal to the feat, singing his hymn and "scraping" the nearly invisible shoreline "just the same as if it had been daylight," as he begins to quiz Twain on the first phase of his piloting education, only to discover that his hapless pupil has made no effort to memorize the navigational landmarks and crossings above New Orleans that they have just negotiated. The result is the first of Mr. B's memorable verbal eruptions: an outburst of enraged exasperation that gradually subsides into a gentle dormancy (OM 2.219). "There's only one way to be a pilot," Mr. B. finally informs his cub, "and that is to get this entire river by heart. You have to know it just like A B C." Despite Mr. B's spectacular temper, self-mastery is the signature of his character. It is the key lesson that he finally teaches his pupil, using a pair of carefully devised practical jokes to undermine Twain's confidence in his growing skills.

All a pilot's experience with the optical challenge of gauging the river's shape under every conceivable atmospheric condition, all his skill in reading the river's surface, all his attentiveness to its rising or falling stages and their complex navigational consequences, however up-to-date his knowledge of snags or wrecks and however deft his "feel" for the boat's ability to "smell" potentially fatal obstacles—if a pilot loses his head and panics at the wheel, all his science will desert him. "I would have felt safe on the brink of Niagara, with Mr. B---- on the hurricane deck," Twain confesses, but only because the magical reassurance provided by B's presence can withstand tests for which knowledge alone has no answer (OM 3.287). With the complicity of a steamboat captain and a team of leadsmen, Mr. B contrives just such a test for Twain's own presence of mind that he fails miserably, dissolving in "coward agony" as his imagination generates dangers that do not exist in a stretch of river that he knows full well is so deep "that I couldn't get bottom there with a church steeple." "You think so, do you?" Mr. B remarks as he pretends to leave Twain alone in the pilot house, whereupon the novice pilot rapidly succumbs to his fears.

In the longest extended episode that Twain writes for "Old Times on the Mississippi," he depicts the extremes of prudence and reckless daring that mark Mr. B's mastery both of himself and of his profession. Shortly after taking on his new cub, Mr. B is hired to pilot a "big New Orleans boat" downriver from St. Louis. This lavishly appointed vessel fills Twain with some of the same childish joy that had marked the arrival of the daily steamboats of his boyhood. Its pilot-house "was a sumptuous glass temple," richly furnished and decorated, with "a wheel as high as my head, costly with inlaid work," and a special waiter to supply snacks and coffee for the pilot and his guests. Looking down the boat's gilded saloon "was like gazing through a splendid tunnel" and even the boiler deck was "as spacious as a church" (OM 2.220).

Amid these luxurious surroundings, Twain's romantic fantasies of piloting recover their appeal, but the minute he quits touring the boat and returns to the pilot-house he realizes that he is hopelessly lost on the river itself. The downstream voyage presents a completely different view of the channel. "My heart broke again," he remembers, as he realizes that he has to learn the Mississippi "*both ways*" just as if it were two distinct rivers. Listening to the conversation of the visiting pilots, as they disclose the "warm personal acquaintanceship" they have acquired with a host of innocuous landmarks at all hours of the day and night, only amplifies his despair: "I wish the piloting business was in Jericho," he declares to himself, "and I had never thought of it" (OM 2.222). During the first stage of this southbound trip, Mr. B responds to the kind of prudential concerns that William James would later attach to Herbert Spencer's evolutionary focus on survival at all costs. He gives the signal to land and ties the steamboat to the riverbank all night rather than run a complicated stretch of channel in the dark with the full force of the current behind him, a situation that makes downstream piloting especially hazardous. The next day, while his cub is still feeling "pretty rusty" with discouragement, Mr. B makes precisely the opposite choice, responding to the irresistible appeal of ideal interests: a luxuriant sense of mastery, in the presence of a knowing audience, that tempts him to run the last perilous crossing north of Cairo, Illinois, just after nightfall.

All the guest pilots who were accompanying the boat were eager to get to Cairo so that they could quickly return to St. Louis, rejoin their own vessels, and put their fresh knowledge of the channel to use. But as the sun sets, they lose hope, much as Twain had earlier lost his own hope of ever mastering the complex science reflected in the pilots' expert talk. For a moment or two they anticipate a repeat of the previous night's decision to tie up safely at the bank. "All the watches closed with a snap," Twain noted at this disappointing juncture, a signal of the crisp conclusions of prudence at work: "everybody sighed and muttered something about its being 'too bad, too bad—ah, if we could *only* have got here half an hour sooner!' and the place was thick with the atmosphere of disappointment" (OM 2.223; emphasis in the original). But Mr. B soon cuts through this mental thickness as deftly as he does the inky shadows of the river.

The decisive signal of his intention to run the crossing ahead occurs when he strikes "two, deep mellow notes" on the steamboat's big bell, alerting the leadsmen to begin sounding the river. Meaningful looks from the other pilots "and nods of surprised admiration" gradually give way to suppressed commentary "in low voices" as Mr. B calmly and in complete silence steers the boat through a series of what seem to Twain like "utterly invisible marks ... in the midst of a wide and gloomy sea."

> Presently I discovered a blacker gloom than that which surrounded us. It was the head of the island. We were closing right down upon it. We entered its deeper shadow, and so imminent seemed the peril that I was likely to suffocate; and I had the strongest impulse to do *something*, anything, to save the vessel. But still Mr. B------ stood by his wheel, silent, intent as a cat, and all the pilots stood shoulder to shoulder at his back. (II, 223; emphasis in the original)

Until the critical moment only the "faint jinglings" of engine room bells and the cries of the leadsmen break the stillness, but as the channel depth falls below eight feet, Mr. B warns the engineer through a speaking tube to stand by. At six and a half feet, the hull scrapes the river bed, and Mr. B springs into action, ringing signal bells and shouting orders: "The boat rasped and ground her way through the sand, hung upon the apex of disaster a single tremendous instant, and then over she went! And such a shout as went up at Mr. B-----'s back never loosened the roof of a pilot-house before!" One of Mr. B's admirers inadvertently underscores the grim stakes of his gamble: "By the Shadow of Death, but he's a lightning pilot!" The psalm to which this splendid compliment alludes is a tribute to the still waters of the soul: a celebration of the mental amplitude that Twain's seven *Atlantic* sketches bring vividly to life.[11]

* * *

The opening chapters of *The Adventures of Tom Sawyer* navigate a profusion of inner worlds every bit as rich as the elaborate structure of awareness on which the science of piloting depends. Surprisingly, when Twain returns to the setting of a sleepy river town to write his first complete novel, he leaves out the grand spectacle of a steamboat arrival with which he had begun "Old Times on the Mississippi." The town's steam ferry plays a minor role in the plot. When Tom's friend Ben Rogers approaches Aunt Polly's long board fence that Tom has begun to whitewash, he comes into sight "personating" a famous steamboat, playing "boat and captain and engine-bells combined" as he brings his imaginary vessel to a stop and prepares to address his friend (TS 12). These are the only glancing references to the world that the *Atlantic* sketches had described, and even so they incorporate a telling error. It is the all-powerful pilot, not the largely ornamental captain, that Ben is actually personating as he mimics the sound of orders and engine room bells that Mr. B manipulates so masterfully in "Old Times." Twain's attention has shifted from the outward technicalities of his Mississippi experience to the inward intensities that he means to explore through the lives of a handful of children during a single momentous summer.[12]

A clear sign of this redirected artistic focus is the opportunity that Twain finds, early in Tom Sawyer's story, for reframing the elaborate experiment in attentiveness that he had proposed in order to illustrate a pilot's complex levels of mental activity. A minor variation in a monotonous series of leadsman's cries will register in a pilot's mind, Twain explains, however deeply engaged in social distractions he might seem to be. That variation instantly becomes a mental seed around which an array of navigational marks will crystalize, allowing him to recreate the steamboat's position, in exacting detail, even weeks later, despite the passage of time and the overlay of unbroken talk that fills a crowded pilot-house.

Tom Sawyer brings the same kind of intelligence to bear on the monotonous verbal forms of a small-town church service.

The ringing of bells marks the various stages in the town's Sunday routine, much as it does the engine room orders of a steamboat pilot. After the congregation has assembled and sung its opening hymn, the minister begins a reading of village notices and news, followed by a long, ritualistic prayer as familiar to Tom as the chorus of "Buffalo Gals" is to Stephen and his anxious steamboat captain:

> The boy whose history this book relates, did not enjoy the prayer, he only endured it—if he even did that much. He was restive, all through it; he kept tally of the details of the prayer, unconsciously—for he was not listening, but he knew the ground of old, and the clergyman's regular route over it—and when a little trifle of new matter was interlarded, his ear detected it and his whole nature resented it; he considered additions unfair, and scoundrelly. In the midst of the prayer a fly had lit on the back of the pew in front of him and tortured his spirit by calmly rubbing its hands together; embracing its head with its arms and polishing it so vigorously that it seemed to almost part company with the body, and the slender thread of a neck was exposed to view; scraping its wings with its hind legs and smoothing them to its body as if they had been coat tails; going through its whole toilet as tranquilly as if it knew it was perfectly safe. As indeed it was; for as sorely as Tom's hands itched to grab for it they did not dare—he believed his soul would be instantly destroyed if he did such a thing while the prayer was going on. But with the closing sentence his hand began to curve and steal forward; and the instant the "Amen" was out the fly was a prisoner of war. (TS 40)

A trifling variation in the minister's performance, like a variation in the leadsman's cry, registers in Tom's consciousness, triggering his resentment at a violation of Sabbath decorum. His ear and hand function like automata, drawing sharp distinctions and executing complex acts that he scarcely needs his will to perform. Restiveness, resentment, unconscious tallying, and tortured desire course through Tom's mind as he absorbs his surroundings with an appreciation for minute detail capable of detecting offensive novelties in the minister's speech, while taking note of the "slender thread" of a fly's neck. Like the fly, Tom had recently been subjected to a thorough Sunday cleaning that began as a spurious performance on his part and ended when his cousin Mary "took him in hand" and made him presentable for church. In the moments before Tom's equally successful effort to take the fly in hand, his head too seems to part company with his body as he enters more and more deeply into his mental world.

Over the course of the story that mental world proves to be an extraordinarily complex place, a deeply submerged or deeply buried existence that expresses itself as often through silence as through words, much as it does while Tom is tallying his internal and external experiences during the Sunday church service. Silence in fact is the opening sign of Tom's presence in the book, the first of many such nonverbal indicators on which the action of the story depends. Aunt Polly calls out her troublesome nephew's name four times at the beginning of Twain's first chapter, an act that the design of the novel's first page effectively amplifies by building an emphatic "Tom!" into its title heading and illustration (see Figure 3.1). On the fourth try she raises her voice "at an angle calculated for distance" and shouts at the top of her lungs before "a slight noise" behind her back betrays the furtive movements of "a small boy" just sneaking out of a pantry closet with jam on his mouth.

In this scene at least Aunt Polly is an almost completely externalized consciousness, wearing spectacles for "style," calculating the trajectories that will carry her voice as far as possible over her garden fence, soliloquizing her concern over Tom's whereabouts, his character, and his future, while Tom himself is suppressing the outer signs of his existence as he steals a treat and plans his escape. "Keep mum" is the mutual promise that Tom and Huckleberry Finn will exchange roughly a third of the way through the book, after they witness Doctor Robinson's murder and swear one another to secrecy out of their fear of Injun Joe. But keeping mum is an indispensable precondition for the psychological unfolding that Twain practices in chapter after chapter, largely though not exclusively on Tom as he probes the labyrinthine inner lives of his characters.[13]

The figure of Tom Sawyer, Twain suggests in his preface, belongs to "the composite order of architecture," a double reference to James Fenimore Cooper's wry account of frontier construction in *The Pioneers* and to the three actual Missouri children from whom Twain claims to have drawn the "characteristics" of his hero. That hero's adventures and experiences—the book's exterior scaffolding to which these preliminary comments and the novel's title draw the reader's attention—give Twain an opportunity to examine more closely the "odd superstitions," the thoughts and feelings, lying beneath the audible talk and behind the "queer enterprises" that motivate his characters. Those motives are elaborate composites in their own right: a tangle of emotions, fantasies, plans, and beliefs as heterogeneous as the collection of precious trash that Tom assembles as he sells off the valuable privilege of whitewashing his Aunt's fence. Those precious objects and creatures, too, are composite signs of the inner and outer lives of the individuals who cherish them.

All Saturday morning and afternoon, boy after boy, "happened along" where Tom was working and contributed his stint of time until the "far-reaching continent" of board fence was done: coating and recoating thirty yards of planks, nine feet high, with a curiously inadequate bucket and brush alone, not so much as a ladder to help a small boy cope with this tall task. The first three assistants purchase their turns with a partly eaten apple, a kite "in good repair," and a dead rat on a string:

> And when the middle of the afternoon came, from being a poor poverty-stricken boy in the morning, Tom was literally rolling in wealth. He had, beside the things before mentioned twelve marbles, part of a jewsharp, a piece of blue bottle-glass to look through, a spool cannon, a key that wouldn't unlock anything, a fragment of chalk, a glass stopper of a decanter, a tin soldier, a couple of tadpoles, six fire-crackers, a kitten with only one eye, a brass door-knob, a dog collar—but no dog—the handle of a knife, four pieces of orange peel, and a dilapidated old window sash. (TS 15)

The process of enticement that ultimately yields this hoard begins in a carefully calibrated silence, as Tom ignores Ben Rogers's steamboat performance, along with his initial smug greeting: "Hi-yi! You're up a stump, ain't you!" Seemingly distracted by the artistic demands of his job, Tom pretends not to notice the interruption, keeping silent as he "gave his brush another gentle sweep and surveyed the result." Only after this apparently thoughtful delay, and a slightly less grating remark from his friend, does Tom allow himself to react as he "wheeled suddenly" in his own version of machine-like personation and answered, "Why, it's you, Ben! I warn't noticing" (TS 13).

Contemplative delays and more thoughtful brushing interrupt the conversation that follows as Tom gradually cultivates Ben's unspoken interest in the hidden attractions of this formidable chore, "Ben watching every move and getting more and more interested, more and more absorbed" (TS 14). Twain describes this tactical success in getting others to do one's own work as a progressive "slaughter of innocents," but none of the participants in the episode are innocent victims. Certainly none of them are helpless. They are attracted to this task by an unexpected desire in their own minds, "a great law of human action," as Twain calls it, not a fixed weakness of human nature. Envy may play a part in the boys' receptivity to Tom's ploy, but it is not Twain's chief interest in the episode. A more complex mental activity is at work—an "action" rather than a vice. The intellect is capable, at a moment's notice, of converting work into play and of resenting the reverse transformation, just as easily as the boys are able to convert broken bits of rubbish into treasure and to neglect the adult economy that tries to attach a system of fixed values to colored tickets in return for memorizing Bible verses.[14]

The symbolic resonance of the debris that Tom accumulates during the whitewashing scene is more elusive than that of the Sunday school tickets, richer with indeterminate promise and completely indifferent to the strict didactic agenda of adult life. Tadpoles and firecrackers suggest the miraculous powers of transformation that are latent in their makeup and fill them with absorbing interest. A piece of blue bottle glass is a similar vehicle of transformation, capable of coloring an entire world and reinvesting familiar places with a measure of enchantment. A key that won't unlock anything seems at first to be utterly useless, though it can also conjure visions of the missing lock that it is meant to open and the hidden secrets that it protects, much as Tom tries to use a marble that he still possesses to find another that he has lost through certain magical procedures and a special incantation: "What hasn't come here, *come*! What's here, *stay* here!" (TS 65; emphases in the original). A lock-less key is part of a very similar invisible partnership.

Absence and presence prey on the minds of most of the principal characters in Twain's story. A sense of obligation to a dead sister is responsible for Aunt Polly's anguish over her efforts to raise Tom properly, but his father's fate never enters into her reflections—an omission that functions like one of the plot's conspicuous silences. Tom never concerns himself with either of his missing parents, except perhaps when he finds himself briefly tempted to worship the formidable figure of Judge Thatcher "because he was *her* parent," the father of the mysterious new girl in town, with blond pigtails, whose name he does not even know (TS 35; emphasis in the original). "Make a man," Becky Thatcher eagerly demands, after Tom first awakens her "human curiosity" by drawing a house on his schoolroom slate, working with the same calculated silence and intensity that first attracted Ben Rogers in the whitewashing exchange. But Tom's own human curiosity concerning absent men is oddly quiescent. The result of Becky's request is a disproportionately gigantic stick figure "that resembled a derrick," but Becky is pleased: "It's a beautiful man," she whispers, "now make me coming along" (TS 55). Huck Finn has vivid memories of the violent relationship between his own parents that lead him to urge Tom to reconsider his marriage plans after the boys find the buried treasure that they have set out to unearth. By contrast Tom's family memories are a vacuum that he is fitfully trying to fill, an absence that would have thrust many of Twain's post–Civil War readers into their own, grief-filled inner worlds.[15]

Other dimensions of the inner life cluster around the remaining items of Tom's whitewashing hoard. A toy cannon made from an empty spool of thread is a reminder of the male and female collaboration that pervades Twain's plot. Thread and string are of particular interest to the boys, both as the means of flying kites or swinging rats and as a way of repairing a collar that has been sewn shut to keep its wearer from going swimming rather than going to school. Both Tom and Huck keep needle and thread pinned to the underside of their lapels, though only one of the two would seem to need them. Aunt Polly uses silk thread tied to the bedpost and a "chunk" of fire to pull Tom's loose tooth, employing a mix of ingenuity and cruelty that startles the unprepared reader as much as it startles Tom when she suddenly thrusts a glowing coal into the boy's face to trigger his reflexive jerk (TS 47). A length of kite line tied to a projecting rock plays a key role in Tom's desperate efforts to find an escape from the depths of McDougal's cave, an echo of the Cretan myth but also a reminder of the devious paths that Tom navigated as he "threaded" his way through the sleeping town to avoid notice before he, Joe Harper, and Huck Finn stage their surprise resurrection at church. A similar circuitous route conducts him to the center of the dense wood behind Cardiff Hill to hide from his schoolmates and nurse his melancholy. Thread is a familiar emblem of inner pathways, the elaborate routes of thought and memory that structure the mental world.

Very few objects are simply inert "matter" in Tom Sawyer's story. Even the one-eyed kitten that he collects from one of his whitewashing friends is a reminder of the kind of acute concentration that leads Mr. B to admonish his cub pilot to "watch her like a cat," as he prepares to execute a complicated bit of steering. A kitten with a missing eye is unlikely to be an effective hunter; it will need careful watching on the part of others in order to survive, and its presence among Tom's pile of wealth is poignant for precisely that reason. A knife handle without its blade is an incitement to the imagination: a theatrical prop that can inflict no harm. A doorknob without a door, a stopper without a decanter, and a dog collar without a dog are all versions of one another, fractured partnerships that evoke a subtle blend of promise and loss. All the items that Twain lists in Tom's fantastic inventory are signs of how the boys think and feel, tokens of the queer mental enterprises with which they fill their world.[16]

By contrast the outward architecture of setting and events that lends its structure to Twain's narrative is comparatively unresponsive to the needs of the imagination and nearly oblivious to its existence. Aunt Polly's family worship service opens with a weighty and inflexible prayer "built from the ground up of solid courses of Scriptural quotations, welded together with a thin mortar of originality," an implacable pyramid supporting "a grim chapter of the Mosaic law" that brings the morning ceremony to a close. Moments later, as Tom is making a vain attempt to memorize a few verses from a more forgiving biblical source—the Sermon on the Mount—his efforts are useless not because his mind is shallow or empty but because it is preoccupied with "traversing the whole field of human thought" while his hands are "busy with distracting recreations" that are entirely independent of his control (TS 26).

A few pages before this scene, Aunt Polly's "potent palm" is only too firmly under her control when she strikes Tom to the floor as punishment for breaking a sugar bowl that his brother Sid had actually knocked off the breakfast table. Tom's quick, aggrieved complaint at this injustice momentarily silences his aunt, but she refuses to apologize "when she got her tongue again" (TS 22). Failures of the tongue—real or pretended—nearly always precede extraordinary inner disclosures in this book. After their emotional flare-up, Tom and Aunt Polly immediately descend into a reciprocal mental drama fueled by self-pity, resentment, and regret. Tom's inner experience is focused with particular intensity on the exploitation and manipulation of nonverbal "signs." Polly begins the joint process of repression and amplification by insisting that Tom "didn't get a lick amiss," when she struck her blow, since he almost certainly gets away with a great deal of unpunished mischief:

> Then her conscience reproached her, and she yearned to say something kind and loving; but she judged that this would be construed into a confession that she had been in the wrong, and discipline forbade that. So she kept silence, and went about her affairs with a troubled heart. Tom sulked in a corner and exalted his woes. He knew that in her heart his aunt was on her knees to him, and he was morosely gratified by the consciousness of it. He would hang out no signals, he would take notice of none. He knew that a yearning glance fell upon him, now and then, through a film of tears, but he refused recognition of it. He pictured himself lying sick unto death and his aunt bending over him beseeching one little forgiving word unsaid. Ah, how would she feel then? And he pictured himself brought home from the river, dead, with his curls all wet, and his poor hands still forever, and his sore heart at rest. How she would throw herself upon him, and how her tears would fall like rain, and her lips pray God to give her back her boy and she would never never abuse him any more! But he would lie there cold and white and make no sign—a poor little sufferer whose griefs were at an end. (TS 22)

Aunt Polly's conscientious mental struggle casts into sharp relief Tom's morose gratitude for the emotional power he has acquired as he weaves a cluster of sentimental clichés into a series of vindictive interior melodramas. Keeping "silence" is a far more elaborate mental activity than merely keeping silent.

As this scene suggests, Twain blends a significant measure of viciousness into Tom's nature, darkening and complicating his interior world in ways that anticipate the twisting depths of McDougal's cave. When his cousin Mary requires him to put on shoes before going to church, he complies while "snarling" with suppressed rage. An accidental dousing with the contents of a washtub, while Tom is lying on the ground beneath Becky Thatcher's window, leads him to spring up with a "curse" as he throws a rock, shattering a windowpane in his reflexive fury (TS 25). Bullying is almost as important to his whirlwind courtship of Becky Thatcher as his skill at drawing stick men and beautiful houses. When she balks at sealing their engagement with the traditional kiss, Tom "clasped her about her neck" as he pleaded his case (TS 60). Moments later, he inadvertently discloses how shallow his own commitments can be when he mentions his former good times with Amy Lawrence. The instant that he first sees Becky, the intense feelings associated with that earlier relationship evaporate without a pang, disappearing "out of his heart like a casual stranger whose visit is done" (TS 20). Amy is able to detect the change in Tom's manner during a Sunday school session, interpreting tell-tale physical indications as deftly as Tom reads the "signs" of latent homesickness in his pirate companions on Jackson's Island (TS 127). Though she never actually speaks to him, a "grain" of trouble and a "dim suspicion" color her thoughts until "a furtive glance told her worlds—and then her heart broke" (TS 34). Tom can be as indifferent to the sorrows of others as he is devoted to petting his own.[17]

Even his friendships among the boys have a strange edge to them. Very little warmth marks the first encounter between Tom and Huck Finn when the two accidentally meet, early in the book, as Tom is going to school. "Hello, Huckleberry!" Tom exclaims, using the full first name of this celebrated "juvenile pariah" much as one of the vigilant town mothers or the schoolmaster might have done: "Hello yourself, and see how you like it," Huck replies (TS 49). The childish taunt closely resembles the verbal hostilities that Tom exchanges with a nameless, citified newcomer whom he meets in the book's first chapter, after eluding Aunt Polly's disciplinary efforts:

"I can lick you!"
"I'd like to see you try it."

Well, I can do it,"
No you can't, either."
Yes I can."
"No you can't."
"I can."
"You can't"
"Can!"
"Can't!"
An uncomfortable pause. Then Tom said:
"What's your name?"
"Tisn't any of your business, maybe." (TS 6)

More is at stake in this exchange than Twain's ability to reconstruct juvenile bickering. These two wary antagonists will eventually work themselves up to a full-scale fight, "rolling and tumbling in the dirt, gripped together like cats," but for an instant, after an "uncomfortable pause," Tom makes a tentative overture that the stranger abruptly snuffs out and then, in an instant, just as abruptly reciprocates with an even more tentative "maybe" that goes virtually unnoticed as the preliminary challenges build to their predictable climax. Neither participant is able to redirect this pointless clash, though neither really wants it.

Only a few moments earlier Tom had been walking down the street with "his mouth full of harmony and his soul full of gratitude" at having mastered a new whistling technique "which he had just acquired from a negro" (TS 5). But this "liquid warble" is a nonverbal form of expression, "produced by touching the tongue to the roof of the mouth at short intervals in the midst of the music." In stark contrast to this melodic accomplishment, the short spoken intervals that lead to Tom's fight with Alfred Temple are incapable of blending outer and inner harmonies. Words seem hopelessly cut off from the most private reservoirs of feeling in two boys who do not even know one another's names before they find themselves "glowering at one another with hate." But an inarticulate manipulation of the tongue, with scarcely any practice, produces the only "strong, deep, unalloyed pleasure" of the book.

Tom's "expiring" laughter at the frantic behavior of Aunt Polly's cat, after he doses the animal with her favorite Pain-Killer, is an instance of pleasure alloyed with petty cruelty—like the suppressed laughter in church when a wandering dog accidentally sits on a pinch-bug, or the "mirth" that disrupts the end of the school's Examination Day ceremony as a desperate cat "suspended around the haunches by a string" descends from a garret scuttle and snatches the school master's wig (TS 160). A simple, uncompounded feeling of any sort is rare in this story. Even the "glad clamor" that breaks out among the picnic party in the vestibule of McDougal's cave results from the rough struggle among the picnickers to extinguish one another's candles and plunge the scene into darkness—a tangle of antagonism and delight that Twain captures in the near-oxymoron with which he describes it (TS 204). The "perceptible twinkle" in Tom's eye as he teases Aunt Polly about her passion for patent medicines implies that a sense of humor, delicately tinged with mutual affection, exists among these characters, but it remains a largely hidden dimension of their emotional lives. Despite the ambivalent start to their relationship in this book, Tom and Huck do share a genuine concern for one another's well-being, but as the two of them make their plans for tracking Injun Joe to his lair, late in the story, Tom insists on doing some of the preliminary scouting on his own because he is reluctant to be seen with the disreputable Huck in public (TS 195).

Tom himself has little understanding of, or appreciation for, the most selfless acts that he performs over the course of the narrative: rescuing Becky Thatcher from a beating when she accidentally tears the schoolmaster's anatomy book, and saving Muff Potter's life when he testifies at his murder trial. In the schoolroom scene Tom's wits are "paralyzed" when the master discovers the torn page and silently scans the students' faces "for signs of guilt" that Tom is well aware Becky is incapable of disguising. Only as Becky begins to crumble, "white with terror," under the master's scrutiny, do Tom's "dismembered faculties" generate a thought that "shot like lightning" through his brain, as he shouts out "I done it!" and prepares for the "merciless flogging" that follows (TS 152).

The process that leads him to break his "Keep mum" pledge with Huck and identify Doctor Robinson's murderer is equally instinctual and completely hidden from the reader. This act too takes place amid a "painful silence" in court, while the accused man "rocked his body softly to and fro," inarticulate with agony (TS 170). The boy's own testimony is briefly thwarted by his resurgent fear as Potter's lawyer begins to question him about his whereabouts on the night of Doctor Robinson's murder: "Tom glanced at Injun Joe's iron face and his tongue failed him. The audience listened breathless, but the words refused to come." A moment later he begins to recover "as he warmed to his subject," while the audience sat "rapt in the ghastly fascinations of the tale." Like Tom's instinctive "I done it" at school, Injun Joe's reaction to the words of this damning witness is "quick as lightning": he leaps through the courtroom window and escapes, while the spectators in turn fall victim to their own dismembered faculties. "Tom, how *could* you be so noble!" Becky exclaims, as she thanks her savior after school is over (TS 152; emphasis in the original). Even Tom can't give her an answer.

Muff Potter's speech to Tom and Huck through the grating of his cell window intensifies their guilty feelings over their initial failure to come to his defense, but they had already begun to suffer over their silence. Potter had shared his food with Huck "when there warn't enough for two." He had mended kites and fishing lines for Tom. When the two boys pay one of their visits to the town jail, the doomed man's words of gratitude amplify their misery:

> Well, boys, I done an awful thing—drunk and crazy at the time—that's the only way I account for it—and now I got to swing for it, and it's right. Right, and *best*, too I reckon—hope so, anyway. Well, we won't talk about that. I don't want to make *you* feel bad; you've befriended me. But what I want to say, is, don't *you* ever get drunk—then you won't ever get here. Stand a little furder west—so—that's it; it's a prime comfort to see faces that's friendly when a body's in such a muck of trouble,—and there don't none come here but yourn. Good friendly faces—good friendly faces. Git up on one another's backs and let me touch 'em. That's it. Shake hands—yourn'll come through the bars, but mine's too big. Little hands, and weak—but they've helped Muff Potter a power, and they'd help him more if they could. (TS 168)

This scene is memorable both for the imposed and the implied silences that it contains: for Muff Potter's unwillingness to speak and for the boys' apparent inability to do so. Despite these limitations, Potter is able to convey the mix of confusion and regret that he feels, along with a surprising measure of tenderness as he aligns his two silent visitors with the setting sun and then stacks them like circus acrobats so that he can touch their hands and faces, a gentle gesture oddly consonant with his name. It is not surprising that Tom comes to Potter's defense after this moment, but it is not a decision that Twain attempts to dramatize, any more than Muff Potter wants to talk about the murder, or the story's narrator tries to account for the long delay before the trial, or to explain Tom's strange indifference to the menace implied by Injun Joe's escape.[18]

Immediately following Potter's acquittal, Tom basks in his fame by day, "but his nights were seasons of horror" as Injun Joe haunts his dreams: "Daily Muff Potter's gratitude made Tom glad he had spoken; but nightly he wished he had sealed up his tongue" (TS 174). Rather than nurse this tension along to a dramatic climax, however, Twain simply notes its natural decay as day after day drifts by and "the weight of apprehension" lifts. Tom and Huck simply turn their attention to treasure hunting, a predictable concern, Twain observes, that breaks out at some point "in every rightly constructed boy's life" (TS 175). By contrast, plot is a superficial construct, an imposition on the ordinary operations of the mind that Twain stresses by having his two rightly constructed boys neglect their anxieties in order to follow a highly artificial script for seeking treasure beneath dead tree limbs at midnight or inside a haunted house, tactics drawn from Tom's reading in various pirate tales.[19]

Muff Potter's dutiful temperance advice for the two boys represents another form of the didactic conventions that structure the book's external world. But having delivered his temperance platitude, Potter is free to disclose a need for comfort that is more intimate, less prescriptive or formulaic, and indifferent to the apparent limitations of "little hands"—a need that will soon recoil on these temporarily liberated powers of speech, turning Potter completely inward as he rocks "softly" back and forth in court, enclosed in a wordless prison. The jail window scene reenacts some elements of the David and Goliath story that Tom invokes, much earlier in the book, during a painful Sunday school quiz about the twelve disciples (TS 36). But the reenactment replaces the comic impact of Tom's gaffe with a degree of psychological delicacy that subsists beneath verbal scripts.

Tom's concern over the sealing and unsealing of his tongue, when he testifies against Injun Joe, is a reminder of how much interest Twain takes in the complicated fabric of words and signs that his characters inhabit: the stylish unstated significance of Aunt Polly's spectacles or the prophetic meaning of an inchworm's movements when it climbs Tom's leg on Jackson's Island, the "mystic sign" of the cross deep in McDougal's cave indicating the location of buried treasure, the figurative "Lord's mark" that the widow Douglas detects in Huck's nature, or the potent energies hidden in the trash that Tom collects as he sells off whitewashing privileges. Becky Thatcher understands the emotional significance of her decision to return Tom's brass andiron knob to his school desk, just as she is able to read the unspoken signals of Tom's despair in McDougal's cave by "a certain indecision in his manner" as he tries one confusing escape route after another or by the abrupt decisiveness that he shows in blowing out Becky's candle to preserve their dwindling sources of light (TS 226).

The cave as a whole has the makings of an elaborate sign. Its upper reaches are reasonably familiar to the giddy young picnic goers who play a version of hide and seek in its passages, stopping occasionally to leave names and messages on its walls with deposits of candle smoke. But as Tom and Becky unwittingly drift deeper into the cave's recesses, they descend below the passages "frescoed" with writing: below the alphabet, in effect, that extends from the cave's A-shaped mouth to the limits of its familiar spaces. Once the two wanderers slip behind a limestone waterfall and follow a "steep natural stairway" leading to "secret depths," they become increasingly involved in a world that is beneath tongues:

> In one place they found a spacious cavern, from whose ceiling depended a multitude of shining stalactites of the length and circumference of a man's leg; they walked all about it, wondering and admiring, and presently left it by one of the numerous passages that opened into it. This shortly brought them to a bewitching spring, whose basin was encrusted with a frost work of glittering crystals; it was in the midst of a cavern whose walls were supported by many fantastic pillars which had been formed by the joining of great stalactites and stalagmites together, the result of the ceaseless water-drip of centuries. (TS 223)

None of these wonders has yet received one of the cloying, tourist names attached to the upper chambers of the cave—The Drawing Room, The Cathedral, Aladdin's Palace—nor are Tom and Becky inclined to supply them. From the point at which they smoke their own names on a portion of the cave wall and descend the hidden stone stairway, they leave the world of surface signs behind. An attack by hundreds of squeaking bats soon drives them further and further through a warren of unknown passages toward a subterranean lake "which stretched its dim length away until its shape was lost in the shadows," a final nameless discovery that Tom hopes to explore once he and Becky take a brief rest. But in a moment "the deep stillness of the place laid a clammy hand upon the spirits of the children," and they realize they are hopelessly lost.

Huck's circuitous surface journey on the night of the picnic, as he follows Injun Joe and his accomplice through the twisting alleyways of town and up Cardiff Hill toward the widow Douglas's house, replicates the underground experience that Tom and Becky undergo, converting their descent beneath tongues into a climb toward urgent speech, when Huck too will unexpectedly break his vow to keep mum in the face of a terrible crisis. Terrified by Joe's savage plan to mutilate the widow out of revenge, Huck runs for help to the nearby home of a Welshman, his wife, and his two stalwart sons: "Let me in—quick! I'll tell everything," he announces as he pounds on the Welshman's door. "Why, who are you?" is the suspicious reply: "Huckleberry Finn—quick, let me in!" (TS 209). At every point in this adventure, Huck recognizes familiar landmarks: the path from the town's side streets up Cardiff Hill, the old Welshman's house, the abandoned quarry where Huck expects Injun Joe to bury his loot. The names reflect a local and accessible geography, rather than the cave's fantastic one, tied together by a single threaded path. Even in the complete darkness of a sumac thicket, where Huck overhears Joe's plot, he "knew where he was" (TS 207).

Familiar though it may be, however, the upper world too is marked by terrible silence, "a thing still more awful than any amount of murderous talk" (TS 208). Like Tom and Becky in the cave's depths, Huck suffers from the clammy hand of fear, as he tries desperately to keep still in the thicket while "shaking as if a dozen agues had taken charge of him." But unlike McDougal's cave, Huck's surroundings are meticulously mapped and navigable, allowing him to turn in his tracks "as carefully as if he were a ship" and run for help. By contrast, the ominous stillness that envelops Tom and Becky answers their feeble cries with hideous echoes and a "ripple" of mocking laughter. "It's all a mixed-up crookedness to me," Tom confesses, as he realizes that he cannot retrace their downward route with the same confidence that Huck displays when he retraces his upward one. This careful interweaving of antagonistic mental states is the most ambitious of Twain's composite goals: a fictional projection of the levels of awareness that every steamboat pilot must master to survive.[20]

* * *

Like *The Adventures of Tom Sawyer*, both *The Innocents Abroad* and *Roughing It* explore the relationship between subterranean and surface worlds. The elaborate crypt of Bishop Borroméo in Milan or the gruesome skeletal exhibits that Twain encounters in the Capuchin Convent in Rome probe psychological interiors that are structured as macabre displays: religious tableaus that falsify rather than illuminate human feeling. The eerie reminiscences of a Capuchin guide, amid the frescos of bone that decorate the convent vault, strike Twain as "grotesque" performances: "I hardly knew whether to smile or shudder" (IA 220). Like Bishop Borroméo's jeweled robes, the honeycomb of mine shafts beneath Virginia City in *Roughing It* is both costly and impoverished, despite the riches that the Comstock Lode contains. Having seen the mines once, Twain writes, and marveled at their elaborate engineering, one never has to visit a second time. They are purely material places.

McDougal's cave is a hybrid form of these preliminary underworld journeys, a provocative mixture of the sordid and the sublime that Twain captures in the hybrid nature of Injun Joe's treasure, hidden "under the cross" in a chamber of the cave not far from where Tom and Becky expect to die. This hoard is an improbable blend of the "swag" that the robbers have accumulated from their career of crime and a mysterious fortune in buried gold that virtually erupts, with a minimum of human assistance, through the dirt floor of the old haunted house where Tom and Huck have gone in search of pirate loot. As the two boys silently watch through holes in the ceiling above, Injun Joe and his accomplice mingle this miraculous windfall with their own bag of silver dollars, much as Oliver Wendell Holmes had insisted that all writers mingle the golden legacy of verbal life with the meager riches of their own imaginations.

The second novel that Twain completes brings a special degree of intensity to bear on the pervasive mental entanglement that Holmes had described. As early as November 1877, a little over a year after the publication of *The Adventures of Tom Sawyer*, Twain had begun to adapt a legend set in sixteenth-century England in order to explore the imaginative amalgamation that Injun Joe's treasure evokes.[21] Like its predecessor, *The Prince and the Pauper* revolves around the interchange between an upper and an underworld, but this second version of the story, from its outset, links the two worlds closely together, both in the minds of its key characters and in the urban setting where the plot unfolds. London becomes a spatial and corporeal labyrinth in Twain's historical romance: both an intricate configuration of narrow, dirty streets like the mineshafts of the Comstock Lode and a network of quasi-intestinal passageways leading to Offal Court, the "foul little pocket" of crowded tenements where the pauper, Tom Canty, and his family live.

A voracious human "swarm" animates both the lower world of the Canty family and the upper world of the English court, where the Prince of Wales has been raised. Each of these communities is engrossed by its own forms of superficial display, but each also harbors a surprising measure of interest in the operations of the mind. The title characters in *The Prince and the Pauper* spend the bulk of the story coping with the imputation of madness and, in the case of Prince Edward, colliding with genuine instances of insanity as he makes his way through an alien social landscape after he and Tom switch clothes and places in life. Tom Canty's struggles are more profound than those of his royal twin, however, since Edward's mental assurance never wavers, while Tom must cope with a more complicated entanglement of interior and exterior demands, imposed by England's collective hunger for a successor to Henry VIII.

With the help of a friendly old priest whom Henry's religious policies had displaced from his parish and thrust into the Canty's urban underworld, Tom learns to understand a smattering of Latin and to read English books. With these tools, and in spite of his degraded surroundings, he schools himself in a potent set of chivalric delusions even before he wanders aimlessly toward Westminster Palace and his first fateful glimpse of an actual prince. Tom's fantasies have partly blinded him to the nature of the outer world, partly intensified the sufferings of poverty, and partly equipped him with a specialized, literary language—a kind of foreign tongue— that gradually earns him the admiration of his childish companions in Offal Court (PP 8). Many of the adults, as well as the children, "brought their perplexities to Tom" as a mediator of their petty disputes. He is both uniquely adapted to and irreversibly alienated from the impoverished swarm amid which he lives, a role that partly anticipates the precocious innocence of Number 44 in the Mysterious Stranger tales, though Tom's mental aptitudes fall far short of Number 44's complex powers.[22]

These mental qualities might well seem to be ideal equipment for accelerating Tom's adaptation to the predicament in which he finds himself when Prince Edward's impetuous blindness to the consequences of a temporary exchange of clothes gets him expelled from the palace grounds and swallowed up by a jeering crowd outside its gates. "Be off, thou crazy rubbish," the royal guard says as he drives the unrecognizable prince deep into the world of madness and filth where he appears to belong (PP 20). The Princess Elizabeth, Lady Jane Grey, and the other members of the Tudor court are far more solicitous in their treatment of Tom, partly because of his royal costume but partly too because he has already pictured this world to himself, in his Offal Court fantasies, and has some glimmering idea of how to cope with its demands. By contrast, the mocking laughter of the mob, as it effectively swallows the real prince, echoes the inhuman noises that terrify Tom and Becky in McDougal's cave.

The crowd outside Westminster Palace makes use of Prince Edward as a source of entertainment, taunting their victim into explosions of royal outrage "that were good stuff to laugh at," until they abandon him at last, deep in the city, when exhaustion forces him to be silent (PP 20). This subterranean initiation parallels, in many respects, the elaborate court rituals that Twain partly mocks and partly celebrates as he describes Tom Canty's gradual lapse into a receptive silence while he adjusts to his bewildering role. The London mob both creates and consumes the great royal festivals staged for its benefit, circulating their own ceremonial loving cup during the Lord Mayor's Guildhall feast and watching "with deep interest" throughout the night as workmen prepare Westminster Abbey for a climactic coronation ceremony. Despite falling outside the circles of court power and influence, they possess a behind-the-scenes familiarity with the apparatus of royal pomp that solicits their interest rather than their scorn. Twain underscores this subtle interplay of perspectives by telling part of the story in the voice of an anonymous "chronicler" who relishes the court's pageantry, in collaboration with a far more confidential narrator whose language is partly tinged with sixteenth-century diction and partly not. This second voice is a self-conscious manipulator of tenses and times whose presence echoes the outside/inside features of Twain's tale.[23]

As these observations imply, tongues have a carefully intertwined part to play in this narrative too. Despite Edward's weary but ultimately politic silence, as the taunting crowd deserts him, he is seldom able to keep mum throughout the book—provoking one group of impoverished citizens after another with his inexplicable behavior, even after the astute and generous Miles Hendon takes him under his wing and repeatedly cautions him to be silent. He is partly fluent in the language of his people and partly not, as an indecipherable song sung in "thieves' dialect" makes plain both to Twain's reader and to the puzzled ears of the young king:

"Bien Darkmans then, Bouse Mort and Ken,
The bien Coves bings awast,
On Chates to trine by Rome Coves dine,
For his long lib at last.
Bing'd out bien Morts and toure, and toure,
Bing out of the Rome vile bine,
And toure the Cove that cloy'd your duds,
Upon the Chates to trine." (PP 147)

Tom Canty's haphazard reading in chivalric romances has better prepared him to bridge the verbal gap between the two worlds he encounters, but this bridge too is imperfect at best: a kind of psychological holding zone much like the self-contained community of London Bridge that Twain briefly introduces into the story. The paradoxical blend of cosmopolitan and provincial life that unfolds among the bridge's denizens ties together, without really joining, the world of royal display north of the Thames with the unruly village and forest existence south of the river. It is an architectural cognate to the thieves' dialect that is designed to tantalize and to thwart unfriendly listeners.[24]

The river itself is an incomparable theater in *The Prince and the Pauper*, a composite scene that recalls the extraordinary vitality of the New Orleans wharf that Twain celebrated in the final magazine installments of "Old Times on the Mississippi." It reflects a curious seasonal composite as well. The events that

Twain recounts in *The Prince and the Pauper* revolve around the death of Henry VIII on January 28, 1547, a time of year that makes Prince Edward's "tanned and brown" appearance when Tom Canty first sees him a strangely incommensurate holdover from Tom Sawyer's momentous summer, bridging without really linking these antithetical worlds (PP 13). The Thames in turn is still another bridge: a staging zone for public energies that dwarf the eruption produced by the arrival of the daily steamboat in Hannibal. Among the earliest of Tom Canty's ordeals as he attempts to impersonate the Prince of Wales is a dinner hosted by the Lord Mayor of London, a ceremonial obligation that entails the first of the story's two floating pageants. When the royal party emerges from the palace to begin its trip to the city, the flotilla of boats gathered to accompany them down the Thames resembles "a glowing and limitless garden of flowers stirred to soft motion by summer winds" (PP 62). The stone terrace leading to the river is covered with soldiers and servants preparing to send off "forty or fifty state barges" filled with the prince's richly costumed entourage. As this "gorgeous fleet" draws near its destination in Barge Yard, "the centre of the ancient city of London," the hoarse cheers from the crowded bank and the boom of celebratory artillery suggest the festival atmosphere of a Mississippi steamboat race that Twain had described in the last of his *Atlantic* sketches. "Racing," he recalled in those pages, "was royal fun."[25]

Tom Canty is not having much fun at this point in his adventure. After the prince's inexplicable disappearance he had found himself undergoing the first of several psychological tests that help sharpen the inward turn of the book. A frantic attempt to identify himself to Lady Jane Grey as "poor Tom Canty of Offal Court" only terrifies the girl, immediately triggering a rumor that the Prince of Wales is mad (PP 29). The news reaches the king with stunning speed, almost as if the palace were a single unified consciousness rather than a conglomerate of courtiers and servants, immediately prompting a royal command to repress "this false and foolish matter" even before Tom is brought into the king's presence. Henry VIII on the final day of his life is a grotesque figure, as Tom first sees him: "a very large and very fat man, with a wide, pulpy face, and a stern expression," one swollen leg wrapped in bandages and propped on a pillow as he reclines on a couch surrounded by silent and deferential attendants. But this formidable invalid turns unexpectedly gentle as Tom approaches, learns his identity, and collapses in fear. "Come to thy father, child," the king gently says, "thou art not well":

> Tom was assisted to his feet, and approached the majesty of England, humble and trembling. The king took the frightened face between his hands, and gazed earnestly and lovingly into it a while, as if seeking some grateful sign of returning reason there, then pressed the curly head against his breast and patted it tenderly. Presently he said—
> "Dost not know thy father, child? Break not mine old heart—say thou knowst me. Thou dost know me, dost thou not?"
> "Yea, thou art my dread lord the king, whom God preserve!"
> "True, true—that is well—be comforted, tremble not so; there is none here would hurt thee; there is none here but loves thee. Thou art better, now; thy ill dream passeth—is't not so? And thou knowest thyself now, also—is't not so? Thou wilt not miscall thyself again, as they say thou didst a little while agone?" (PP 33)

This is not the sort of behavior that Prince Edward had led Tom to expect from the irascible king when the two boys were first getting acquainted in the prince's cabinet. "Fathers be alike, mayhap," Edward had observed after hearing Tom describe the daily beatings he received at home. "Mine hath not a doll's temper," the prince continues, "He smiteth with a heavy hand, yet spareth me; he spareth me not always with his tongue though" (PP 16). As Henry patiently reassures Tom that he is in no danger, the king's tongue seems quite different from the punitive instrument that Edward had described, an echo of the tentative and reflective voice of Muff Potter in the St. Petersburg jail.

In a few moments an acquaintance with foreign tongues becomes the means that Henry chooses to test the depth of Tom's delusion:

> The king was silent and thoughtful a while, and his face betrayed a growing distress and uneasiness. Presently he said, with something of hope in his voice—
> "Perchance he is but mad upon this one strain, and hath his wits unmarred as toucheth other matters. God send it may be so! We will make trial."

Then he asked Tom a question in Latin, and Tom answered him lamely in the same tongue. The king was delighted, and showed it. The lords and doctors manifested their gratification also. The king said—

"Twas not according to his schooling and ability, but sheweth that his mind is but diseased, not stricken fatally. How say you sir?"

The physician addressed bowed low and replied—

"It jumpeth with mine own conviction, sire, that thou hast divined aright."

The king looked pleased with this encouragement, coming as it did from so excellent authority, and continued with good heart—

"Now mark ye all—we will try him further."

He put a question to Tom in French. Tom stood silent a moment, embarrassed by having so many eyes centred upon him, then said, diffidently—

"I have no knowledge of this tongue, so please your majesty." (PP 34–5)

This puzzling result is a blow to the king's hopes, but he prescribes rest and sports to restore his son's health, and terrifies the surrounding members of his court by declaring, as "baleful lightnings" flicker in his eyes, that Edward will succeed him, "mad or sane," and anyone who speaks of the prince's illness will hang. The Duke of Norfolk's imminent execution, however, dismays Tom so deeply when he hears of it that Henry's kinder instincts briefly reemerge: "I know thy heart is still the same, even though thy mind hath suffered hurt," Henry tells the boy, "for thou wert ever of a gentle spirit" (PP 37).

Making "trial" as the king does in this scene is a recurring feature of Twain's story, a tactic resorted to by an intriguing variety of characters to assess the inner lives of others. The two great noblemen whom Henry assigns as temporary caretakers for his seemingly mad son, St. John and Hertford, are both confused by the strange blend of tangible similarities and intangible differences in the makeup of their young prince before and after the onset of what they consider his mysterious disease, but the fear of even listening to treasonous suspicions paralyzes them. By contrast Tom Canty's mother is not at all deterred from testing her misgivings about the identity of the boy whom her husband has dragged back to their tenement, enraged by his stubborn insistence that he is the Prince of

Wales. An "undefinable something" in the child's manner troubles her. Three times in the middle of the night Goodwife Canty tries to elicit from the sleeping prince a startle reflex unique to her son, but with no success. "O, this is a heavy day for me!" she concludes, echoing the king's heavy sigh when he first confronts the terrified Tom Canty in Westminster Palace (PP 71). Neither parent is emotionally willing to relinquish a claim to either troubled boy, but both appeal to ingenious diagnostic trials to probe the condition of their minds.[26]

Miles Hendon initially decides to humor the "diseased ravings" of the mad beggar who believes himself to be Prince Edward, not out of a desire to cure him but simply because the act of saving the boy from another jeering mob outside the Guildhall dinner has already awakened Hendon's affection—a psychological propensity that August Feldner too will experience when he rescues Number 44 from the persecutions of Heinrich Stein's printers. In the process of tending to his new charge, however, Hendon also makes an accidental trial of the boy's mental state when he discovers that the mad "prince" is inexplicably able to incorporate the news of Henry VIII's death into his delusion by insisting that he is now the new king. Hendon is surprised that a mind so completely absorbed in an inner world could remain so alert to changes in the outer one and so quick to assimilate them (PP 93). During Edward's subsequent wanderings among the villages south of the Thames, he meets a farmer's widow who contrives "devices" aimed at assessing the interests of her "demented" visitor, closely observing the ebb and flow of his attention in order to determine whose runaway servant he might be. Like Henry VIII she is a deft inventor of trials.

Back at court, the Princess Elizabeth tactfully thwarts Lady Jane Grey's repeated efforts to probe Tom Canty's nonexistent knowledge of Greek. Tom himself will eventually apply his own array of mental tests to others when he interrupts the proceedings of a shouting mob outside the palace windows, who are helping the city sheriff convey a group of prisoners to execution. A mix of boyish curiosity, innate sympathy, and common sense, gradually leads Tom to overcome his ingrained reverence for authority and his superstitious fears as he frees a man who had been condemned to be boiled to death in punishment for poisoning a neighbor and a woman condemned to hang for witchcraft. Upon learning that the accused witch is able to raise terrible storms simply by pulling off her stockings, Tom's curiosity completely overwhelms his dread of the dark arts and reaches "fever heat": "Exert thy power," he cries enthusiastically to the friendless woman, "I would see a storm" (PP 133). When this trial yields the same outcome as King Henry's French test, Tom frees the woman and her nine-year-old daughter: "There, good soul, trouble thyself no further, thy power is departed out of thee. Go thy way in peace; and if it return to thee at any time, forget me not, but fetch me a storm" (PP 134). The assembled courtiers quietly delight in these signs of the prince's returning "mental health."

At this point in the story, Twain's narrator observes, Tom Canty is still an "ash cat" making a slow but steady adjustment to his strange environment: "A child's facility in accommodating itself to circumstances was never more strikingly illustrated" (PP 135). Equally striking is the extent to which *The Prince and the Pauper* has taken on the attributes of a clinical study, stressing at some length the psychological acuity of its characters, regardless of their place in England's social hierarchy. This inward focus reaches its peak during the book's crucial scene in Westminster Abbey, when Tom brings his fully matured skills to bear in order to rescue the true king from the punitive zeal of the rest of the Tudor court who have assembled, along with a church full of lesser citizens, to see Edward VI crowned. The true king marches down the center aisle of the Abbey to interrupt the coronation, just as Tom, Huck, and Joe had marched triumphantly into church to interrupt the minister's eulogy at their funeral service. Unlike the magically resurrected boys, however, Edward has to prove his identity to the satisfaction of the Lord Protector or risk a public whipping.

The members of the court in particular are in a panic at Edward's startling performance, their "tangled minds" completely overwhelmed by the regal bearing of this mysterious beggar and the instantaneous deference with which the boy whom they had come to regard as their new king welcomes the intruder (PP 268). Edward's seemingly uncanny ability to answer correctly all the questions about court life that the Lord Protector poses—his mastery of all outward "trials"—fails to convince the nobles that he is who he claims to be. Only the recovery of the Great Seal of England, missing since Henry's death, will save Edward from a beating, a test that nearly proves his undoing. On the day the two boys had exchanged clothes in the prince's cabinet, Edward had hastily hidden the Seal in an unusual spot rather than replacing it in the secret "jewel-closet" where it belonged. Tom Canty had long ago discovered the seal but didn't grasp its use or importance until he realizes that Edward must be coaxed into remembering its hiding place, in the presence of the assembled court, in order to rescue them both from their respective predicaments. Edward can easily pinpoint the location of the jewel-closet, and explain how to open it, but when the lord St. John goes to retrieve the Seal, it isn't there—a weird outcome that only deepens the general perplexity at the same time that it sharpens the distinction between outer display and inner essence underlying the entire story. Even a secret jewel-closet is an article of costume rather than an emblem of interior riches or of character.

Only Tom's desperate determination, and his patience with Edward's balky memory, prevents a disaster: "List to what I say," he urges the true king, as the two of them stand on the coronation platform, surrounded by a suspenseful entourage of courtiers: "follow every word—I am going to bring that morning back again, every hap just as it happened" (PP 273). Step by step Tom reconstructs the scene that took place at the beginning of the book, until Edward's mind is able to "focalize" itself, much as Twain's did when he finally grasped the circumstances that led to his adaptation of Oliver Wendell Holmes's dedication for his own use in *The Innocents Abroad*:

> "For a jest, my prince, we did exchange garments. Then we stood before a mirror; and so alike were we that both said it seemed as if there had been no change made—yes, you remember that. Then you noticed that the soldier had hurt my hand—look! here it is, I cannot yet even write with it, the fingers are so stiff. At this your highness sprang up, vowing vengeance upon that soldier, and ran toward the door—you passed a table—that thing you call the Seal lay on that table—you snatched it up and looked eagerly about, as if for a place to hide it—your eye caught sight of—"
>
> "There, 'tis sufficient!—and the dear God be thanked!" exclaimed the ragged claimant, in a mighty excitement. "Go, my good St. John,—in an armpiece of the Milanese armor that hangs on the wall thou'lt find the Seal!"

In the moments preceding this realization, the court remained torn by "uneasiness, apprehension, and consuming excitement." At one point Edward's startling assurance and Tom's fierce conviction produce an effect that Twain's narrator compares to a slowly turning kaleidoscope, as the richly dressed courtiers gradually tumble into realignment surrounding Edward, leaving Tom "wholly alone and isolated from the world, a conspicuous figure, occupying an eloquent vacancy" (PP 271). The vacuum quickly refills, however, when the jewel-closet too proves vacant. At first Edward's mind is similarly empty and full as he searches "among a thronging multitude of valueless recollections for one single little elusive fact" to prove his identity. "Follow me still," Tom quickly reassures him: "you shall recall everything" (PP 273). Through his own series of valueless recollections, Tom rebuilds Edward's memory chamber—a final mental trial in the series of introspective spectacles that shape Twain's story.[27]

* * *

In *A Tramp Abroad*, Twain sets aside the incomplete manuscripts of two novels—*The Prince and the Pauper* and the *Adventures of Huckleberry Finn*—in order to write a book about the natural and cultural resources of Europe that he and his family encountered during a sixteen-month-long excursion in which Twain sought to distance himself from a number of professional frustrations in the United States. Between April 1878 and the end of August 1879, the Clemens family along with a handful of servants, guides, and companions lived in half a dozen different cities on the continent and in England, while Twain sorted through the layers of his emotional life, exploring the boundaries between outer and inner experience that had seized his attention as he dramatized the complex skill of piloting, the composite being of Tom Sawyer, and began thinking about the trials of Tom Canty.[28]

For a little over a month in the late summer of 1878, Twain's Hartford friend, Joseph Twichell, joined him for a walking tour of the Black Forest and the Alps, a slender narrative pretext for the book that Twain hoped would repeat the commercial success of *The Innocents Abroad* and help put behind him the memory of his Whittier birthday speech. But the *Quaker City* tour or the flush times in Nevada and California had each provided a much firmer scaffolding for the anecdotal performances of Twain's two previous travel books. To fulfill his contract for *A Tramp Abroad*, inward rather than outward movement would have to replace the structural matrix that geographical extension had supplied for the earlier narratives.[29] A sleepless night in a German inn provides a dramatic illustration of this commitment to introspective form.

Twain and his fictional walking companion, Mr. Harris, paid a memorable visit to the town of Heilbronn during the early stages of their tour. After admiring the town's ornate municipal clock, viewing the engraved tablets and rude effigies in the local church, collecting legends at a nearby castle, and examining the grooves that generations of barefoot children had worn in the stone pavement beneath a chain-link swing, the two adventurers returned to their inn room for dinner. It was an "immense" and garish space, Twain writes, with two narrow beds at opposite ends and a round table "as large as King Arthur's" in the center—a kind of clock dial echoing the various measuring devices that fill this visit, including the pedometers that Twain and Harris intend to use to keep track of their progress (TA 65). This curious room soon proves to be the setting for an elaborate exercise in psychic measurement that Twain conducts throughout the disorienting night that follows.

After their strenuous day of sightseeing, Harris quickly falls asleep, but Twain "hangs fire," his restless thoughts racing through "the beginning of every subject which has ever been thought of" without pausing for a moment's focus: "At the end of an hour my head was in a perfect whirl and I was dead tired, fagged out." An extraordinary interior spectacle promptly follows. Over several painstaking pages Twain's "brain-territory" becomes the site of an erratic mental tour among various states of semiconsciousness, ending at the threshold of a "dreamless stupor" that is suddenly shattered by an indefinable noise:

> My dulled faculties dragged themselves partly back to life and took a receptive attitude. Now out of an immense, a limitless distance, came a something which grew and grew, and approached, and presently was recognizable as a sound,—it had rather seemed to be a feeling, before. This sound was a mile away now—perhaps it was the murmur of a storm; and now it was nearer,—not a quarter of a mile away; was it the muffled rasping and grinding of distant machinery? No, it came still nearer; was

it the measured tramp of a marching troop? But it came nearer still, and still nearer—and at last it was right in the room: it was merely a mouse gnawing the wood-work. (TA 72)

This mysterious and expansive "something," half outward sensation and half inward feeling, ultimately shrinks from a distant storm or a marching army into a mouse as restless as Twain himself. In his newly receptive attitude, he begins "unconsciously counting" the sounds the mouse makes, deriving "exquisite suffering" as his unnaturally acute hearing seems responsive to the slightest noise. In an effort to silence the creature, Twain hurls his shoes "at random" in the complete darkness, wakens Harris twice, shatters a mirror, and eventually devotes what seems like hours, in a "venomous access of irritation," trying to locate his clothes and dress in the dark in the hope of taking a walk to settle his nerves.

Eventually his blundering efforts to avoid the room's furniture disturb all the inhabitants of the inn. When the landlord, the chambermaid, and the other guests appear at opposite doors, holding candles, Twain discovers that he has confused a single chair with a long inventory of nonexistent obstacles, "revolving around it like a planet, and colliding with it like a comet half the night," as he searched for his clothes, and all the while covering a distance of forty-seven miles according to his pedometer (TA 76). This ludicrous detail pits a spurious objectivity against the tempestuous subjective events of Twain's sleepless night: a series of vivid delusions that his pages chart in meticulous detail. The book's outward walking tour may be largely facetious, but its inward one is capable of compressing a considerable mental landscape into a tightly circumscribed space, responding with extravagant outbursts of energy to the tantalizing vacuity with which it sometimes finds itself surrounded.[30]

The "true charm of pedestrianism," Twain ultimately confesses, as he and Harris eventually set out to explore the Black Forest, is the welcome occasion that it offers for aimless conversation, inviting an unhurried intimacy with the tourist's interior scenery. "The walking is good to time the movement of the tongue by," Twain writes, a comparison that converts the body into a kind of cognitive pedometer: a cleverly engineered instrument for keeping "the blood and the brain stirred up and active," absorbed in the random stream of impressions that movement elicits (TA 146). Woodsy smells, lovely summer weather, and fresh air are a welcome sensory background to this interior ramble, but they are "unconscious and unobtrusive" auxiliaries, much like the extraneous data that the steamboat pilot learns to screen away from the central focus of his attention. The "supreme pleasure" of a walking tour "comes from the talk":

> And what a motley variety of subjects a couple of people will casually rake over in the course of a day's tramp! There being no constraint, a change of subject is always in order, and so a body is not likely to keep pegging at a single topic until it grows tiresome. We discussed everything we knew, during the first fifteen or twenty minutes, that morning, and then branched out into the glad, free, boundless realm of the things we were not certain about. (TA 146)

Both men relish the feeling of "entire emancipation" that they experience, including emancipation from the mind's tedious certainties.

Pegging at single topics, however, soon proves to be the defining preoccupation of Black Forest life. In stark contrast to the fairytale wonders that Twain and Harris had half expected to experience in this legendary place, they encounter an actual population of farmers and villagers who advertise their station in life by the formidable piles of manure that they display around their houses, an "Alpine pomp" of fertilizer that Twain treats as a ponderous index to the ordinary imagination's earthy limitations (TA 138). "What is man, without manure?" he wonders in the facetious sketch for a Black Forest novel that summarizes his disappointment, casting the title of Old Man's Socratic dialogue as a scatological joke. Twain had already begun to draft portions of *What Is Man?* shortly before leaving on his European tramp. Within a few months of his return to America, he would test some of its doctrines during meetings of the Monday Evening Club, a Hartford reading group that included Harris's real-life precursor, Joseph Twichell, among its members.[31] The disorienting night in the Heilbronn inn is one sign of Twain's growing interest in the volatile states of consciousness that Old Man will associate with the behavior of an Interior Master who, like Twain and Harris, relishes boundless rather than bounded mental realms.

Throughout their Black Forest stroll, Harris and Twain gradually grow indifferent to the distinction between "wisdom or nonsense" and more keenly in tune with a "sober truth" that Twain announces in one of the book's appendixes: that man is "a most ridiculous mixture" (TA 394). Under the hypnotic influence of their stride, they find themselves dwelling on the overrated intellect of ants, on grammar and dentistry, on doctors, death, and skeletons, until the last topic unexpectedly "resurrects" Nicodemus Dodge from "the deep grave of my memory" (TA 148). This ungainly figure, a "countrified cub of sixteen" wearing a faded slouch hat and a pair of "mighty brogans," appeared one day in the Missouri printing office where Twain was working and asked to see the "boss" in the hope of getting a job. After a brief interview, the editor in charge concludes that Nicodemus is a particularly intriguing variation on the ridiculous mixtures of man: a surprisingly complex human mechanism who has come to town to learn a trade now that his father—"the pizenest kind of a Free-will Babtis'"—can no longer afford to "run" him. "I'm strong and hearty," Nicodemus declares, "and I don't turn my back on no kind of work, hard nur soft," a brief but engaging self-portrait that suggests a measure of appreciation for the mental challenges of "soft" work that his mighty brogans would seem to belie. "We'll give you a trial," the editor announces, despite the bemused resentment that Twain and the other office apprentices clearly feel for this seemingly awkward interloper.

Their initial smugness quickly gives way to a belief among the village "smarties" that Nicodemus is bound to be an ideal butt for practical jokes. When the newcomer proves impervious to persecution, however, and surprisingly adept at retaliating against his persecutors, the town's young doctor proposes to scare him to death by putting a medical display skeleton into his bed. This plot too misfires. The intended victim simply sells the expensive office exhibit to a "traveling quack" for three dollars and purchases a hoard of treats that he enjoys in the abandoned smokehouse behind the print shop where he lives: "a new jewsharp, a new top, a solid india-rubber ball, a handful of painted marbles, five pounds of 'store' candy, and a well-gnawed slab of gingerbread as big and thick as a volume of sheet music" (TA 151). When the conspirators sneak up to the smokehouse window at midnight to observe the results of their final joke, they find Nicodemus sitting on his bed in a nightshirt with these homely treasures by his side, humming

"Camptown Races" through a mouth-comb. The village smarties in this episode play the role of the quizzical Pharisee for whom Nicodemus's pious father had named him, stalking this resilient stranger by night only to encounter the provocative riddle of his formidable innocence.

One of the earliest of the vignettes that Twain inserts into *A Tramp Abroad*, Jim Baker's "perfectly true fact" about the behavior of some California blue jays, underscores the book's focus on the kind of psychological resources that Nicodemus Dodge displays.[32] Baker, a "middle-aged, simple-hearted miner" like some of the most memorable figures in *Roughing It*, was sitting in front of his mountain cabin one Sunday morning, "thinking of the home away yonder in the States that I hadn't heard from in thirteen years," when he noticed a blue jay studying a knot-hole in the roof of an abandoned cabin nearby. "I'm of the opinion it's a totally new kind of hole," this ambitious bird announces to himself, as he prepares to fill two complementary cavities at once: Jim Baker's profound loneliness and the deserted dwelling of his last human companion, another miner who had left the mountains seven years earlier.

Dropping acorn after acorn into the empty cabin, without the slightest sign of progress, ultimately drives the jay into an emotional frenzy, "walking up and down the comb of the roof and shaking his head and muttering to himself," anticipating Twain's "venomous access of irritation," in the Heilbronn inn. "I never see a bird take on so about a little thing," Jim Baker recalls (TA 16). Eventually the jay's fruitless efforts leave him "pale with rage," leaning against the cabin chimney and emitting a stream of profanity "to free his mind" from frustration. The noise attracts a flock of his companions. "There must have been five thousand of them," Jim Baker guesses, enough birds to give a "blue flush" to the region, all disputing over the nature of the insatiable hole. Finally one old jay happens to glance through the cabin door, solves the mystery of the disappearing acorns, and announces "the whole absurdity of the contract" to the entire flock: "Well, sir," Baker concludes, "they roosted around here on the house-top and the trees for an hour, and guffawed over that thing like human beings" (TA 17). In time birds from throughout the United States turn the cabin into a tourist attraction, much like the Alpine peaks from which Twain and Harris will survey "the empty universe" as their walking tour unfolds (TA 195). Like Jim Baker and his ambitious jay, they too will find ways to fill the emptiness with their own imaginative abundance. The tale that the old miner tells is, in effect, a miniaturized version of *A Tramp Abroad* as a whole: a form of vacancy, like Twain's immense room at Heilbronn, that awakens the limitless mechanism of the mind.

This realization lies at the heart of Jim Baker's conviction that he can understand the language of animals. Mental energy is crucial both to human and to blue jay nature. "There's more *to* a blue jay," the old miner insists, "than any other creature":

> He has got more moods, and more different kinds of feelings than other creatures; and mind you, whatever a blue-jay feels, he can put into language. And no mere commonplace language, either, but rattling, out-and-out book-talk—and bristling with metaphor, too—just bristling! And as for command of language— why you never see a blue-jay get stuck for a word. No man ever did. They just boil out of him ... A jay's gifts, and instincts, and feelings, and interests, cover the whole ground. A jay hasn't got any more principle than a Congressman. A jay will lie, a jay will steal, a jay will deceive, a jay will betray; and four times out of five, a jay will go back on his solemnest promise ... Yes, sir, a jay is everything that a man is. A jay can cry, a jay can laugh, a jay can feel shame, a jay can reason and plan and discuss, a jay likes gossip and scandal, a jay has got a sense of humor, a jay knows when he is an ass just as well you do—maybe better. If a jay ain't human, he better take in his sign, that's all. (TA 13–14)

This tribute to animal intelligence, like the cabin-filling episode that follows, is a key to the introspective orientation of the entire book. The definitive human "sign" in Twain's narrative is the overflow of inward experience into outward display: the eruption of instincts, feelings, and interests, in all their ridiculous inconsistency, that repeatedly breaks through the superficial veneer of Twain's European walking tour.

A young American student Twain encounters in Baden-Baden is another species of human "gem" for just this reason. Cholly Adams, from western New York, had spent two years in Germany, supported by his father, learning to be a "horse-doctor," but when he overhears Twain, Harris, and another American acquaintance speaking his native dialect, he can't resist the chance to pour out his delights and frustrations. The result is a "surf-beat" of slang and profanity that completely engulfs Twain and his friends, who stifle their own powers of speech in order to accommodate the young man's desperate need for release. The relentless German instructional system, and two years of immersion in foreign languages in order to pursue his studies, had driven him to distraction: "Here you've got to peg and peg and peg and there just ain't any let-up," Cholly complains, in his heavily censored outburst, "and what you learn here, you've got to *know*, dontchuknow,—or else you'll have one of these ---------- spavined, spectacled, ring-boned, knock-kneed old professors in your hair.... I'm getting blessed tired of it, mind I *tell* you" (TA 127; emphases in the original). Like the rejuvenating laughter of Jim Baker's blue jays, the familiar "clack" of American speech briefly frees Cholly Adams from what he considers the mindless absurdity of his life.

What one knows, as Twain and Harris had discovered during their Black Forest ramble, can be exhausted in fifteen or twenty minutes of dutiful conversation. The glad, free, boundless realm of uncertainty—an inner landscape of unfettered possibility—yields an inexhaustible surf-beat of words. Like Cholly Adams, Twain and Harris too had come to Europe to study. The nominal motive behind their trip had included both a spurious walking tour and painting lessons, which they had begun during their protracted stay in Heidelberg. In order to gauge his artistic progress, Twain decides to display his first ambitious oil canvas anonymously in the Heidelberg city Art Exhibition. The "marked individuality" of this work, "Heidelberg Castle Illuminated," draws spectators "as by a lodestone," Twain proudly reports, when they mistake its chaotic incompetence for a Turner (TA 60). As *A Tramp Abroad* unfolds, a mix of earnest and facetious aesthetic verdicts offers Twain still another point of access to the introspective sphere of experience— one that he had already begun to exploit in vivid expressionistic descriptions of the "luminous spray" of afternoon sunlight striking Heidelberg Castle or the "intricate cobweb" of the city's gas-lit streets and bridges flinging "lances of light" into the deep shadows of the Neckar River (TA 10).

Turner's work, Twain subsequently admits, used to enrage him (TA 158). Now that he has begun painting on his own, however, John Ruskin's *Modern Painters* has taught him to see Turner's famous "Slave Ship" in a different light. Indeed (Twain continues) Ruskin's "rigid cultivation" allowed the seasoned critic "to find truth in a lie" as he gazed at Turner's canvas, a lesson that Twain too now claims to have absorbed. Formerly he had delighted in a review by a Boston reporter who compared Turner's "fierce conflagration of reds and yellows," on exhibit in the city after its purchase by an American collector, to "a tortoise-shell cat having a fit in a platter of tomatoes" (see Figure 3.2). But *Modern Painters* had convinced Twain otherwise: "Mr. Ruskin would have said: This person is an ass. That is what I would say, now." Twain's pseudo-conversion manages to emulate both aesthetic extremes. Each extravagant falsehood—Turner's oceanic conflagration and the reporter's ludicrous platter of tomatoes—is an index to the transformative power of perception.[33]

Reason, Twain will ultimately conclude, is largely useless in the analysis of beauty, an insight that extends the protracted engagement with lies and truth that Jim Baker, John Ruskin, and Turner all address. "There are women who have an indefinable charm in their faces which makes them beautiful to their intimates," Twain writes late in *A Tramp Abroad*, "but a cold stranger who tried to reason the matter out and find this beauty would fail":

> He would say of one of these women: This chin is too short, this nose is too long, this forehead is too high, this hair is too red, this complexion is too pallid, the perspective of the entire composition is incorrect; conclusion, the woman is not beautiful. But her nearest friend might say, and say truly, "Your premises are right, your logic is faultless, but your conclusion is wrong, nevertheless; she is an Old Master—she is beautiful, but only to such as know her; it is a beauty which cannot be formulated, but it is there, just the same." (TA 357)

No objective conception of beauty can hope to explain the subjective experience of its presence. The sphere of unformulated feeling resists the application of faultless logic, inviting the mix of deference and mockery that Twain brings to bear on the connoisseurship of John Ruskin and that prompts him to make a perverse intervention in the illustration of his book.

Throughout his career Twain made extensive use of scores of plates to entice subscription purchasers and to entertain the reader, but *A Tramp Abroad* is the only volume in which Twain insisted on including thirteen of his own crude drawings, and three equally inept ones by Joseph Twichell, among the more than three hundred professional illustrations that appeared in the book's 1880 edition.[34] Most of these personal contributions are childish scrawls: the "little sketch" of an old military tower in Wimpfen, a "study" of the horse and carriage that Twain and Harris borrow from their Heilbronn landlord, the ludicrous cartoon of a Blue China Cat statuette imbedded directly in Twain's manuscript page as if to underscore its unmediated purity (see Figure 3.3). Old Blue China (Twain implies) is as authentic as its creator's handwriting. Much to his regret, however, he has to leave the cat's remarkable color out of his book: "that old sensuous, pervading, ramifying, interpolating, transboreal blue which is the despair of modern art" (TA 124). This cascade of adjectives is in itself a reminder of the stubborn gap between inner and outer vision that no amount of descriptive fervor can bridge. Only a painter like Turner could really hope to re-create the blue flush of five thousand birds surrounding Jim Baker's lonely mountain cabin.

The first of Twain's crude sketches in *A Tramp Abroad* is the life-size "tracing" of a sword fragment from the Heidelberg University dueling clubs (see Figure 3.4). Twain devotes three grim chapters, early in the book, to these wrenching student rituals, as if to establish at the outset of the narrative a fascination with the boundless mental interiors that his chapters will undertake to address. He and Harris had intended to study a meeting of the dueling clubs "in the interest of science," but the note of wry detachment that this expression implies doesn't survive the first actual contest that Twain witnesses. Ultimately the insights he acquires into this brutal tradition are as two-dimensional and fragmentary as the sword tracing. Silence—a "dignified gravity and repression," Twain calls it—punctuated by explosive outbreaks of "wonderful turmoil" characterize the student duels themselves, a contrast that is as mesmerizing as it is ridiculous:

> The combatants were watching each other with alert eyes; a perfect stillness, a breathless interest reigned. I felt that I was going to see some wary work. But not so. The instant the word was given, the two apparitions sprang forward and began to rain blows down upon each other with such lightning rapidity that I could not quite tell whether I saw the swords or only the flashes they made in the air; the rattling din of these blows,

as they struck steel or paddings was something wonderfully stirring, and they were struck with such terrific force that I could not understand why the opposing sword was not beaten down under the assault. Presently, in the midst of the sword-flashes, I saw a handful of hair skip into the air as if it had lain loose on the victim's head and a breath of wind had puffed it suddenly away. (TA 26)

A pair of seconds and a surgeon periodically call a halt to the fighting to examine and briefly bandage fresh wounds or to stop the contest if the injuries to the duelists seem dangerous. A timekeeper with a "memorandum book" keeps records of each battle. Traditional usages and a system of colored caps prescribe the behavior of club members, on and off the dueling grounds, and even through the excruciating medical repair of their lacerated faces, custom dictates that the duelists keep mum (TA 37). The handful of hair that "skips" away from a young man's scalp, in the first battle that Twain witnesses, is the only reminder that these frantic but deeply repressed human machines are actually children in disguise—apparitional versions of Tom Sawyer and Joe Harper, playacting with wooden swords on Cardiff Hill.

For the most part *A Tramp Abroad* exults in explosive departures from wary work, though in most instances those departures take the form of comic shams: mocking the kind of masculine cults that the dueling clubs exemplify. Twain's account of his Riffelberg climbing expedition, for instance, is aimed at the mountaineering excesses of British adventurers and their pursuit of risk. Over two long chapters Twain purports to describe a seven-day Alpine assault involving scores of pack animals, seventeen guides, four surgeons, three chaplains, fifteen barkeepers, and a Latinist, all to complete a three-hour hike to a tourist hotel. In quest of further exploits to add to his pages, Twain sends Harris on a proxy expedition through some rugged Alpine terrain, an account of which Harris cribs from the work of other writers, weaving in Fiji, Choctaw, Zulu, and Chinese terms "to adorn my page" (TA 211). On a later occasion, faced with another dangerous proxy mountaineering assignment, Harris subcontracts the work to a local adventurer for three francs (TA 255). The universal plagiarism of verbal life that Oliver Wendell Holmes had explained to Twain a few years earlier is the catalyst for these fantastic displays.

You never see a blue jay get stuck for a word, Jim Baker observed, any more than Twain's hyper-alert mind gets stuck for fresh subjects as it rushes "with a frantic speed" from topic to topic in a ceaseless onslaught of unfinished beginnings during his sleepless night in Heilbronn. Perfect stillness and lightning movement, the mental extremes of the dueling club, are a kind of mirror for Twain's own artistic consciousness, just as the rage of Jim Baker's ambitious blue jay mirrors Twain's own compositional frustrations as he struggled to fulfill his contract for *A Tramp Abroad*. Similar introspective mirrors occur throughout the book, from the enchanting little German girl at a performance of *Lohengrin* who is so fidgety that she believes she is infested with five hundred fleas, to the extraordinary account of an Alpine sky near Mt. Blanc that elicits another of Twain's experiments in producing a verbal equivalent for Turner's kinetic images:

> While we were still on very high ground, and before the descent toward Argentiere began, we looked up toward a neighboring mountain-top, and saw exquisite prismatic colors playing about some white clouds which were so delicate as to almost resemble gossamer webs. The faint pinks and greens were peculiarly beautiful; none of the colors were deep, they were the lightest shades. They were bewitchingly commingled. We sat down to study and enjoy this singular spectacle. The tints remained during several minutes—flitting, changing, melting into each other; paling almost away, for a moment, then reflushing,— a shifting, restless, unstable succession of soft opaline gleams, shimmering over that airy film of white cloud, and turning into a fabric dainty enough to clothe an angel with. (TA 316)

The experience, Twain concluded, "was suggestive of a soap-bubble split open, and spread out in the sun," a formulation that is both delicate and violent, like the paradoxical dimensions of the student duels that so engrossed Twain's attention.

Mt. Blanc itself, "a vast dome of snow," had seemed at first to dominate the entire sky, framed "in a strong V-shaped gateway of the mountains" as Twain and Harris approached it. But even this overbearing monolith proves capable of the same prismatic imaginative effects that Twain had witnessed on the high slopes above Argentiere, a variation on the kaleidoscopic fluidity that unfolds in Westminster Abbey as the members of the Tudor court watch Tom Canty patiently realign the details of Edward's memory until he is able to recall the location of the royal seal and recover his throne. The Alps pose an expressive challenge that Twain partly addresses and partly evades throughout *A Tramp Abroad* as he finds himself "groping" toward an account of the "deep, nameless influence" that the mountains exert: "a longing which is like homesickness" he writes, "a grieving, haunting yearning, which will plead, implore, and persecute till it has its will" (TA 231–2). Such moments belong among the many instances of unformulated feeling that perplex and enrich mental life.

Midway through Twain's book, he finds himself drawn to a particularly improbable introspective mirror: a pair of Arkansas newlyweds, in the Jungfrau Hotel, who combine to reenact the wonderful turmoil of the Heidelberg dueling clubs. The young couple take possession of a broken-down piano in the hotel drawing room—"the very worst miscarriage in the way of a piano that the world has seen," Twain writes—and convert it into a medium for their feelings that quickly purges the room of all solemnity and restraint, and of all the other timid guests as well. With her worshipful groom to turn the sheet music pages, Twain notes, "the boss of that instrument" began to play:

> The bride fetched a swoop with her fingers from one end of the keyboard to the other, just to get her bearings, as it were, and you could see the congregation set their teeth with the agony of it. Then, without any more preliminaries, she turned on all the horrors of the "Battle of Prague," that venerable shivaree, and waded chin deep in the blood of the slain. She made a fair and honorable average of two false notes in every five, but her soul was in arms and she never stopped to correct. The audience stood it with pretty fair grit for a while, but when the cannonade waxed hotter and fiercer, and the discord-average rose to four in five, the procession began to move. A few stragglers held their ground ten minutes longer, but when the girl began to wring the true inwardness out of the "cries of the wounded," they struck their colors and retired in a kind of panic. (TA 224)

Twain himself stays for the entire performance out of "reverence" for the perfection of this complete commitment to true inwardness.

The young couple eventually depart as "gorged" with inner exultation as young Cholly Adams after unleashing his surf-beat of slang. This aesthetic display too is part of the book's introspective cast. Low-grade music, Twain observed after taking in a band performance in Baden-Baden, exalts even an uncultured "oyster" like himself. The higher reaches of opera require a keener intellect and special training to appreciate. "Yet if base music gives certain of us wings," he wonders, "why should we want any other?" (TA 157). The sole "scientific" discovery that Twain claims to have made on his trip both echoes and inverts this realization: "*above a certain point*," he concludes, after studying the optical illusions of the Alpine horizon, "*the higher a point seems to be the lower it actually is* (TA 287). Perception, Twain implies, is simply another name for our mental wings. Throughout *A Tramp Abroad*, diminished actualities—like the constraints of what one knows—give way to the boundless allure of the inner world.

4

Shadings

Between September 1879, when the Clemens family returned to the United States, and September 1883, Mark Twain finished four books and published three of them: *A Tramp Abroad*, *The Prince and the Pauper*, and *Life on the Mississippi*. The last of these incorporated the 1875 *Atlantic Monthly* sketches on the science of piloting, as well as one chapter from an incomplete manuscript of the *Adventures of Huckleberry Finn*, which Twain would finish late in 1883. Portions from the manuscript of *A Tramp Abroad* would also find their way into *Life on the Mississippi*, underscoring how entangled with one another these books ultimately prove to be.[1] At the heart of this remarkable period lies *A Tramp Abroad*, in the pages of which Twain seemed determined to explore the fertile disorder of his mental life. The alps themselves become an evocative form of introspective instrumentation, as Twain's tramp unfolds, calibrated by geological forces to record inconceivable vistas of time that both subdue and exalt the observer with a sharp conviction of human insignificance. A visit to Milan cathedral, a building that had completely engrossed Twain's attention during the *Quaker City* tour twelve years earlier, takes on a similar instrumental cast:

> We spent an impressive hour in the noble cathedral, where long shafts of tinted light were cleaving through the solemn dimness from the lofty windows and falling on a pillar here, a picture there, and a kneeling worshiper yonder. The organ was muttering, censers were swinging, candles were glinting on the distant altar, and robed priests were filing silently past them; the scene was one to sweep all frivolous thoughts away and steep the soul in a holy calm. A trim young American lady paused a yard or two

from me, fixed her eyes on the mellow sparks flecking the far-off altar, bent her head reverently a moment, then straightened up, kicked her train into the air with her heel, caught it deftly in her hand, and marched briskly out. (TA 356)

Twain treats the church's vast interior like a sublime kaleidoscope, tinting its jumbled contents in mesmerizing shafts of light. Bishop Borromeo's ponderous crypt and the statue of the flayed man are nowhere in evidence. Instead, the young tourist who catches Twain's eye is yet another introspective mirror of Twain himself, responsive to the surrounding atmosphere of holy calm, yet as volatile as the altar's mellow sparks. Her ceremonial dress only partly impedes the mix of reverence and irreverence that she displays.

As Twain leaves the church, he realizes that he has finally come to appreciate the "subdued splendor" of the Old Masters as an instance of complex, subjective instrumentation. Time modifies their surfaces in ways that the original artists could never have anticipated, conferring on them "a mellow richness ... which is to the eye what muffled and mellowed sound is to the ear" (TA 356). When he revisits his 1875 *Atlantic Monthly* sketches on the science of piloting, he adapts the expressive lessons of *A Tramp Abroad* to capture the same subtle interplay between objective and subjective life that he senses in his brief return to Milan Cathedral. Initially at least *Life on the Mississippi* sets out to document a whimsical research exercise: tabulating the physical and cultural changes that have taken place in the Mississippi Valley both in Twain's lifetime and across the centuries of European exploration and settlement. But the book quickly evolves into a study of the unexpected collisions between inward and outward forms of vision. Touring New Orleans in the company of George Washington Cable—an authority whom Twain considers a "masterly delineator" of the South's "interior life"—can expose the "fine shades" of inner experience that elude an uninstructed imagination. Cable has the ability to foster in others "a vivid *sense* as of unseen or dimly seen things" (LM 269; emphasis in the original). *Life on the Mississippi* will undertake a similar tour of interior life, a blend of outer and inner senses as subtle as the science of piloting turned out to be.[2]

* * *

In 1882 Twain returned to the Mississippi much better equipped to exploit the experience than he was when he began his training twenty-five years earlier as Horace Bixby's cub. Instead of the little notebook where Bixby insisted that his hapless apprentice record all the channel marks and place names of the river—the pilot's ABC—Twain brings along a small secretarial staff, a poet and a stenographer, to help with the process of expanding his seven magazine articles into a book. This informal partnership reflects the systematic collaboration between feelings and facts that Twain proposes to explore as his chapters unfold. Supplementing the original *Atlantic* sketches called for Twain to steep himself in the testimony of other observers who might deepen his own appreciation for dimly seen things. Even for the work of a seasoned journalist, *Life on the Mississippi* is unusually rich in transcription and quotation, beginning with a long epigraph from an 1863 issue of *Harper's Magazine* that tries to shape the reader's geographical "conception" of the river by comparing its extent to that of the La Plata, the Nile, the Ganges, or the Rhine, a foretaste of the representational challenges that the poet/stenographer will confront.[3]

The river's "physical history," as Twain calls it in the book's opening pages, is closely allied to the pilot's relentless concentration on the changing course of the channel or the shape of the bank, the sand bars, and islands that the current builds or obliterates as it rewrites the geographical and political "facts" that attempt to define it. The true pilot's indifference to every concern of human life other than the river mirrors the restless indifference of the river itself. By contrast, the Mississippi's "historical history" accounts for much of the new material with which Twain decides to introduce the original *Atlantic* sketches in their new setting. In doing so, however, he depicts history itself as equally shifting and subjective, a disorderly confluence of facts and feelings. It makes no sense, for instance, to report that Hernando De Soto first saw the Mississippi in 1542; the date itself means nothing, Twain insists, without the addition of "perspective and color"—painterly impressions that reproduce time in imaginative form. "When De Soto took his glimpse of the river," Twain wrote:

> Ignatius Loyola was an obscure name; the order of the Jesuits was not yet a year old; Michael Angelo's paint was not yet dry on the Last Judgment in the Sistine Chapel; Mary Queen of Scots was

not yet born, but would be before the year closed. Catherine de Medici was a child; Elizabeth of England was not yet in her teens; Calvin, Benvenuto Cellini, and the Emperor Charles V. were at the top of their fame, and each was manufacturing history after his own peculiar fashion; Margaret of Navarre was writing the "Heptameron" and some religious books,—the first survives, the others are forgotten, wit and indelicacy being sometimes better literature-preservers than holiness ... the Council of Trent was being called; the Spanish Inquisition was roasting, and racking, and burning, with a free hand; elsewhere on the continent the nations were being persuaded to holy living by the sword and fire ... Rabelais was not yet published; "Don Quixote" was not yet written; Shakespeare was not yet born; a hundred long years must still elapse before Englishmen would hear the name of Oliver Cromwell. (LM 14–15)

These reference points "mellow and modify" the newness of American history, Twain suggests, much like time enriches the impact of the Old Masters, giving the country "a most respectable outside-aspect of rustiness and antiquity" (LM 15). But a respectable outside, like manufactured history, is a misleading imposition on the unruly interior that Twain's examples implicitly celebrate: the inextinguishable vigor of wit and indelicacy that persists despite the brutal prescriptions of "holy living." Facts and figures alone (like those that the *Harper's* editors deploy) cannot generate a "distinct realization" in the mind, a vivid inner perception of beauty or meaning (LM 13). To explore these inward experiences requires imaginative gifts like those that G. W. Cable displays as he probes the hidden emotional shadings of New Orleans.

Twain's brief review of the two French expeditions that survey the Mississippi's course after De Soto's death underscores this difference between an objective grasp of outside conditions and the intensity of distinct realization. For this second venture into the historical record, Francis Parkman's narrative in *La Salle and the Discovery of the Great West* helps sharpen Twain's vision. "Joliet the merchant and Marquette the priest," as Twain calls them, are the precursors for the stenographer and the poet who contribute to completing *Life on the Mississippi*: the first hoping to find a profitable short cut to the Gulf of California and the second seeking Catholic converts among the native peoples living on the banks of the "Conception," Marquette's pious name for the river that De Soto had discovered. A few decades later La Salle and his lieutenant, Henri de Tonty, explored the river all the way to the Gulf of Mexico, setting up ceremonial crosses at various points and claiming the Mississippi valley for France. "Nobody smiled at these colossal ironies," Twain bitterly observes, after describing how La Salle and his priests indoctrinated the local tribes and "drew from these simple children of the forest acknowledgments of fealty to Louis the Putrid, over the water" (LM 20):

> The voyagers journeyed on, touching here and there; "passed the sites, since become historic, of Vicksburg and Grand Gulf;" and visited an imposing Indian monarch in the Teche country, whose capital city was a substantial one of sun-baked bricks mixed with straw—better houses than many that exist there now. The chief's house contained an audience room forty feet square; and there he received Tonty in State, surrounded by sixty old men clothed in white cloaks. There was a temple in the town, with a mud wall about it ornamented with the skulls of enemies sacrificed to the sun. (LM 21)

This implicit contrast between two Sun Kings, each presiding over a ceremonial court, intensifies Twain's appreciation for the colossal ironies of history, a realization that emerges much more vividly in *Life on the Mississippi* than it does in Francis Parkman's decorous feeling for historic "sites." Each of these opposed mental worlds—the court of Louis the Putrid at Versailles and the Teche monarch's temple of skulls, Parkman's patriotic composure and Twain's caustic emotion—is a partial index to the complex psychological currents circulating through the American interior.

A pilot's notebook (as Horace Bixby had taken pains to point out) is an indispensable tool for converting ephemeral details or impressions into a navigational record, disciplining as well as enhancing the powers of attention that the pilot brings to his work. Mastering the ever-changing but unbroken continuity of the channel is the essence of the pilot's profession. With the bulk of *Life on the Mississippi*, by contrast, vivid discontinuities appeal to the mind at every turn, giving a distinctive shape to the portions of the book that Twain adds to the 1875 piloting episodes.[4] This form of dispersed attention gathers momentum through the review of Francis Parkman's history and comes violently to life in the psychotic personality of Mr. Brown, the first subject that Twain takes up when he links the "Old Times" chapters with the story of his 1882 excursion by describing the destruction of the *Pennsylvania*, one of the most lavish and most famous steamboats of piloting's golden age.

Mr. Brown had originally appeared in the *Atlantic* sketches as the victim of an indiscriminate memory, an inborn trait rather than the carefully disciplined mental aptitude that a pilot required. He was incapable of forgetting anything or of distinguishing between trivial memories and important ones. Much like Jim Blaine in *Roughing It*, he "would start out with the honest intention of telling you a vastly funny anecdote about a dog," Twain notes, and soon wander off into a consideration of the dog's breed, its owner's family history, accounts of the weather or the annual crop statistics that happened to coincide with the weddings and funerals that he had begun to review, adding "extracts from sermons he had heard years before about the efficacy of prayer as a means of grace" (OM 5.572). During these interminable monologues, Brown would gradually succumb to the hypnotic tedium of his own performance, muttering to himself as he went off watch much as if he too, like Jim Blaine, were drifting off to sleep.

This hapless figure from 1875 bears little relation to the volatile tyrant Twain describes in 1882 when he resurrects Brown "out of the shadows of that vanished time" to begin building his magazine articles into a book.[5] It is Mr. Brown, not Horace Bixby, who comes most vividly to mind, twenty-five years later, as Twain recalls the "sharp" psychological schooling that the river provided (LM 128). His appreciation for a well-drawn literary character, he believes, derives from this incomparable on-the-job education. Bixby had temporarily loaned his cub's services to Brown, one of the pilots on the *Pennsylvania*, while Bixby himself set out to master the Missouri River, adding still new mental feats to his formidable professional knowledge. The change at first delighted Twain when he found himself assigned to "the executive family of so fast and famous a boat" (LM 129). But this euphoria comes to an abrupt end. "It must have been all of fifteen minutes—fifteen minutes of dull homesick silence" in the *Pennsylvania* pilot house, Twain remembered, before Brown suddenly dropped the mask of contemptuous indifference that he had displayed when Twain first met him to reveal a shrieking monster, his face "as red as fire, and every muscle in it working," as he attacks his new cub (LM 130). Twain "stood as in a dream, all my senses stupefied" under Brown's vicious verbal assault, a pattern that repeats itself day after day "during a stretch of months" that are filled with constant dread. "The moment I was in the presence," Twain wrote, "even in the darkest night, I could feel those yellow eyes upon me, and knew their owner was watching for a pretext to spit out some venom on me" (LM 131).

This encounter reflects an altogether different order of remembrance from the unruly associative links that had held Brown's mind captive in the *Atlantic* sketches. Predatory focus rather than a hapless susceptibility to distraction is now the distinguishing feature of his intelligence. Brown's original survey of crops, livestock, circuses, and prayer were indiscriminate expressions of the stenographic mind. More explosive mental processes characterize his malignant "presence" in *Life on the Mississippi*. Nightly revenge fantasies provide Twain with a meager comic compensation for the savagery that Brown repeatedly displays. In defense of his younger brother Henry, who is a clerk on the boat, Twain administers one satisfactory pummeling to Brown that delights the *Pennsylvania*'s captain but results in Twain's being dismissed from its crew when no substitute pilot to replace the psychotically vindictive Brown proves available. Henry remains on the boat when it leaves New Orleans without his older brother (LM 138).

When the *Pennsylvania* explodes and burns, on this fatal upriver trip, Henry Clemens dies from internal injuries he suffers while trying to help other injured crew members and passengers.[6] One of the mates is horribly burned but manages to survive. Brown, however, along with the boat's chief clerk was "never seen or heard of after the explosion," as if he were simply obliterated during a disaster in one of the Pennsylvania coal mines from which Twain claims he was originally "extracted." This startling disappearance underscores the complex psychological background that Twain attaches to Mr. Brown when he reintroduces him to readers of *Life on the Mississippi*: the "bastard dialect" that betrays Brown's mining past, his ludicrously principled refusal to use any curse word stronger than "dod derned" during his frightening outbursts, the fierce class resentments that erupt when he attacks his new cub's educational pretensions, the reflexive professional instinct with which he jumps back to the *Pennsylvania*'s untended wheel the instant after Twain has finished pummeling him.

The boat's other pilot, George Ealer—with his fondness for Goldsmith and Shakespeare, his flute-playing, and his devotion to chess—is in every respect a more appealing figure than Brown. But Brown is the more haunting presence, a richer mental resource from which Twain in turn is able to extract a complex of powerful feelings ranging from his own species of personal venom to the sheer stupefied paralysis that grips him during Brown's first attack. This dramatic movement between emotional extremes echoes the psychological complexity of the Heidelberg dueling clubs, the explosive potential of Mr. Bixby's customarily restrained character, or the surreal contrasts between peacetime routine and wartime horrors that the Vicksburg survivors recall when Twain arrives at the city on his 1882 downriver voyage.

Brown's abrupt disappearance in the aftermath of the boat's deadly explosion belongs to a larger pattern of extinction intrinsic to the Mississippi. Towns and individuals, islands and sandbars, simply vanish from the river and from the narrative, leaving evocative absences that are part of the sharp schooling Twain has set out to depict. When he passes the site of the *Pennsylvania* disaster on his return trip to the river in 1882, he notes that the channel no longer flows over the wreck's location. An island where many of the survivors had sought shelter decades earlier "has joined itself compactly to the main shore," Twain notes, burying the riverbed and with it all signs of the sunken steamboat and its victims. "Some farmer will turn up her bones with his plow one day," he notes, "and be surprised"—a prediction that joins the long list of startling discontinuities that Twain envisions or explores (LM 197).

From the beginning *Life on the Mississippi* brings a quasi-scientific perspective to bear on Twain's experience that entangles objective and subjective perception. On the train trip west from New York, he measures distances not as matters of miles, speed, or time but as contrasts in dress and behavior. The region of eastern fashion yields to what Twain terms "the region of full goatees," up-to-date styles give way to "obsolete and uncomely" ones, and railway station loafers begin to put both hands, rather than one, in their trouser pockets. "This is an important fact in geography," Twain facetiously declares. The inhabitants of provincial cities may have access to New York tailors and dressmakers, he observes, but not to the "godless grace, and snap, and style" that lie beneath them (LM 146). Each of these intangible attributes becomes a form of subjective calibration: an index to perceptual differences that resist conventional measurement.

Other forms of snap and style compensate for the loss of Eastern sophistication once the downriver trip begins. Like a cultural anthropologist, Twain is eager to collect instances and samples of life along the Mississippi River: the colorful ethnic myths of an Irish book vendor on a St. Louis dock, the fantastic lies that he briefly coaxes out of an apparently obliging pilot, matter-of-fact anecdotes that dramatically understate the dangers of piloting during the war. Twain's stenographic temperament prompts him to record at some length the "impressions" of a favorite confidante, Uncle Mumford, second mate of the *Gold Dust*, with a minimum of censorship, capturing the old veteran's lively orders to his crew as he castigates the government's postwar attempts to engineer the river, an instance of the stenographic intelligence at work on an institutional scale:

> As long as I have been mate of a steamboat,—thirty years—I have watched this river and studied it. Maybe I could have learnt more about it at West Point, but if I believe it I wish I may be WHAT *are you sucking your fingers there for?—Collar that kag of nails!* Four years at West Point, and plenty of books and schooling, will learn a man a good deal, I reckon, but it won't learn him the river. You turn one of those little European rivers over to this Commission, with its hard bottom and clear water, and it would just be a holiday job for them to wall it, pile it, and dike it, and tame it down, and boss it around, and make it go wherever they wanted it to, and stay where they put it, and do just as they said, every time. But this ain't that kind of a river. They have started in here with big confidence, and the best intentions in the world; but they are going to get left. What does Ecclesiastes vii. 13 say? Says enough to knock their little game galley-west, don't it? (LM 183)

What God has made crooked no one can make straight, Uncle Mumford believes, particularly when that crookedness refers to the restless coils of the Mississippi.[7] But nearly everyone whom Twain meets on his trip has set aside the wisdom of Ecclesiastes in favor of the intoxicating confidence of the Federal government's river Commission. In all Twain encounters at least five contending theories for controlling the Mississippi's shifting channel and its catastrophic floods, each capable of seizing on a listener like an infectious disease only to give way to the appeal of the next (LM 185). Steer by the river in your head, Horace Bixby had once admonished his cub (OM 3.284), but twenty-five years later that painstakingly constructed interior channel has spawned a spectrum of mental rivers, with Ecclesiastes at one extreme, the freightage and profit calculations of the *Cincinnati Commercial* at the other, and five theoretical Mississippis in between, each imaginatively engineered to dazzle the listener with its particular species of wisdom but none capable of holding permanent sway over the mind. Among the four appendixes that Twain adds to *Life on the Mississippi*, he includes a detailed report on Federal river management as a sample of the government commission's sophisticated engineering ambitions.

Along with this technical proposal for the "reconstruction" of the river and a New Orleans newspaper report on flood relief, these appendixes include a long Indian legend entitled "The Undying Head" that Twain admires for what he terms its "weird conceits" and "energy of movement" (LM 361). As the volatile figures of Mr. Brown or Uncle Mumford suggest, the head is a source of weird energy throughout Twain's book, the origin of more than one sort of mental inundation that overflows his pages like the great 1882 flood overflows the levees and dikes of the nation's civil engineers. Some of this narrative excess takes the form of several self-contained stories that Twain inserts into *Life on the Mississippi*. In the first of these, "A Thumb-Print and What Came of It," he purports to record the dying confession of a consumptive German named Karl Ritter whom Twain claims to have met some time ago in Munich.[8] Ritter and his small family had emigrated to America and were living near Napoleon, Arkansas, as the Civil War drew to a close when a pair of Union privates broke into their house, chloroformed them as they slept, and clubbed Ritter's wife and daughter to death after the two unexpectedly awoke from their drugged sleep.

Startled by a cavalry patrol, the killers fled, but Ritter had awakened from his own "sodden lethargy" in time to notice that one of the men lacked a thumb and the other had left behind a bloody fingerprint on a document—evidence that ultimately enables Ritter to identify them, when he disguises himself as a fortune-teller and visits nearby Union army camps. "Did I appeal to the law—I?" the dying man exclaims to Twain: "Does it quench the pauper's thirst if the King drink for him? Oh, no, no, no—I wanted no impertinent interference of the law. Laws and the gallows could not pay the debt that was owing to me! Let the laws leave the matter in my hands, and have no fears: I would find the debtor and collect the debt" (LM 208). But sixteen years elapse before Ritter finally encounters the more brutal of the two robbers in a Munich morgue, where Ritter is responsible for aiding any of the "dead" that might happen to awaken from a deep coma. When one corpse does unexpectedly stir from its death-like lethargy, it proves to be the former Union soldier who had beaten Ritter's family to death. Through nods and shakes "the shrouded face" confirms his identity, accompanying the information with "a spectral smile of such peculiar devilishness," Ritter remembers, "that it struck an awakening light through my dull brain," a final instance of semi-anesthetized awareness in this brief tale (LM 234). Over the next "three hours and six minutes," Ritter watches in an ecstasy of pleasure, scrupulously timing the murderer's eventual death.

Like the Indian legend of "The Undying Head" from the book's appendix, Twain's own story is full of weird conceits and uncanny energy as it alternates between the states of drugged stupor and sustained rage that Ritter describes, a feature of the narrative that mirrors the peculiar presence of chloroform in the possession of two vagrant soldiers. Fortune-telling and finger-print analysis form an equally peculiar combination in the story's plot. Twain's two companions on the 1882 trip, the stenographer and the poet, "break into a fusillade of excited and admiring ejaculations" when Twain finishes his tale, but all three men gradually drop into "an abysmal reverie" over the disposition of the treasure that the dying Ritter had entrusted to Twain. Gradually they succeed in chloroforming their own scruples as they decide to split the $10,000 in gold among themselves, rather than convey it to the young German family that Ritter had hoped to support, but abysmal reverie ultimately triumphs when they learn that the money's hiding place in the town of Napoleon had long ago been washed into the Mississippi and disappeared (LM 218–20).

This half-gruesome and half-ludicrous episode is a burlesque of the heightened and smothered emotions that Twain immediately begins to explore as he and his companions reach Vicksburg and revisit the experience of the siege that preceded the city's capture by Union troops in 1863. The few civilians who had been unable to evacuate dug shelters to protect their families from several weeks of constant bombardment: "mere holes," as one survivor described them to Twain, "tunnels driven into the perpendicular clay bank" where he and his neighbors retreated when the shells began to fall. "Left to tell their own story, in their own way," Twain observed, "those people told it without fire, almost without interest," an initial signal of the uncanny anesthetic effect of their terrible experience (LM 229). The cave refuges that they dug eventually became unbearable interiors in several senses, concentrations of feeling and memory that ultimately prove as fatal as the Union shrapnel. "Twice we had sixteen people in our cave," Twain's informant continues:

> "and a number of times we had a dozen. Pretty suffocating in there. We always had eight; eight belonged there. Hunger and misery and sickness and fright and sorrow, and I don't know what all, got so loaded into them that none of them were ever rightly their old selves after the siege. They all died but three of us within a couple of years. One night a shell burst in front of the hole and caved it in and stopped it up. It was lively times, for a while, digging out. Some of us came near smothering. After that we made two openings—ought to have thought of it at first."
>
> "Mule meat? No, we only got down to that the last day or two. Of course it was good; anything is good when you are starving." (LM 231)

In response to a pair of implied questions, Twain's informant suddenly seems impatient with the superficial nature of the curiosity that they reflect. An ability to survive on mule meat is the least of the discoveries that he associates with the "terrific" transformations of the siege. People can adapt to almost any "queer combination" of experiences, he insists, when doing so is a matter of survival. But some queer combinations leave a deeper psychological mark than others.

On one occasion Twain's informant was in the process of inviting a friend to share some scarce whiskey in his cave when a sudden shell burst cut off his friend's arm as the two were shaking hands. "And do you know the thing that is going to stick the longest in my memory," he continues, "and outlast everything else, little and big, I reckon, is the mean thought I had then? It was 'the whiskey *is saved'*" (emphasis in the original). The memory of this reflexive reaction is part of the mental legacy that got loaded into the survivors of the siege caves: a sign of the trauma that severs this speaker from his old self as brutally as the shrapnel amputates his friend's arm (LM 231). His thought is "mean" only in the sense that it is trivial, rather than callous, but its queerness clearly troubles him, without inciting any of the fire or interest that Twain misses in his long narrative. A kind of chloroform mutes this speaker's emotions without entirely blunting his grasp of the surreal nature of his experience. Like the "unseen or dimly seen things" that the streets of New Orleans conceal, this passage touches on shades of inner experience that only a master delineator can hope to capture.

In another of *Life on the Mississippi*'s self-contained stories, "A Burning Brand," Twain explores the inverse of this complex psychological state: the capacity of a skillful fiction to trigger wildly disproportionate displays of feeling. The brand of the title is an ex-convict who has not quite been snatched from the burning. The elaborate tale of redemption that he purportedly writes to a friend who is still in prison prompts a dramatic public catharsis once the letter begins to circulate among eastern church congregations who are desperate for emotional release. "Here was true eloquence; irresistible eloquence," Twain writes after listening to a clergyman friend rehearse a presentation of the ex-convict's poignant letter that he hopes to be able to make without breaking down:

> I have seldom been so deeply stirred by any piece of writing. The reader of it halted, all the way through, on a lame and broken voice; yet he had tried to fortify his feelings by several private readings of the letter before venturing into company with it. He was practicing upon me to see if there was any hope of his being able to read the document to his prayer-meeting with anything like a decent command over his feelings. The result was not promising. However, he determined to risk it; and did. He got through tolerably well; but his audience broke down early, and stayed in that condition to the end. (LM 316)

Charles Dudley Warner is the first listener who manages to keep his composure as the letter is read at a Sunday service. Warner quietly suggests to the clergyman at the church door that the letter might be an extremely skillful deception, as in fact it proves to be: a clever ruse aimed at exploiting gullible religious sympathies and, ultimately, securing a pardon for its imprisoned recipient who is actually its Harvard-educated author. It is a "rounded, symmetrical, complete, colossal" swindle, Twain exclaims, half in outrage and half in delight at the extraordinary psychological acuity it displays.[9]

Life on the Mississippi is an elaborate study in just such convoluted streams of feeling, both those that Twain experiences directly and those that he hears or reads about. In a chapter blandly entitled "Some Imported Articles" he reviews half a century of traveler's testimony on the wildly divergent psychological impact of the river: its grandeur, its horrors, its majestic power, its moral and physical pollution. Dante might have incorporated images of the Mississippi in the *Inferno*, Mrs. Trollope suggests in 1827. An English barrister later in the century views the river "with that reverence with which everyone must regard a great feature of external nature" (LM 178). Basil Hall compares it to a painting of the deluge. Captain Marryat, writing ten years after Mrs. Trollop's visit, calls it "the great common sewer of the western America," a "turbulent and bloodstained" scene of crime and desolation (LM 177).

"As a panorama of the emotions," Twain admits that Marryat's outburst has a degree of psychological value that leads him to print a long extract from it in his pages. Equally complex emotional panoramas prompt him to a chapter-length assault on the furnishings of a prosperous Southern home (LM 241), a brutal account of Murel's murderous river gang (LM 189), and a portrait of the black tenant families that were stranded by the remnants of the 1882 flood. "We were getting down now into the migrating negro region," Twain writes:

> These poor people could never travel when they were slaves; so they make up for the privation now. They stay on a plantation till the desire to travel seizes them; then they pack up, hail a steamboat, and clear out. Not for any particular place; no, nearly any place will answer; they only want to be moving. The amount of money on hand will answer the rest of the conundrum for them. If it will take them fifty miles, very well; let it be fifty. If not, a shorter flight will do.
>
> During a couple of days we frequently answered these hails. Sometimes there was a group of high-water-stained, tumble-down

cabins, populous with colored folk, and no whites visible; with grassless patches of dry ground here and there; a few felled trees, with skeleton cattle, mules, and horses, eating the leaves and gnawing the bark—no other food for them in the flood-wasted land. Sometimes there was a single lonely landing-cabin; near it the colored family that had hailed us; little and big, old and young, roosting on the scant pile of household goods; these consisting of a rusty gun, some bedticks, chests, tinware, stools, a crippled looking-glass, a venerable arm-chair, and six or eight base-born and spiritless yellow curs, attached to the family by strings. They must have their dogs; can't go without their dogs. Yet the dogs are never willing; they always object; so, one after another, in ridiculous procession, they are dragged aboard ... Sometimes a child is forgotten and left on the bank; but never a dog. (LM 197)

This description itself is a kind of crippled looking glass in which Twain half-recognizes the hunger for "moving" that marked his own restless imagination. Ridiculous though this migrant procession may be, Twain understands the emotional world it represents.

His Saturday afternoon visit to a New Orleans cockpit introduces another emotional panorama as potent as those of the migrating tenant families or the Heidelberg dueling clubs. "I had never seen a cock-fight before," Twain reports, so he is all the more surprised when he arrives to find a group of spectators as heterogeneous as the birds they have come to watch: men and boys "of all ages and all colors, and of many languages and nationalities" gathered around the ring of the cockpit, preserving at first all the decorum of a prayer meeting (LM 277). "There were no brutal faces" in the group, he notes, as "a negro and a white man" prepared their fighting cocks for battle. The instant that the two birds attacked one another, "the Babel of many-tongued shoutings broke out, and ceased not thenceforth":

> When the cocks had been fighting some little time, I was expecting them momently to drop dead, for both were blind, red with blood, and so exhausted that they frequently fell down. Yet they would not give up, neither would they die. The negro and the white man would pick them up every few seconds, wipe them off, blow cold water on them in a fine spray, and take their heads in their mouths and hold them

there a moment—to warm back the perishing life perhaps; I do not know. Then, being set down again, the dying creatures would totter gropingly about, with dragging wings, find each other, strike a guess-work blow or two, and fall exhausted once more. (LM 277)

Unlike the Heidelberg episodes in *A Tramp Abroad*, where Twain's fascination with the dueling ritual never entirely dissipates, he cannot bear to watch the conclusion of this fight, but its brutal intimacy seems to him less objectionable than the aristocratic cruelty of fox-hunting. Even the cocks (he imagines) "experience, as well as confer enjoyment," a dubious claim that draws Twain too into the spectators' frenzied circle (LM 278).

A long, painterly description of a Mississippi River sunrise that Twain includes in a chapter entitled "Sketches By the Way" begins in an atmosphere of deep silence that resembles the initial solemnity of the cockfight. A sense of "loneliness, isolation, remoteness from the worry and bustle of the world" fills the predawn hush as "the solid walls of black forest soften to gray" and vistas of smooth water gradually appear. But this momentary calm too will come to a brutal end:

> When the light has become a little stronger, you have one of the fairest and softest pictures imaginable. You have the intense green of the massed and crowded foliage near by; you see it paling shade by shade in front of you; upon the next projecting cape, a mile off or more, the tint has lightened to the tender young green of spring; the cape beyond that one has almost lost color, and the furthest one, miles away under the horizon, sleeps upon the water a mere dim vapor, and hardly separable from the sky above it and about it. And all this stretch of river is a mirror, and you have the shadowy reflections of the leafage and the curving shores and the receding capes pictured in it. Well, that is all beautiful; soft and rich and beautiful; and when the sun gets well up, and distributes a pink flush here and a powder of gold yonder and a purple haze where it will yield the best effect, you grant that you have seen something that is worth remembering. (LM 201)

Twain's spurious painting lessons in *A Tramp Abroad* may have encouraged him to replicate what he called the "Turner spell" in words.¹⁰ He imposes an imaginary recession of the seasons on this river scene as the intense green of summer, "massed and crowded" on the bank, gives way to the paler hues of spring in the middle distance before melting into an almost colorless dormancy on the horizon. The view is both memorable and a picture of memory, its emotional coloration ending in the dim, indeterminate vapor and "shadowy reflections" characteristic of the extraordinary watercolors that were part of the Turner Bequest, a rich collection of the artist's work that held Twain's interest, in the National Gallery, to a degree that the "Slave Ship" could not match (see Figure 4.1).

The very next paragraph shatters this visionary "sleep" with the anecdote of a river captain who accidentally kills his wife in her stateroom berth when he frantically tries to free her from a sinking boat by cutting through the deck with an axe. The mind is a contriver of weird conceits and queer combinations, a source of lyric coherence and of mutilation that coalesce with particular intensity in the series of chapters that describe Twain's visit to Hannibal, as *Life on the Mississippi* comes to a close.¹¹ He arrives at the town's landing early on a Sunday morning and walks through its vacant streets afflicted with the same sense of psychic disorientation that Vicksburg's citizens had experienced amid the bizarre juxtapositions of the 1863 siege: a "realizing sense," Twain calls it, of how a prisoner abruptly released from the Bastille might have felt after years of captivity (LM 323). Despite possessing what he describes as a photographically exact memory, Twain struggles to accommodate himself to the factual changes that twenty-nine years have brought to pass, even when an obliging old gentleman meets him on top of Holliday's Hill and offers to bring much of his knowledge up to date. Some of Twain's contemporaries, he learns, have made a success of life, while others "have gone to the dogs." Some are still in Hannibal—"town littered with their children," the old man reports—while others have disappeared in Mexico or prospered in St. Louis. "Killed in the war" is the "brief and simple" answer to many of Twain's questions about a childhood acquaintance.

The three chapters that follow this hilltop panorama generate a series of vignettes capturing the tenacity and the fragility of the mind: a schoolgirl acquaintance apparently driven mad by a foolish childhood prank (LM 326); a boy named Dutchy, celebrated for his "prodigious memory," drowned in a muddy creek (LM 331);

an "interesting cave a mile or two below Hannibal" containing the corpse of a fourteen-year-old girl, preserved in a copper cylinder that gawkers sometimes open to examine her face. This startling detail mirrors with uncanny accuracy Twain's own scrutiny of the aging and seemingly ageless faces that he encounters during this visit to his old hometown (LM 338). No vignette from these chapters is more startling than the picture of a vagrant burning to death in the town jail that Twain's photographic memory and acute sense of guilt have combined to preserve. Shortly before the tramp's arrest Twain had taken pity on his plight and loaned him some matches to light his pipe. In the middle of the following night, the church bells sound a fire alarm and the entire village collects at the jail:

> The tramp had used his matches disastrously: he had set his straw bed on fire, and the oaken sheathing of the room had caught. When I reached the ground, two hundred men, women, and children stood massed together, transfixed with horror, and staring at the grated windows of the jail. Behind the iron bars, and tugging frantically at them, and screaming for help, stood the tramp; he seemed like a black object set against a sun, so white and intense was the light at his back. (LM 340)

The town marshal, with the jail's only key, is the only citizen who doesn't answer the frantic alarm: "It was said that the man's death-grip still held fast to the bars after he was dead; and that in this position the fires wrapped him about and consumed him. As to this I do not know. What was seen after I recognized the face that was pleading through the bars was seen by others, not by me." Twain's memory, however, maintains its own death-grip on these events, an introspective mirror framed by the jail's grated window that signals the tenacity of the poetic imagination.

* * *

A unique collaboration between stenographic discipline and poetic insight is partly responsible for the erratic growth of the *Adventures of Huckleberry Finn*. Capturing its language (Twain insisted in one of his prefaces) called for a careful discrimination among Mississippi valley dialects: a form of attentiveness that drew heavily on Twain's intimate acquaintance with the vocal currents of his boyhood. His ear, in turn, becomes the reader's guide to savoring the distinct voices that compose his book. But the traditional generic scaffolding of prose fiction—its large ethical or dramatic claims—elicited from Twain a mock threat against any reader who tried to impose a plot, a motive, or a moral on Huck's story. "Picks is the thing, moral or no moral," Twain's highly practical narrator will exclaim when he is fed up with trying to dig a hole using table knives, just to satisfy Tom Sawyer's literary tastes: "I don't care shucks for the morality of it, nohow" (HF 307).

Twain too pays a great deal of attention to his tools and comparatively little to exalted principles. The scrupulously weighted vocal "shadings" that he weaves into his pages echo the pervasive mental exercises that preoccupy his narrator from the moment that Huck begins his own book by weighing the accuracy displayed by "Mr. Mark Twain" in *The Adventures of Tom Sawyer*. In the most crucial passages of Huck's story, he too is drawing on the resources of a meticulous ear, along with his full array of senses and instincts, listening—quite often as if his life depended on it—and struggling to interpret the sounds that he hears. He is probing his thoughts and reporting on the introspective results, examining his feelings and making closely calibrated choices as painstaking as those that Twain himself employs as he orchestrates the language of Huck's book. The threatening "Notice" with which Twain prefaces the story is more than simply a warning sign posted between the title page and the text. It is an implicit invitation to participate in the intricate work of noticing.[12]

Huck brings an exacting level of attention to bear on the smallest details of his experience. "I didn't notice anything at first, but next I did," he remarks, as he stoops down to examine some puzzling tracks in a dusting of snow just outside the widow Douglass's fence. A closer look reveals the pattern of a cross nailed into "the left boot heel," a talisman (as Huck immediately recognizes) to ward off the devil (HF 19). This acute alertness to a potent sign launches a train of adventures that will end only when the book does. "I was up in a second and shinning down the hill," Huck continues, without a moment of explanation, enacting the fits and starts that plagued his creator, as he explored the rich interplay between noticing and choosing that Huck's haste both highlights and obscures.

Huckleberry Finn needed no introduction to readers of *Life on the Mississippi* when Twain used an excerpt from Huck's downriver journey to illustrate the vestiges of keelboat life displayed by the crews of the commercial lumber rafts that "flaked" the river during his boyhood. Most of the chapter entitled "Frescoes from the Past" precedes Twain's tribute to the science of piloting with a lengthy account of a surreptitious visit that Huck pays to one of these rafts, a "vast level" formed by "an acre or so of white, sweet-smelling boards," carrying the "two dozen men or more" who are necessary to maneuver it downriver toward the New Orleans market (LM 23). *The Adventures of Tom Sawyer* had been in print for seven years when Twain describes Tom's old companion as "an ignorant village boy" who has escaped "from his persecuting father, and from a persecuting good widow" to float down the Mississippi with a runaway slave toward the mouth of the Ohio at Cairo. During an especially dark and oppressive night, the two travelers find themselves trailing behind "a monstrous long raft" and wondering how close they are to their goal.[13]

Nearly every feature of Twain's brief introduction to the excerpt misrepresents the complex intelligence that Huck had quickly displayed once he began to narrate his own story. The passage that appears in *Life on the Mississippi* is missing the first two paragraphs of the long manuscript chapter from the *Adventures of Huckleberry Finn* in which the lumber raft episode originally appears. Those paragraphs make plain how interested Twain had become in the mental collaboration between his book's unlikely partners, and in the meticulous study of consciousness that Huck's aptitude for introspection provides. The night before they sight the "monstrous log raft," Huck and Jim survive a frightening encounter with the disorienting effects of darkness and dense fog in the midst of cluster of snags and islands that combine to make the essential work of noticing nearly impossible to practice.

Huck is attempting to secure the raft to a sapling until the fog lifts when the force of the current suddenly uproots the small tree and sweeps Jim and the raft out of sight, leaving Huck behind on a little tow-head of sand and shrubs, "so sick and scared I couldn't budge for most a half a minute it seemed to me" (HF 99). Without fixed reference points in the fog, he is helpless to catch up in their canoe. Sound, speed, and direction lose all meaning, much as they had when Twain found himself beset by complete darkness and mysterious noises in his Heilbronn hotel room. "Thinks I, it won't do to paddle," Huck tells himself: "first I know I'll run into the bank or a tow-head or something." His hearing is the only sense he can use as he whoops and listens for a faint reply to guide him: "I got to set still and float," Huck realizes, "and yet it's mighty fidgety business to have to hold your hands still at such a time" (HF 100).

The current spins the drifting canoe around so slowly that Huck can only detect its movement by the apparent change in the direction of Jim's cries—if (as he notes) they even are Jim's cries and not those of some other panicked raftsman. Adding to his bewilderment, the river carries him past the "smoky ghosts of big trees" along the bank and finally shoots him down a narrow channel filled with snags that "fairly roared, the current was tearing by them so swift":

> I kept quiet, with my ears cocked, about fifteen minutes, I reckon. I was floating along, of course, four or five mile an hour; but you don't ever think of that. No, you *feel* like you are laying dead still on the water; and if a little glimpse of a snag slips by, you don't think to yourself how fast *you're* going, but you catch your breath and think, My! how that snag is tearing along. If you think it ain't dismal and lonesome out in a fog that way, by yourself, in the night, you try it once—you'll see.
>
> Next, for about half an hour, I whoops now and then; at last I hears the answer a long ways off, and tries to follow it, but I couldn't do it, and directly I judged I'd got into a nest of tow-heads, for I had little dim glimpses of them on both sides of me, sometimes, just a narrow channel between; and some I couldn't see, I knowed was there, because I'd hear the wash of the current against the old dead brush and trash that hung over the banks. Well, I warn't long losing the whoops down amongst the tow-heads and I only tried to chase them a little while, anyway, because it was worse than chasing a jack-o-lantern. You never knowed a sound dodge around so and swap places so quick and so much. (HF 101; emphases in the original)

A keen sense of measurement marks Huck's thinking at every turn, as if he were periodically checking a wristwatch to maintain some vestige of control over his movements. His language too veers in and out of dialect as different scales of accuracy compete with one another. The passing minutes and seconds mingle Huck's fragile objective grasp of these confusing circumstances with an acute appreciation for the subjective illusion that accounts for the apparent movement of the snags and for the equally swift transition from that startling outward detail into the dismal loneliness that he feels. This intense absorption in the processing of sights, sounds, and feelings underlies the fine distinctions that Huck draws among a variety of mental states as the passage unfolds, each as subtly shaded as the vocal distinctions that Twain carefully draws at the outset of the story: to reckon, to think, to feel, to judge, and to know.

When the roar of the current finally recedes and Huck senses that he is back in the open river, the whoops have ceased. One of the treacherous snags, he concludes, must have claimed Jim's life: "I was good and tired," he recalls, "so I laid down in the canoe and said I wouldn't bother no more," quietly voicing a blend of exhaustion and resignation that masks the psychic entanglement of his struggle. From the beginning of the book, Huck has shown himself to be an economist of anxiety: losing interest in the adventures of Moses when the widow remarks that he has been dead "a considerable long time"; deciding not to try for heaven once he learns that Miss Watson intends to go there; abandoning his fruitless effort to understand the religious differences between Miss Watson and the widow. But this instance of mental exhaustion amid the solid white silence of the fog has no comic or pragmatic dimension. A subtle emotional shading sets it apart from Huck's impatience with the social nuances of civilized life. Life itself seemed little more than a bother to him now, and he persuades himself to give in to his fatigue by reasoning that "I would take just one little cat-nap" (HF 102).

This is not the first time in the book that Twain invites the reader to consider sleep as a version of death and the startling return to consciousness as a disconcerting and illuminating rebirth. A bit earlier in the story, Huck and Jim sleep "like dead people" after a harrowing brush with robbers on a wrecked steamboat, and wake up to sort through some salvaged loot, discuss the history of monarchy, and debate the wisdom of Solomon—the most pronounced of several instances in which an encounter with death dramatically deepens the mental life that Twain's characters display (HF 93–8). During pap's homicidal bout with delirium tremens, Huck barricades himself behind a turnip barrel with his father's gun but falls asleep on watch. The next morning it takes him a moment or two "to make out where I was" when pap wakes him. This frightening reminder of his father's nature is the catalyst for Huck's meticulous escape plan, planting a series of misleading clues to convince the entire village that he is dead. When Huck's unexpectedly long cat-nap ends, in this latest episode, he is similarly startled to find himself still alive and "spinning" stern first down "a monstrous big river," under a starlit sky. The experiences of the recent past "seemed to come up dim out of last week," a form of interior fog that takes some moments to disperse.

Chasing one distant black "speck" after another, Huck finally catches up with the badly damaged raft and his sleeping companion just before dawn. Jim's experience during the fog proves to have been the precise duplicate of Huck's: bewilderment, desperation, and despair, all leading to an exhausted sleep that Huck reflexively exploits in a kind of callous thought experiment aimed at the vulnerability of a waking mind. Without any more hesitation than he displayed when he detected pap's boot print in the snow, he sets out to convince Jim that the fog, the snags, and the loneliness were all a dream that Jim's imagination had invented in a ten-minute nap. "Dad fetch it," Jim objects, "how is I gwyne to dream all dat in ten minutes?" (HF 104). But Jim, in fact, is quite familiar with the propensity of dreams to alter the perception of time and space. After "studying" the problem over for five minutes, he sets out to interpret the elaborate vision that Huck insists he had, just as he had relished exploring the circumstances of his witch-ride on the night when Tom hung his hat in a tree or deciphered the advice of an oracular hair-ball in order to reassure Huck that his father would not beat him to death. In each of these episodes, Jim's is the more mobile imagination: psychologically more insightful than Huck and far more ingenious as he makes use of trivialities, curiosities, and rubbish to probe his own anxieties or ease those of someone else.[14]

Jim first reconstructs the terrifying events in the fog, employing the same mix of truth and "stretchers" that Huck had detected in *The Adventures of Tom Sawyer*: he "told me the whole thing right through, just as it happened," Huck observed, "only he painted it up considerable." With the details fresh in mind, Jim sets out to examine the array of warnings that they must contain, until dawn gradually reveals the raft's broken oar, along with the leaves, branches, and dirt it had accumulated as it collided with the riverbank during the night. "'O, well, that's all interpreted well enough, as far as it goes, Jim,' I says, 'but what does these things stand for?'" To Jim's mind the dream had summarized the complex psychological challenges ahead: the good intentions of some men whom he and Huck might conceivably encounter in their attempt to reach the free states, neutralized by the uncertain motives of others; warnings that would require a determined effort from both of them to understand; "quarrelsome people and all kinds of mean folks" who would need to be handled with great tact if their plan to head up the Ohio were to succeed. For Jim the dream was an occasion to explore the mental snags ahead, not the physical obstacles to his freedom. Huck's disingenuous question as the morning light reveals the tell-tale "rubbish" is oblivious to these deeper currents:

> Jim looked at the trash, and then looked at me, and back at the trash again. He had got the dream fixed so strong in his head that he couldn't seem to shake it loose and get the facts back into its place again, right away. But when he did get the thing straightened around, he looked at me steady, without ever smiling, and says:
> "What do dey stan' for? I's gwyne to tell you. When I got all wore out, wid work, en wid de callin' for you, en went to sleep, my heart wuz mos' broke bekase you wuz los', en I didn' k'yer no mo' what become er me en de raf'. En when I wake' up en fine you back agin, all safe en soun', de tears come en I could a got down on my knees en kiss' yo' foot I's so thankful. En all you wuz thinkin' 'bout, wuz how you could make a fool uv ole Jim wid a lie. Dat truck dah is trash; en trash is what people is dat puts dirt on de head er dey fren's en makes 'em ashamed."
> Then he got up, slow, and walked to the wigwam, and went in there, without saying anything but that. But that was enough. It made me feel so mean I could almost kissed *his* foot to get him take it back. (HF 105; emphasis in the original)

After yet another strangely precise fifteen-minute interval, Huck manages to apologize, but the mood of the passage has irretrievably changed. Jim's dream interpretation is a different order of disclosure than his opinions on the wisdom of Solomon, the oddities of the French, or the ominous significance of touching a snake skin. Once he shakes loose the grip of his vision, he realizes that he has opened a window into emotional layers that are ordinarily as hidden as the motives of the strangers he knows he will have to read as their journey proceeds.

When Tom Sawyer exploited Aunt Polly's feelings with an earlier bogus dream, incorporating the details of the conversation he had overheard as he was hiding under his aunt's bed, he was attempting to excuse his willingness to let her suffer, while he and his companions planned a dramatic resurrection at their own funeral. When Aunt Polly discovers the ruse, she anticipates Jim's powerful rebuke: "O, child you never think," she tells Tom: "You never think of anything but your own selfishness. You could think to come all the way over here from Jackson's Island in the night to laugh at our troubles, and you could think to fool me with a lie about a dream; but you couldn't ever think to pity us and save us from sorrow" (TS 144). In revisiting the scene for Huck's book, Twain casts Jim in Aunt Polly's role but sets aside the self-pity she expresses, as well as her pious delight when she first believes in the visions that Tom claims to have had: "Tom! The sperrit was upon you! You was a-prophecying—that's what you was doing!" By contrast, Huck's trick was (as he admits) gratuitously "mean"—a petty hoax—and Jim's sense of violation far more potent than Aunt Polly's weary grievance.

The night after the fog incident finds Huck and Jim trailing the huge lumber raft that Huck decides to board in order to cope with a nagging source of uncertainty that has begun to occur to them both: how to recognize Cairo if they pass it in the night and the houses are dark? How to distinguish the mouth of the Ohio from the "same old" Mississippi reemerging from behind the foot of a big island to form a single channel once more? Jim agrees with the plan to eavesdrop on the raftsmen's conversation in the hope that they will mention putting ashore for supplies or a spree when they get to Cairo. The uncertainty of their predicament has grown unbearable. In language that seems quite foreign to the idiom of an ignorant village boy, Huck confesses that "a young person can't wait very well when he is impatient to find a thing out" (HF 107), so he "shook" the rags from his body, "jumped into the river, and struck out for the raft's light."

This transition too represents a rebirth of mental energies. Huck doesn't simply report throwing his clothes into a convenient pile, with the idea of retrieving them when he returns to the raft. He sheds them like a useless excrescence or the materials of a cocoon, marking a phase of interior development that he has outgrown. Once he catches up to the lumber raft and cautiously conceals himself among some shingles where he can safely listen to the crew's conversation, all his boyish impatience seems to have washed away. The keelboat talk and manners that Twain promised to present in *Life on the Mississippi* do dominate the following pages, but they are filtered through the acute and appreciative intelligence of the listener who is hidden near the raftsmen's campfire, where the watch on duty have gathered to drink and sing.[15]

Not once over the next fifteen pages does Huck disclose any anxiety to hear about Cairo. Just as Twain had advised his own readers to do in the book's dismissive "Notice," Huck abandons for the time being all interest in motive, moral, or plot to record the shifting textures of the crew's collective mental life. At first they seem an unpromising group, a "mighty rough looking lot" of thirteen men passing a jug as they stand their watch on deck. But looks can be deceiving. The men are drinking from tin cups, Huck notes, not directly from the jug's spout as they listen to one man offer a loud, nasal rendition of an obscene song, "roaring" out lyrics that Huck himself is too polite to record but which the raftsmen greet with "a kind of Injun war-whoop" of approval. It "warn't a nice song," Huck admits, "for a parlor anyway," hinting that his own opinion falls somewhere in between a war-whoop and shocked disapproval (HF 107). Shadings of this kind fill every page of Huck's story.

Another singer follows the first with fourteen verses of a song that even Huck recognizes to be "kind of poor," a conclusion that the raftsmen plainly share, though they show a considerable measure of patience before they object on the threshold of verse fifteen: "one of them said it was the tune the old cow died on; and another one said, 'O, give us a rest;' and another one told him to take a walk," three nicely discriminated varieties of exasperation that combine to enrage the performer. "They made fun of him till he got mad and jumped up and begun to cuss the crowd, and said he could lam any thief in the lot." This challenge immediately prompts yet another sudden shift in mood as the aggrieved singer and the biggest man in the audience square off for an apparent battle to the death. The crew clearly relish the threatening speeches that each of the opponents makes as much as they did the first obscene song that Huck overheard, but when the two men eventually begin "edging away in different directions," muttering colorful but empty threats, a "little, black-whiskered chap" loses patience with the show and promptly whips them both. This unexpected outcome draws the loudest applause of all, as the two braggarts shake hands "very solemn," wash their "red noses and black eyes" in the river like a pair of lugubrious circus clowns and join their comrades at the raft's long sweeps as it steers through a channel crossing.

"You lay thar tell the chawin-up's done," one of the mock antagonists had declared, as he threw down "a buckskin coat that was all hung with fringes," followed by a hat "which was all over ribbons," in anticipation of the fearful battle that never takes place (HF 109). The long steering oars that the crew employs to keep the raft in the channel are another sort of fringe in this elaborate scene. In some respects so are the shingles that Huck is hiding behind on the margins of the campfire circle, and Huck's visit to the raft itself is little more than a fringe episode loosely linked to the larger narrative he has set out to tell. As the previous night's hazardous adventure in the fog had made plain, the river itself is fringed with obstacles and opportunities, both of which Twain will eagerly exploit as he strives to fill the remaining pages of the book. It is a dilemma that the crew of the lumber raft shares. The social and aesthetic complexity of their minds remains a latent presence in the story even when they briefly desert their campfire to work the sweeps, leaving behind a freshly lit pipe from which Huck is able to steal a smoke during the fifteen-minute absence that he tabulates on his ubiquitous mental timepiece. No sooner do the crew return from their navigational chore than they "went to talking and singing again" (HF 111).

An extraordinary inventory of gifts and interests immediately dominates the scene around the campfire: fiddle-playing, patting Juba, and a keel-boat breakdown so lively that the men soon grow winded with the frantic dance and sit down to resume drinking as they talk. Huck notes the range of topics that they consider with a stenographer's attention to detail: the habits and differences among hogs, the "different ways" of women and the best ways to put out house fires, the management of Indian affairs, the workings of monarchy, how to make cats fight, what to do about epileptic fits, and the "differences betwixt clear-water rivers and muddy-water ones" (HF 112). Nearly every subject appears to involve addressing numerous increments of difference, the fractional shadings of judgment that invariably fascinate the active intelligence. One would think the proximity of Cairo would at least cross Huck's mind when the crew discuss "how Ohio water didn't like to mix with Mississippi water," but it doesn't. Instead he is engrossed in mixtures rather than differences: the blend of precision and imprecision, fact and fable, that the men circulate along with their whiskey. The talk soon turns to the topic of how to keep tobacco from "getting mouldy" and then to ghosts, when a crew member named Ed breaks into the second-hand accounts of ghost sightings that his friends have been sharing to present an original experience of his own.

Huck takes in Ed's tale about a mysterious floating barrel, two nights of deadly thunder storms, and the "stark naked" corpse of a baby with the same attentive care that he gave to the raftsmen's bawdy songs, but Ed and his companions are paying attention to verbal nuances that, for the moment, Huck seems to miss. When the story's main character, Dick Allbright, confesses to having accidently strangled his infant son, Charles William, and hidden the body in a barrel, Ed registers some parenthetical admiration for Allbright's ability to "curl his tongue around the bulliest words in the language when he was a mind to, and lay them before you without a j'int started anywhere"—a reminder of the complex aesthetic appetites that the crew repeatedly displays. Ed admires this verbal flair even in a murderer. "Yes," he continues:

> he said he used to live up at the head of this bend, and one night he choked his child, which was crying, not intending to kill it, which was prob'ly a lie, and then he was scared, and buried it in a bar'l, before his wife got home, and off he went, and struck the northern trail and went to rafting, and this was the third year that the bar'l had chased him. He said the bad luck always begun light, and lasted till four men was killed, and then the bar'l didn't come any more after that. He said if the men would stand it one more night—and was agoing on like that, but the men had got enough. They started to get out a boat to take him ashore and lynch him, but he grabbed the little child all of a sudden and jumped overboard with it hugged up to his breast and shedding tears, and we never see him again in this life, poor old suffering soul, nor Charles William neither. (HF 118)

Without a moment's hesitation, a raftsman named Bob jumps on Ed's garbled syntax to ask whether Allbright or the dead Charles William was shedding tears. When Ed fires back that the baby had been dead three years and couldn't possibly cry, Davy, the black-whiskered man who had thrashed the two braggarts, immediately asks how the corpse could possibly keep that long. Listener after listener badgers Ed with one objection after another, varying his name as they do so—Edward, Eddy, Edmund, Edwin—with the predictable result among these exquisitely sensitive roughs: "Ed got up mad and said they could all go to some place which he ripped out pretty savage, and then walked off aft cussing to himself, and they yelling and jeering at him and roaring and laughing so you could hear them a mile" (HF 119).

Within moments they discover Huck among the shingles and briefly consider painting him sky-blue and throwing him overboard, before Huck's tears—real or contrived—prompt Davy to protect him. Huck's own split-second decision to answer "Charles William Allbright" when Davy asks his name suggests how quickly he is able to grasp at the trailing fringe of Ed's story and adapt it to his plight. The crew's prompt, appreciative laughter displays a much different emotional flavor from their jeering mockery an instant before. "I was mighty glad I said that," Huck admits as he senses the atmospheric change, "because maybe laughing would get them in a better humor" (HF 121).

A belated attempt on Huck's part to pick up some last-minute information about Cairo only arouses the men's scornful disbelief: "O, come!" they scoff, and "O, your grandmother," quite mild expressions of disgust after Ed's savage curses a few sentences earlier. Their extraordinary range of moods and eclectic array of interests, their appetite for racy songs and lucid syntax, the mix of patience and impatience that they display would appear to include a measure of Davy's implicit sensitivity to the presence of an impressionable "cub" in their midst. Huck returns to Jim as uncertain as ever about the location of Cairo, but his own moods now begin to fluctuate as dramatically as those of the raftsmen when he realizes that reaching the mouth of the Ohio River will mean that Jim is in fact "most free," a scrupulously weighed distinction, in Huck's mind, between his own apprehensive grasp of their situation and Jim's euphoric faith that the instant he sees Cairo, "he'd be a free man" (HF 123).

Huck fidgets around the raft, wrestling with his conscience and feeling "so mean and so miserable I most wished I was dead":

Jim talked out loud all the time while I was talking to myself. He was saying how the first thing he would do when he got to a free State he would go to saving up money and never spend a single cent, and when he got enough he would buy his wife, which was owned on a farm close to where Miss Watson lived; and then they would both work to buy the two children; and if their master wouldn't sell them, they'd get an ab'litionist to go and steal them.

It most froze me to hear such talk. He wouldn't ever dared to talk such talk in his life before. Just see what a difference it made in him the minute he judged he was about free. It was according to the old saying, "Give a nigger an inch and he'll take an ell." Thinks I, this is what comes of my not thinking. Here was this nigger which I had as good as helped to run away, coming right out flat-footed and saying he would steal his children—children that belonged to a man I didn't even know; a man that hadn't ever done me no harm.

I was sorry to hear Jim say that, it was such a lowering of him. My conscience got to stirring me up hotter than ever, until at last I says to it, "Let up on me—it ain't too late, yet—I'll paddle ashore at the first light and tell." I felt easy and happy and light as a feather right off. All my troubles was gone. I went to looking out sharp for a light and sort of singing to myself. By and by one showed. Jim sings out:

"We's safe, Huck, we's safe! Jump up and crack yo' heels, dat's de good ole Cairo at las' I jis' knows it!" (HF 124)

Singing out and singing in are concise indexes to the elaborate mental counterpoint of this passage—"Thinks I, this is what comes of my not thinking"—but when Huck tries to harness his newfound inward ease and betray his friend to a pair of slave hunters, his resolution shreds with the first words out of his mouth: "What's that yonder?" one of the slave hunters asks when they intercept Huck paddling toward shore in his canoe, "'A piece of a raft.' I says" (HF 125). The first stage of this famous deception on Huck's part is far from fluent, not a procession of bully words strung elegantly together like Dick Allbright's confession but a piece of Huck's fragmented mental state, a verbal rag that he shakes off in the process of seeking some tolerable equilibrium between the fears that "most froze" him when he listened to Jim's unguarded joy and the fiery rebuke of his conscience.

Once the slave hunters have been successfully duped, however, Huck returns to the raft and examines his thoughts like a practiced introspective psychologist:

> They went off, and I got aboard the raft, feeling bad and low, because I knowed very well I had done wrong, and I see it warn't no use for me to try to learn to do right; a body that don't get started right when he's little, ain't got no show—when the pinch comes there ain't nothing to back him up and keep him to his work, and so he gets beat. Then I thought a minute, and says to myself, hold on,—s'pose you'd a done right and give Jim up; would you felt better than what you do now? No, says I, I'd feel bad—I'd feel just the same way I do now. Well, then, says I, what's the use you learning to do right, when it's troublesome to do right and ain't no trouble to do wrong, and the wages is just the same? I was stuck. I couldn't answer that. So I reckoned I wouldn't bother no more about it, but after this always do whichever come handiest at the time. (HF 127)

These are the words of the economist of anxiety once more, anticipating Huck's ultimate determination to go to hell rather than return Jim to slavery, near the end of the book, and recapitulating his decision not to try for heaven, once he discovers in his opening chapter that Miss Watson intends to go there. From this standpoint, Huck is treading water throughout his story, rather than drifting toward a decisive moral transformation.

By contrast, Twain repeatedly insists that the reader pay close attention to the active nature of Huck's mental life: to his habit of weighing, comparing, distinguishing, and choosing as he considers his own actions and feelings or tries to assess those of other people. "I set down, one time, back in the woods, and had a long think about it," he explains, when he tries to make sense of the efficacy of prayer after a confusing talk with Miss Watson. When the widow complicates the issue by introducing the idea of "spiritual gifts," Huck returned to the woods "and turned it over in my mind a long time" before settling on the concept of two incompatible Providences that still bewilders him even after he has "thought it all out" (HF 14). These reflective activities are clearly related to one another and just as clearly different. A "long think" is nearly independent of any discrete mental object or idea. It is a purely transitive experience. As soon as distinct images or ideas begin to emerge from this generative process, they invite a kind of tactile inspection as we turn them over in the mind. In time they can evolve into a map or a path that one follows out to a temporary resting place, exactly as Huck does with his theological dilemma, once he concludes that the wages of acts are actually feelings, an intangible currency that he intuitively substitutes for the proverbial wages of sin, without realizing that (like Twain) he is an unconscious plagiarist.

Throughout the course of the story, Huck often finds himself immersed in making up his mind. Sometimes the process is nearly instantaneous, as when he blurts out "Charles William Allbright" to Davy's question on the lumber raft. More often he wrestles with a nest of invisible mental tow-heads, as he does when he finds that he is unable to "answer up prompt" to a menacing question from the slave hunters: "Is your man white, or black?" "I must lay it by in my mind," Huck decides, "and think it over some time or other," as he reflects on the surprising value of telling the truth to Mary Jane Wilks but postpones a more probing consideration of the discovery. Mary Jane's younger sister poses a different challenge when Huck is trying to maintain his improbable identity as an English valet, pretending to choke on chicken bones in order to gain time to have "another think" when his questioner catches him in an obvious lie (HF 222–3).

He deceives himself almost as easily as he deceives Jim's hair-ball when he is terrified by the tracks that signal his father's ominous reappearance outside the widow's fence. No sooner does he discover pap waiting in his bedroom one night than he recognizes a change in his feelings: "I had shut the door to. Then I turned around, and there he was. I used to be scared of him all the time, he tanned me so much. I reckoned I was scared now, too; but in a minute I see I was mistaken. That is, after the first jolt, as you may say, when my breath sort of hitched—he being so unexpected; but right away after, I see I warn't scared of him worth bothering about" (HF 23). Very quickly Huck is able to distinguish the hitch of surprise from the deep-seated fear he used to feel—a matter of interior degrees rather than a complete transformation in the relationship. The persecuting father and the persecuting good widow to whom Twain simplistically refers when he introduces the lumber raft episode into *Life on the Mississippi* are both embedded in a more complex emotional fringe that borders the story, a halo of dimly sensed feeling that Huck begins to explore as he meticulously examines his father's appearance, while pap in turn gives his son an "all over" scrutiny.[16]

Huck has put on "frills," pap notices, since living with the widow—fringes and ribbons that prompt his latent resentment—while pap increasingly seems to belong to the fringe of rubbish brushing the banks of the river. His tangled hair and mixed-up whiskers, Huck observes, overhang his face "like he was behind vines," masking the "fish-belly white" of his skin. "He was most fifty, and he looked it," Huck remembered, with a retrospective sensitivity to the aging process that seems at the very least precocious in a thirteen- or fourteen-year-old boy, while pap displays some of the same unguarded enthusiasm about books that Huck originally does when the widow first takes him in, listening to his son read aloud "about half a minute" before he "fetched the book a whack with his hand and knocked it across the house" (HF 24).

Huck's narrative is remarkably rich in sounds and poor in color, an attribute that Twain seems to acknowledge when, in the next moment or two, he has pap tear up the prize print that Huck had won in school, "a little blue and yaller picture of some cows and a boy." Like the sky-blue pot of paint on the lumber raft, this inconsequential detail effectively intensifies the book's pervasive commitment to the rich system of shadings on which Huck's language depends, the blacks and grays that dominate his palette. Emmeline Grangerford's drawings, he notes, are "blacker, mostly, than is common," with the exception of the "white slim ancles" that she gives to her sorrowing maidens. When Huck and Jim tie up the raft and sit in the shallow water near the river bank to watch "the daylight come," he describes the experience largely by ear, and though the east "reddens up" as sunrise approaches, the shifting qualities of "paleness," "blackness," and a slowly "softened up" gray dominate the visual world (HF 156). A kaleidoscope of relative values rather than different hues characterizes Huck's description, with the same mix of subtle and coarse gradations that mark the book's vernacular speech. Even the passionate redhead, Mary Jane Wilks, chiefly impresses Huck with the way that her eyes "was all lit up like glory" when he first meets her (HF 211). She is not a vividly colored presence in the story until Huck reveals the plot of the king and the Duke, when her face slowly caught fire "like sunset" with indignation. For that very reason, Huck wants her out of the way until his own counterplot has a chance to unfold, because her facial expression is as clear as black and white on the pages of his book: "A body can read it off," he notes, "like coarse print" (HF 242).

Sally Phelps—after Jim and Huck the most complex emotional intelligence in the story—is less easily readable, but like Mary Jane Wilks she is a volatile compound of outbursts that leave her alternately blazing "like a house afire" with outrage or joy, mingled with bouts of tenderness and grief that mitigate her fiery nature. When she tactfully quizzes Huck on the whereabouts of "Sid" after the boys have successfully freed Jim in the closing chapters of the story, she makes a point of allowing him the time he needs to make up his own mind about how he will answer. It has gradually dawned on Aunt Sally that Huck and Tom could easily have escaped from their bedroom on the night of the Evasion, when a posse of armed neighbors had gathered in her house to fight off the gang of cutthroats threatening to steal Jim, but the knowledge only leaves her "in a kind of brown study," for the time being, a state of imperfect illumination that lasts well into the next evening:

> And then when I went up to bed, she come up with me, and fetched her candle, and tucked me in, and mothered me so good I felt mean and like I couldn't look her in the face; and she set down on the bed and talked with me a long time, and said what a splendid boy Sid was, and didn't seem to want to ever stop talking about him; and kept asking me every now and then, if I reckoned he could a got lost, or hurt, or maybe drownded, and might be laying at this minute, somewhere, suffering or dead, and she not by him to help him; and so the tears would drip down, silent, and I would tell her that Sid was all right, and would be home in the morning, sure; and she would squeeze my hand, or maybe kiss me, and tell me to say it again, and keep on saying it, because it done her good, and she in so much trouble. (HF 350)

This passage restages Jim's account of his heartbreak when he fears that Huck has been drowned in the fog, as well as the immense relief that Mary Jane Wilks experiences when Huck assures her that the family's slaves will not be sold away to satisfy the greed of the king and the Duke. Along with Huck's feelings for Buck Grangerford, these are the most acute, affective moments in the book, singling out the characters whose inner worlds are most vital to the growth of Huck's own:

> And when she was going away, she looked down in my eyes, so steady and gentle, and says:
> "The door ain't going to be locked, Tom; and there's the window and the rod; but you'll be good, *won't* you? And you won't go? For *my* sake."
> Laws knows I *wanted* to go, bad enough, to see about Tom, and was all intending to go; but after that, I wouldn't a went, not for kingdoms. (Emphases in the original)

Like Huck, Tom, and pap, Aunt Sally is fully aware of the various ways of entering and leaving a bedroom, depending on the purposes one has in mind, and equally aware that Huck knows more about Tom's whereabouts than he is willing to tell. But she takes no further steps to civilize her make-believe nephew. When Huck does slide down the lightning rod three times during the night, trying to decide what course of action to pursue, her expectant presence in the window with her candle prompts him to swear to himself "that I wouldn't do nothing to grieve her any more" (HF 350).

As the book draws to a close, Huck finds himself once more suspended between two worlds that are represented, at this stage of the story, by pap Finn at one extreme and Sally Phelps at the other. His three trips up and down the lightning rod suggest how sensitive his mental equilibrium has become. This is precisely the predicament that characterizes Huck's life at the widow's when his adventures began. In time, he recalled of that earlier period, despite the discomforts of starchy clothes and table manners, it gradually got easier to attend school, to learn his lessons, and to take his punishment whenever he grew "uncommon tired" and played hooky. Civilized life grew less "raspy": "I liked the old ways best," Huck remembered, "but I was getting so I liked the new ones too, a little bit. The widow said I was coming along slow but sure, and doing very satisfactory. She said she warn't ashamed of me"

(HF 18). Distinguishing among the shades of feeling that compose this delicate emotional ensemble, both in the widow and in himself, is the mark of Huck's keen, introspective intelligence.

* * *

The state of psychological suspension that Huck describes at many key moments in his story—his ability to live in more than one world at a time and to relish the ways of each—echoes the imperfect integration of old times and new times that *Life on the Mississippi* depicts and that pervades some of the most suggestive moments in *A Tramp Abroad*. The French town of Chambery, on a stifling Sunday afternoon, seems to Twain "as quaint and crooked as Heilbronn" when he and Harris spend a night there at the end of their alpine adventure. But their brief tour of the town is also a miniature retrospective of Twain's career: a blend of the hypnotic lassitude of a Missouri village with troubling psychic signals from the outer world. Chambery, at first, seems under a spell:

> A drowsy reposeful quiet reigned in the back streets which made strolling through them very pleasant, barring the almost unbearable heat of the sun. In one of these streets which was eight feet wide, gracefully curved, and built up with small antiquated houses, I saw three fat hogs lying asleep, and a boy (also asleep), taking care of them. From queer old-fashioned windows along the curve, projected boxes of bright flowers and over the edge of one of these boxes hung the head and shoulders of a cat—asleep. The five sleeping creatures were the only living things visible in that street. There was not a sound; absolute stillness prevailed. It was Sunday; one is not used to such dreamy Sundays on the Continent. In our part of the town it was different that night. A regiment of brown and battered soldiers had arrived home from Algiers, and I judged they got thirsty on the way. They sang and drank till dawn, in the pleasant open air. (TA 347–8)

The riverine curve of Chambery's back streets bears a dreamlike similarity to St. Petersburg or Bricksville, the somnolent settings of *Huckleberry Finn*'s experience. The uncanny stillness that Twain and Harris encounter anticipates the lonely precincts of the Phelps farm, when Huck first arrives there to the mournful song of a spinning wheel. Even the brown and battered Algerian veterans seem to mirror pap Finn's insatiable thirst and racist passions. These contrasting worlds address overlapping dimensions of Twain's imaginative life, much like the different flavors of the widow Douglass's cooking improve (to Huck's taste) when they can mix with and modify one another—an early emblem of Huck's instinctive preference for the fluid continuum of experience. Sharp distinctions have little interest for him. "I see it warn't nothing but a dictionary," he notices, when Joanna Wilks asks him to swear that he has been telling her the truth, "so I laid my hand on it and said it" (HF 224). A dictionary artificially separates and numbers the ingredients of the verbal stream. It exerts no reverential claim.

Consciousness, as William James characterizes it, has a processional life; it is not a collection of neatly labeled packages but a shimmering confluence of mental currents, like the variegated circulation of interests and feelings that Huck savors as he listens to the crew of the lumber raft that he visits. Huck grasps James's insight, even if he might not be able to articulate it, when he senses that his raspy discomfort with civilized ways had begun to diminish as he moved back and forth along the continuum between his old existence and his new one. In Twain's fiction, this interest in the mind's pervasive transitive states plays an especially vivid role in *A Connecticut Yankee in King Arthur's Court*, a book that Twain had already begun to plan while he was on tour with George Washington Cable promoting the *Adventures of Huckleberry Finn*.[17] The burlesque collision between science and superstition, aristocracy and democracy, over which the "Yankee" presides is only superficially programmatic. Many of the illustrations that accompany the narrative split the verbal currents of Twain's page with competing streams of images that challenge the reader's powers of integration (see Figure 4.2). They often amount to editorial cartoons, a product of what the narrator dismissively recognizes as "the circus-side of my nature" (CY 1). But Twain's opening "Word of Explanation" for a manuscript that its author actually calls "The Tale of the Lost Land" displays very little of the burlesque or circus-loving sensibility.

During a guided tour of Warwick Castle, Twain claims to have encountered a "curious stranger" among the castle's visitors who "at once began to say things which interested me" (CY 1). He is a knowledgeable, candid, hypnotic presence, capable of weaving a spell about his listener "as he talked along, softly, pleasantly, flowingly" before abruptly administering a jolt of "electric surprise" by implying that he is personally familiar with the relics of King Arthur's day that their guide is presenting in a formulaic, "droning voice." After this startling disclosure, the stranger promptly disappears, but that evening he knocks at Twain's door in the Warwick Arms to explain himself. At the time of this unexpected visit, Twain had once more submitted to a verbal spell, "steeped in a dream of the olden time" that he had manufactured for himself by browsing in "old Sir Thomas Malory's enchanting book" (CY 2). While a rainstorm "beat upon the windows" of the room, he relished the book's "rich feast of prodigies and adventures, breathed-in the fragrance of its obsolete names, and dreamed again."[18]

By midnight Twain is ready for a final tale that he transcribes at some length for his reader, a long episode in which Malory records two of Sir Launcelot's many legendary feats. In the first Launcelot kills two giants who have imprisoned sixty "great gentlewomen born" and forced them to manufacture silk—a kind of sixth-century sweatshop inflicted on aristocratic rather than immigrant workers. Although the giants are well armed, their heads are curiously exposed to view, a detail that suggests the head might well be Malory's target as well. Launcelot "clave" the skull of the first giant in two and split his companion down the middle, when he tried to flee "for fear of the horrible strokes." Each description resonates with the divided nature of the episode that Twain chooses to transcribe and with the splitting of roles that soon takes place after Launcelot acknowledges the gratitude of the liberated prisoners and "betaught them unto God." In the second phase of his adventure, he goes to the aid of a single knight who is attacked by three others just outside the chamber window where Launcelot (rather like Twain himself) has been sleeping: "Truly, said Sir Launcelot, yonder one knight shall I help, for it were shame for me to see three knights on one, and if he be slain I am partner of his death" (CY 3).

The two are already partners in fact, however, much like the ill-fated giants, for once Launcelot takes his weapons and descends from his chamber window "by a sheet" to offer his help, the one knight proves to be Sir Kay, a fellow member of Arthur's court, who at Launcelot's insistence allows his famous ally to carry on the unequal fight alone. In "six strokes" the three attackers fall "to the earth" and yield to Launcelot "as man of might matchless." No sooner do they somewhat reluctantly negotiate the terms of their submission than Launcelot dismisses them and absconds with Sir Kay's armor, leaving his own armor and shield for Sir Kay to use as he returns to Camelot, unmolested by any more assailants who will be intimidated by the formidable insignia of the matchless man, an extension of the intertwined nature of partnership that the tale has begun to explore. The next moment, "my stranger" knocks at Twain's door and after four nightcaps of "hot Scotch whiskey" begins his story.

These preliminaries are more than just the conventional bridge between actual and imaginary life with which authors sometimes introduce a work of fiction. They echo the opening of the *Adventures of Huckleberry Finn*, where that narrator too introduces himself both as an inhabitant and a reader of books. The "erratic genius," Henry Clay Dean, in *Life on the Mississippi*, lives like a tramp on the curbstones of Keokuk, Iowa, utterly absorbed in his eclectic reading, until a desperate theater manager asks him to address a mass meeting on the verge of the Civil War, and Dean dazzles the restive audience with the explosive energy of his intelligence (LM 347). *A Connecticut Yankee in King Arthur's Court* begins in a similar zone of intersection between inner and outer worlds, a zone that Twain proposes to explore rather than abandon, once the Yankee's actual tale begins. His superficially innocuous "Word of Explanation," like the pleasant stream of his narrator's speech, touches immediately on a surprising collection of interesting things. Continuity, rather than rupture, is the experience that it strives to explain.

These transitive energies announce themselves with a sharp blow. Twain's stranger, like one of the doomed giants in Launcelot's double exploit, has his head cracked open by a crowbar in an altercation with an enormous Hartford factory worker named Hercules, a blow that "seemed to spring every joint in my skull and make it overlap its neighbor" (CY 5). Curious narrative overlaps continue once the stranger awakens in a beautiful country landscape to find himself challenged and then captured by a knight who proves to be the same Sir Kay the Seneschal of Malory's tale. Concluding that his assailant must have escaped from a circus or an asylum, the stranger negotiates the terms of his submission, just as Launcelot's three captives do, and the two march "comfortably" together through the deserted countryside toward a town that proves to be Camelot. At this point Twain's visitor grows too sleepy to continue his story, and he loans Twain the manuscript of his adventures—a palimpsest of overlapping narratives in which this Yankee of the Yankees describes the rich feast, the vivid silks, and the oddly stylized brutality of Malory's fragrant prose, all brought to life at King Arthur's court.[19]

"I am a partner of his death," Launcelot had observed to himself as he watched Sir Kay fend off his three attackers, an expression suggesting that a failure to act on Sir Kay's behalf would amount to a kind of death, as well as a degree of culpability in Sir Kay's fate: in effect, a psychological partnership with both the victim and his victimizers. An equally fluid relationship forms with electric suddenness between Twain and the curious tourist with the "obsolete smile" whom he quickly designates "my stranger" the moment that he enters Twain's rooms at the Warwick Inn. The book begins, then, with a series of subtle variations on the idea of interwoven mental identities, partly mediated by, but not confined to, the mind's propensity to immerse itself in nourishing verbal streams. A continuum of thought and feeling flows steadily, and almost invisibly, beneath the superficial contrasts and crude oppositions of the Yankee's tale.[20]

"I am an American," Twain's enigmatic visitor declares as he settles down to introduce himself without once mentioning his name—an oversight that he will never directly correct anywhere in the long manuscript describing his transmigrated experience. Instead he emphasizes the intensely practical nature of his mind, pronouncing himself "nearly barren of sentiment, I suppose—or poetry, in other words" (CY 4). Before Twain's practical visitor has traveled very far through the "reposeful, summer landscape" of sixth-century Britain, however, his barren mental condition begins to change, starting with another note of electric surprise that he produces in a "fair slip of a girl" that he and his captor pass on the road to Camelot. Other than a "hoop of flame-red poppies" decorating her "cascade of golden hair," the narrator remembers, she is completely naked and completely indifferent to the presence of Sir Kay (the "circus man") and his prisoner:

> She walked indolently along, with a mind at rest, its peace reflected in her innocent face. The circus man paid no attention to her; didn't even seem to see her. And she—she was no more

startled at his fantastic make-up than if she was used to his like every day of her life. She was going by as indifferently as she might have gone by a couple of cows; but when she happened to notice me, *then* there was a change! Up went her hands and she was turned to stone; her mouth dropped open, her eyes stared wide and timorously, she was the picture of astonished curiosity touched with fear. And there she stood gazing, in a sort of stupefied fascination, till we turned a corner of the wood and were lost to her view. That she should be startled at me instead of at the other man, was too many for me; I couldn't make head or tail of it. And that she should seem to consider me a spectacle, and totally overlook her own merits in that respect, was another puzzling thing, and display of magnanimity, too, that was surprising in one so young. There was food for thought here. I moved along as one in a dream. (CY 11; emphasis in the original)

The Yankee's dream, like Twain's preliminary reading in Malory's book, has instantly become a kind of mental feast as he itemizes the emotional turmoil that he awakens in the girl. Timidity, astonishment, fear, curiosity, stupefaction, and fascination instantly replace the restful vacancy in her face, as if the narcotic influence of the poppies she is wearing had only the most superficial effect on her intelligence. The feelings themselves tumble out in a vivid cascade that is not easy for the narrator to characterize or classify, in spite of his Yankee practicality. The affective categories "touch" one another, as Huck thinks the dishes in a good meal should do, rather than maintaining the crisp distinctions of a coin toss. In the space of a few sentences, the narrator's own thoughts participate in the kind of reverie that had appeared to absorb the girl's complete attention in the moments before she registers his presence. The two minds are effectively mirrors of one another: partners rather than products of antagonistic worlds.

This brief encounter in the opening stages of the Yankee's tale quickly proves to be a model for the many portraits of consciousness that follow once he arrives at Arthur's castle. Despite the "loud contrasts" that characterize the scene, it too seems to mingle mental indolence with a hunger for rapt astonishment captured in the "guileless relish" with which Arthur's nobles consume "tales of blood and suffering," or the "delighted ejaculations" with which they greet the dogfights that break out over the spent bones of a Round Table feast (CY 19). States of apparent mental vacancy alternate with outbreaks of electrified awareness whenever an irresistible combination of interests unexpectedly stirs the intelligence. Twain depicts these processes within the narrator himself in a type of slow motion when the "airy" page he names Clarence first informs him that he has arrived in King Arthur's court. "I waited a minute," the narrator notes, "to let that idea shudder its way home" before asking the date. "528—nineteenth of June," Clarence replies, cheerfully precise and cheerfully inaccurate, as events turn out, but the mixed information sets off a brief struggle in the narrator's mind that calls into play a number of the qualities that will eventually enable him to begin a remarkable adaptation to this seemingly alien world:

> *Something* in me seemed to believe him—my consciousness, as you may say; but my reason didn't. My reason straightway began to clamor; that was natural. I didn't know how to go about satisfying it, because I knew that the testimony of men wouldn't serve—my reason would say they were lunatics, and throw out their evidence. But all of a sudden I stumbled on the very thing, just by luck. I knew that the only total eclipse of the sun in the first half of the sixth century occurred on the 21st of June, A. D. 528, O. S., and began at 3 minutes after 12 noon. I also knew that no total eclipse of the sun was due in what to *me* was the present year—*i.e.* 1879. So, if I could keep my anxiety and curiosity from eating the heart out of me for forty-eight hours, I should then find out for certain whether this boy was telling me the truth or not. (CY 16–17; emphases in the original)

The Yankee's innate practicality reasserts its sway once he singles out an arcane fact to cling to. He proves himself to be every bit the economist of anxiety that Huck is by putting the mystery surrounding his strange whereabouts "clear out of my mind" until the presence or absence of what he will soon call "his" eclipse can resolve it. But like Huck, he too is a remarkable mental compound, sorting through a consortium of interior voices that compete for attention and influence.

An idea can "shudder" its way into a measure of mental acceptance that is impossible to account for on reasonable grounds. Luck can be as useful as logic in addressing the interior conflict that breaks out between a receptive mental "something" and its outraged opponent. Anxiety and curiosity coexist in this troubled "I," each capable of eating out the heart with their deeply corrosive uncertainties, but doing so for very different reasons and with very different tools. Worry and wonder give rise to their own distinct forms of suspense. All of these vivid interior energies seem to impinge on one another in the narrator's state of suspended judgment, much as a similar emotional impingement turned the slip of a girl he had seen on the road into stone.

This brief introspective process takes a more intense form a handful of chapters later, when the narrator is waiting in Arthur's dungeons to learn the effect of the terrible calamity that he has threatened to inflict on the kingdom. In a second instance of sudden inspiration, he has decided to exploit the eclipse that is about to take place in order to terrify Arthur's court and secure his status as a formidable magician, sending Clarence back to the king with the news that if any harm should come to him he intends to blot out the sun. Once he is alone, an unexpected mental eclipse immediately begins to eat out his heart, shuddering its way home much as the original conviction of Clarence's truthfulness had done: "the knowledge that I was in deadly danger," he explained, "took to itself deeper and deeper meaning all the time; a something which was realization crept inch by inch through my veins and turned me cold" (CY 44). The vivid colors and endemic violence of the castle's "upper world" have so imbedded themselves in the narrator's imagination as to suggest a figurative vocabulary for the operations of the mind. By contrast to the world of courtly display where his captors have just stripped him naked, dungeons and mental interiors are the natural storehouses for forbidden thoughts. Depth is an equally natural emblem of psychic intensity. In the remote recesses of consciousness, hidden away amid a "maze of underground corridors" beneath the castle's public spaces, realization gradually takes hold.

The sensory assault that the narrator associates with the outer world—the "gay display of moving and intermingling colors" that he first notices in the castle courtyard—repeats itself in the "fierce glare of daylight" when he finally emerges from his dungeon to confront the multitudes of spectators who are gathered in terrified silence to witness his execution, arranged in "sloping terraces that were rich with color." These images are far from the psychic monotones of Huckleberry Finn's experience. Though the narrator's cell had maintained "the complexion of midnight to a shade," it takes his mind "but a second" to traverse the startling interior distances represented by these antagonistic environments, bounding up with "revulsion" from its own state of frozen dread at one moment, but plunging just as swiftly into near-idiotic confusion when Arthur's guards arrive to take him to his death. The narrator had coolly resolved to put out of his mind the nagging puzzle of his predicament until a sixth-century eclipse could settle the question. What remains behind after this superficial mental purge is a remarkably rich introspective web of knowledge and feeling, aptly captured in the intermingling sensations of Arthur's world.

Clarence introduces two odd inaccuracies into the texture of the Yankee's dream that set the stage for these mental extremes. The first proves to be a mistake about the day of the month that will ultimately save the narrator's life, but not before it almost completely deprives him of his reason. The second occurs when Clarence proposes to visit him in the dungeon and help get word to the friends who will ransom him, once Sir Kay has told the customary, elaborate lie about the narrator's capture and set the traditional terms of his liberation (CY 18). Like the narrator himself, Clarence appears to be making, at best, an imperfect adjustment to the demands of this sixth-century scene. "Oh, call me pet names, dearest, call me a marine!" the airy page will exclaim when Sir Kay first begins to exaggerate his knightly adventures, a clear verbal signal that Clarence too belongs among the overlapping seams of Twain's story, equipped with the proper costume but not the proper speech for his part (CY 23).

Quite unexpectedly, however, Sir Kay declares his intention to burn this exotic prisoner at the stake, rather than hold him for ransom, a chilling verdict that he delivers before the assembled knights of the Round Table with a barely suppressed yawn that also overlaps with the sleepy consciousness of his creator. Of all the sixth-century figures whom the Yankee encounters, only Sir Kay and Merlin appear to possess a subliminal awareness that this strange visitor does not belong in their fictional fabric of giants, ogres, knights, and magicians. They share a grim determination to be rid of him. He is a heretic—a perpetrator of mental crimes—and must be destroyed as quickly as possible, with the singularly savage punishment that the medieval law of heresy demands. Clarence quickly "fell to making fun of my sorry plight," when he pays his promised visit to the narrator's cell, but he succumbs just as quickly to the antagonistic appeals of desire and fear when he discovers that, like Merlin, the narrator too is a master magician (CY 38). The blend of old ways and new ways that compose his character figures largely in the self-congratulatory explanation that he offers to the narrator when he is unexpectedly led to the stake a day ahead of the scheduled eclipse that he had counted on to intimidate Arthur into releasing him. "Tis through me the change was wrought!" Clarence exults:

> And main hard have I worked to do it, too. But when I revealed to them the calamity in store, and saw how mighty was the terror it did engender, then saw I also that this was the time to strike! Wherefore I diligently pretended, unto this and that and the other one, that your power against the sun could not reach its full until the morrow; and so if any would save the sun and the world, you must be slain to-day, whilst your enchantments are but in the weaving, and lack potency. Odsbodkins it was but a dull lie, a most indifferent invention, but you should have seen them seize it and swallow it, in the frenzy of their fright, as it were salvation sent from heaven; and all the while was I laughing in my sleeve the one moment, to see them so cheaply deceived, and glorifying God the next, that He was content to let the meanest of His creatures be His instrument to the saving of thy life. Ah, how happy has the matter sped! You will not need to do the sun a *real* hurt—ah, forget not that, on your soul forget it not! Only make a little darkness—only the littlest darkness, mind, and cease with that. It will be sufficient....Go to thy triumph, now! but remember—ah, good friend, I implore thee remember my supplication, and do the blessed sun no hurt. For *my* sake, thy true friend. (CY 46; emphases in the original)

Like the Yankee, Clarence too is a careful student of the psychic vulnerability of others. He is an astute judge of the best moment to strike a paralyzed intelligence in order to have the maximum impact on its thinking. At the same time, he is a sly tactician who knows that he needs to insinuate his own plan with "this, that, and the other one" rather than proclaim it directly, just as the narrator will soon begin to insinuate bits of modern technology into the nooks and crannies of Arthur's realm while he prepares the minds of the population for the dramatic cultural revolution that he intends to foment.

Yet this instantaneous sympathy with, and mirroring of, the narrator's mental practices overlaps, in Clarence's consciousness, with the superstitious terror and deep piety of his sixth-century nature, just as Twain's contemporary intelligence responds with pleasure to the archaic fragrance of Malory's prose. The opening chapters of "The Tale of the Lost Land" depict a mental continuum of past and present, of inner and outer life, that helps explain the narrator's immediate appreciation for the paradoxical delicacy of these superficially indelicate knights and ladies (CY 34), for the beautiful simplicity of Merlin's familiar tale about the Lady of the Lake (CY 30), for the "loftiness and sweetness" in the faces of the courtiers "that rebuked your belittling criticisms" (CY 23), and for their surprising gifts as "good and serious listeners" (CY 20). All these mitigating instances of taste and perception suggest that the narrator is remarkably well-equipped to appreciate the virtues of the world in which he finds himself and to savor its "pleasant stir and noise and confusion."[21]

This receptivity to the unpredictable appeal of interest is the governing principle of the book: an antidote to the droning voice of tour guides, the tedium of a stale joke, or the soporific influence of an old and familiar story. No sooner does the narrator find himself installed as Arthur's chief minister than he sets about to "invent, contrive, create; reorganize things; set brain and hand to work, and keep them busy" (CY 54). His urgency is only partly motivated by a desire to make life bearable amid the society of "more or less tame animals" with which he believes he is surrounded. Minds and hands demand to be kept busy as a condition of their survival. Morgan Le Fay's dungeons illustrate the power of mental focus and the dangers of mental stagnation in a number of perverse ways, when the narrator eventually inspects them some years after his transformation into The Boss.

At the end of a long banquet during which Le Fay had been trying to ingratiate herself with her distinguished guest, she offers to show him the "blithe sight" of her torture chambers in action. Following his hostess and her guards on a "chill, uncanny journey" through passageways "of imprisoned night"—another descent into the chambers of consciousness—the narrator discovers there a young father stretched on the rack, trapped by an odd legal contingency that is an institutional correlate for the grim machine that is killing him. If he dies under torture without confessing to the crime of killing a royal stag—an offense that he actually has committed—the Queen will be unable to evict his small family from their farm and doom them to starvation. "It is truly a stubborn soul, and endureth long," the Queen had confessed, with barely concealed admiration, when the young man's "muffled shriek" first "bored its way up through the stillness" of her banquet chamber (CY 153).

But in another instance of the book's uncanny partnerships, Morgan Le Fay too is caught in a mental dilemma. To have a guilty prisoner die in her dungeons, without access to the Church's rite of confession and absolution, would be a mortal sin for which the Queen's own soul would have to answer. Hence the presence of two priests beside the executioner's brutal "machine" ready to administer prompt absolution to the doomed man the moment that they have something to absolve. But Church doctrine also dictates that if she tortures to death an innocent victim who steadfastly refuses to confess to a crime that he did not commit, her soul is safe. The presence of the prisoner's wife and child in the "rack-cell" adds further layers of psychological complexity to an already tortured set of circumstances, since their cries of distress might either stiffen or weaken his resolve to keep silent.[22]

"I could not let this horror go on," the narrator declares, "it would have killed me to see it," adding a final twist to the multiple forms of racking that the scene depicts. It takes The Boss himself some moments to make sense of the intricate psychological fabric on display in the dungeon chamber. Once he learns the young couple's story, he comes to share the Queen's warped admiration for their mental fortitude: "I'll book you both for my colony," he informs them, "you'll like it there: it's a Factory where I'm going to turn groping and grubbing automata into *men*" (CY 157; emphasis in the original). Morgan Le Fay's dungeons are the opposite kind of factory: a device for turning men into grubbing automata. But the device is not entirely of her making. Some of her prisoners are legacies, inherited from prior regimes and held so long that not even the prisoners themselves or the priests who visit them can remember their crimes. The most recent of her victims is also the most modern in spirit: a subject who had declared that men were "about all alike, and one man as good as another." "He said he believed that if you were to strip the nation naked and send a stranger through the crowd, he couldn't tell the king from a quack doctor, nor a duke from a hotel clerk," cheerfully irreverent sentiments that mirror the narrator's own (CY 167). The Queen's prisoners are effectively layered like a schematic cross-section of cultural change, with the oldest of them completely steeped in an "imprisoned night" to which no one can attach a date and the latest virtually free of the mental encumbrances that The Boss's revolutionary colony is intended to correct.

One special victim spends decades in a chamber from which he is able to glimpse his former home, at a great distance, through an arrow-slit in the walls. The Queen had deliberately set out to "scorch his heart" by staging mock funerals at his cottage door that were meant to destroy him with anxiety. The strategy backfires, however, for it gives her prisoner an excruciating mental interest, "half a ray" of absorbing intellectual light, on which his mind is able to feed until the narrator frees him and reunites him with his family (CY 168). Even the rack-cell proves to harbor a residue of intellectual light when the narrator learns that the priests were "generously hot" to have the executioner punished for mistreating the prisoner's wife, while he coolly tortured her husband. A sympathetic priesthood, however, is both a reassuring and a frustrating discovery from the narrator's point of view, "for it was just the sort of thing to keep a people reconciled to an Established Church" (CY 161). He would prefer that the traits of ruthlessness and mercy be hermetically sealed off from one another, but that is not the kind of world in which he finds himself.

"What a jump I had made!" the Yankee exults, when he first assumes his new status in the kingdom, after the happy accident of his eclipse. In fact, a restless proclivity for mental jumps of all sorts pervades his nature from the outset of his story. The strange society that surrounds him is exactly the sort of stimulus his mental equipment demands: "I couldn't keep from thinking about it, and contemplating it, just as one does who has struck oil" (CY 63). He is, in effect, a version of Morgan Le Fay's captive: both a victim of the ingenious forms of cruelty that her mind devises and a beneficiary of the all-engrossing interests that her psychological tactics awaken. Like the Queen's two priests, Twain's narrator is generously hot in his mental enthusiasms. Even the discouragingly abject state of Britain's people and the insidious domination of the Church scarcely dampen his zeal for observation, sampling, study, and reflection.[23]

He makes a point of being present at jousting tournaments, despite his contempt for the "ridiculous human bull-fights" that they entail, both because it is impolitic to "hold himself aloof from the things which his friends and his community have at heart" and because he wants to "study the tournament" with an eye to making improvements (CY 72). He experiments with the literary talents of an intelligent priest to see what sort of "reporter-material" he might be able to exploit when he establishes a newspaper. He sets up surreptitious schools and factories throughout the kingdom and cultivates "a complete variety of Protestant congregations" both as a hedge against his eventual assault on the Catholic monopoly and because of his belief that variety is "a law of human nature." No single religious garment, he is convinced, could possibly satisfy the range of "spiritual wants and instincts" that are as diverse as our "physical appetites, complexions and features" (CY 81), a familiar Enlightenment insight that will reappear at the conclusion of *What Is Man?*[24]

Indeed, for an engineer and an inventor, this Yankee of Yankees is surprisingly indifferent to the practical details of engineering and inventing, much as a child at play is indifferent to the impractical nature of an engrossing fantasy. He never goes into particulars about his mines or factories with anything like the degree of attention that he devotes to the qualities of lively journalism. He never elaborates on the steps by which he introduces the telephone to Clarence and his other close associates, never comments on the recipe for blasting powder or how he manages to produce enough of it on short notice to blow up Merlin's massive Roman tower, never accounts for the origin of the dragoon pistols that he uses when he meets Sir Sagramour in a final tournament, dressed more like a ballet dancer than the cowboy he appears to want to imitate. Technology and Yankee know-how are little more than the stage props of his dream. Its energy and variety spring from thoughts, ideas, feelings, and from the fervor with which the narrator seizes on all these forms of mental life and plays with them, much like Young Man's Interior Master will do in the course of his thought experiments.[25]

Twain makes this point quite explicit late in the story, as his narrator is struggling to train Arthur to imitate the behavior of a commoner during their ill-fated adventure of traveling about the kingdom in disguise:

There are wise people who talk ever so knowingly and complacently about "the working classes," and satisfy themselves that a day's hard intellectual work is very much harder than a day's hard manual toil, and is righteously entitled to much bigger pay. Why, they really think that, you know, because they know all about the one, but haven't tried the other. But I know all about both; and as far as I am concerned, there isn't money enough in the universe to hire me to swing a pickaxe thirty days, but I will do the hardest kind of intellectual work for just as near nothing as you can cipher it down—and I will be satisfied, too. Intellectual "work" is misnamed; it is a pleasure, a dissipation, and is its own highest reward. The poorest paid architect, engineer, general, author, sculptor, painter, lecturer, advocate, legislator, actor, preacher, singer, is constructively in heaven when he is at work; and as for the magician with the fiddle-bow in his hand who sits in the midst of a great orchestra with the ebbing and flowing tides of divine sound washing over him—why certainly, he is at work, if you wish to call it that, but lord, it's a sarcasm just the same. (CY 279)

The constructive heaven of consciousness—its endless variety of appetites and interests, the flowing tide of activity that it generates—is everywhere in evidence in the Yankee's story, waiting for him to recognize its presence and harness its potential from the moment that he awakens amid the "polished up court of Comanches" that medieval chivalry seems to resemble. Even the jousting tournament conceals surprising interior reserves, despite the narrator's withering contempt for the institution. Wasteful though it may be, it is also a visible embodiment of intense emotional commitments, a fact that Launcelot recognizes when he declines to challenge Sir Gareth's eminence on a day when the succession of different colors under which Sir Gareth vanquished opponent after opponent signaled the unique psychological urgency that "enforceth him to do great deeds" (CY 76). "This day he shall have the honour," Launcelot explains to the king, who is urging him to answer Gareth's general challenge: "though it lay in my power to put him from it, I would not." These words appear in a trial version of the narrator's newspaper, a disappointing experiment that lacks "the whoop and crash and lurid description" he expects of modern journalism. The generosity of Launcelot's position suggests, however, that in this instance it is the narrator and not Arthur's knights who has the temperament of a polished Comanche.

"We don't reason, where we feel; we just feel," the Yankee observes to himself at one point, as he sighs over the centuries that separate him from the Hartford telephone operator whom he loves (CY 94). Precisely the same explanation accounts for the seemingly irrational gullibility of Arthur and his court when they accept on faith the testimony of strangers, before setting off on improbable chivalric quests. Maps are as superfluous as corroboration or credentials when a knight departs on such a journey. The process supersedes the end, just as the interminable stories that Sandy tells during the narrator's own mission to liberate forty-five damsels from "cruel captivity" require no preface and finish with no result (CY 127). They are transitive tales.

Brains would have been a liability in Camelot, the narrator believes, not because it is a civilization without ideas but because it is full of them: "inherited ideas" that "flowed in ruts worn deep by time and habit," just as the narrator recognizes that his own ideas do. Both cultural legacies (as Old Man would observe in the pages of Twain's late dialogue) are stubbornly resistant to change. The "intellectual moles" of Arthur's kingdom find a way to accommodate the Yankee's presence among them, just as readily as he accommodates himself to theirs; "the account was square, the books balanced, everybody was satisfied," the narrator declares (CY 69). But the books don't balance as neatly as he implies, since it is the common people who confer the narrator's title, not the officials of the court or the narrator himself. The term that he translates as The Boss "fell casually from the lips of a blacksmith, one day, in a village; was caught up as a happy thought and tossed from mouth to mouth with a laugh and an affirmative vote; in ten days it had swept the kingdom, and was become as familiar as the king's name" (CY 69). The Yankee's miraculous telephone system could not have dispersed this happy thought any more swiftly throughout Britain than the receptive minds and oral circuitry of these intellectual moles succeed in doing.

Less efficient but no less meaningful instances of mental receptivity emerge elsewhere in the narrator's experience. It takes a moment or two for one of the freemen he encounters during his quest with Sandy to absorb the idea of democracy, but once the principle had a chance to "soak into his understanding" he was instantly on fire with excitement (CY 112). One of the Yankee's advertising knights experiences a setback at Morgan Le Fay's castle, but when the narrator suggests a clever adaptation of the slogan he is using in his campaign to popularize Persimmons's Soap, the knight promptly appreciates the twist: "Verily, it is wonderly bethought! (CY 142). The loss of a sale or two, the Yankee had assured his discouraged agent, is not a disaster. "We have brains, you and I," the narrator remarked, "and for such as have brains there are no defeats."

Even the monks in the Valley of Holiness—a citadel of religious superstition in Arthur's realm—show unexpected inner resources and mental agility. The majestic Latin chant that they contribute to the narrator's carefully orchestrated restoration of their Holy Fountain is an outgrowth of their own spiritual experience and musical gifts. It is not one of the narrator's "invented" effects—the fireworks and phony incantations he deploys to dazzle the population and intimidate Merlin. When the Fountain that the narrator's trained experts had repaired once more begins to flow, the spectators gathered in the Valley to witness the miracle fondle the stream like a long-lost child. "Yes, it was pretty to see," the narrator grudgingly admits of this curiously intimate gesture, "and made me think more of them than I had done before" (CY 224). One of his recently instituted news journals happens to arrive in the Valley of Holiness during his stay, and though the monks briefly fear that its printed pages may be a "dark work of enchantment," they are thrilled with the "marvelous exactness" of its descriptions when the narrator reads a few passages aloud:

> And might they take this strange thing in their hands, and feel of it and examine it?—they would be very careful. Yes. So they took it, handling it as cautiously and devoutly as if it had been some holy thing come from some supernatural region; and gently felt of its texture, caressed its pleasant smooth surface with lingering touch, and scanned the mysterious characters with fascinated eyes. These grouped bent heads, these charmed faces, these speaking eyes—how beautiful to me! (CY 262)

The narrator is not always so successful or so generous a teacher. He completely fails in his repeated attempts to explain the concept of purchasing power to a group of tradesmen with whom he and the king are visiting during their tour in disguise. The sluggish minds of his pupils eventually enrage him, but in subjects other than economics they are far from sluggish.

One of these pupils, a seemingly abject charcoal burner named Marco whom the narrator originally befriends, explodes with revolutionary fervor once the narrator's leading remarks tempt him to do so. "I have said the words, I have said the words!" he cries, when he renounces the brutal caste system that has degraded him: "the only ones that ever tasted good in my mouth, and the reward of that taste is sufficient. Lead on, an ye will, be it even to the scaffold; for I am ready" (CY 299). A self-satisfied blacksmith, a mason, and a wheelwright, all of whom the frustrated narrator sets out to humiliate, prove to be far from simpletons when the narrator traps them in a legal snare that could send all three to the pillory:

> Pale, shaky, dumb, pitiful? Why, they weren't any better than so many dead men. It was very uncomfortable. Of course I thought they would appeal to me to keep mum, and then we would shake hands, and take a drink all around, and laugh it off, and there an end. But no; you see I was an unknown person, among a cruelly oppressed and suspicious people, a people always accustomed to having advantage taken of their helplessness, and never expecting just or kind treatment from any but their own families and very closest intimates. Appeal to *me* to be gentle, to be fair, to be generous? Of course they wanted to, but they couldn't dare. (CY 333; emphasis in the original)

These men may be slow to grasp the meaning of purchasing power, but the narrator is forced to acknowledge that their social and political educations are far from negligible.

Arthur is by far the most obtuse intelligence in this extended episode of the book. His inept effort to prove himself an experienced and successful farmer ultimately results in his enslavement, when the villagers to whom he is speaking conclude that he and the narrator are a pair of treacherous madmen and attempt to hunt them down. But even the king is prone to periods of deep musing and elaborate dreams, disrupted by the provocative intrusion of "randoming" thoughts (CY 266). Though his thinking sometimes appears to the narrator as congested as the trickle of sand through an hourglass, at other moments even the narrator is brought to admire the way in which the king "works" his intellect (CY 269). The experience of slavery both humiliates and educates him, stripping away the "mere artificiality" of his royal prerogatives to expose the genuinely human feelings within (CY 351).

Sandy's musings and feelings run deeper still. The long extracts from Malory's book that Twain puts into her mouth have, at first, a narcotic effect on the narrator's spirit, but when he occasionally interrupts the thread of her story with some instance of American slang, Sandy will repeat his alien expressions quietly to herself as she memorizes their sounds and meaning, "turning the words daintily over her tongue" and remarking on their "fair and winsome grace" (CY 127). Her resourcefulness and quick wit stand the narrator in good stead at Morgan Le Fay's court, and though she firmly believes that a herd of swine are in fact a collection of captive princesses, her distress at the narrator's inability to see their true nature leads her to reflect on the mysterious differences that divide one human being's perception from that of another—exactly the point that the narrator himself will make, a few pages later, when he recognizes that Sandy is not a lunatic (CY 183, 191).

Her own psychological acuity and tact far exceed the narrator's own. When he bluntly and thoughtlessly dismisses one of her attempts to assimilate his slang, she offers an account of her feelings that is a metaphorical tapestry of gentle rebuke and emotional insight, just verging on sarcasm before registering in a nearly bewildering verbal display what she terms the subtle "complexion" of her mind:

> I would I might please thee, sir, and it is to me dole and sorrow that I fail, albeit sith I am but a simple damsel and taught of none, being from the cradle unbaptized in those deep waters of learning that do anoint with a sovereignty him that partaketh of that most noble sacrament, investing him with reverend state to the mental eye of the humble mortal who, by bar and lack of that great consecration seeth in his own unlearned estate but a symbol of that other sort of lack and loss which men do publish to the pitying eye with sackcloth trappings whereon the ashes of grief do lie bepowdered and bestrewn, and so, when such shall in the darkness of his mind encounter these golden phrases of high mystery, these shut-up shops, and draw the game, and

bank the fires, it is but by the grace of God that he burst not for
envy of the mind that can beget, and tongue that can deliver so
great and mellow-sounding miracles of speech, and if there do
ensue confusion in that humbler mind ... wit ye well it is the very
substance of worshipful dear homage and may not lightly be
misprized, nor had been, an ye had noted this complexion of my
mood and mind and understood that that I would I could not,
and that I could not I might not, nor yet nor might *nor* could, nor
might-not nor could-not, might be by advantage turned to the
desired *would*, and so I pray you mercy of my fault, and that ye
will of your kindness and your charity forgive it, good my master
and most dear lord. (CY 212; emphases in the original)

In her fragrant, sixth-century prose, Sandy is recasting Huck's
realization that a "body that don't get *started* right when he's little,
ain't got no show" (HF 127; emphasis in the original). Like Huck
too she is trapped by the incompatibility between what she believes
she ought to do and what she is capable of doing. But in this passage
Sandy is able to articulate the intricate operations of her "mental
eye" with a dramatic potency rarely matched even by Jim in Twain's
earlier book.[26]

The narrator responds to this speech with the first signs of a
"shuddery reverence" that will ultimately reconfigure his relations
with Sandy, but this is not the first of the remarkable interior
discoveries that he makes as "The Tale of the Lost Land" unfolds.
Much to his surprise, he recognizes that "a passion for art had got
worked into the fabric of my being" by the cheap colored lithographs
in his Hartford house, a passion that the barren chambers of
Arthur's castle cannot satisfy (CY 52). His aesthetic tastes extend
to writing as well. Good journalism requires variety and emotional
scope to give it life, "to disguise repetitiousness of fact under variety
of form" and prompt a reader to "drain the whole column" of an
elaborate newspaper article "with a good appetite, and perhaps
never notice that it's a barrel of soup made out of a single bean,"
though noticing this dubious professional achievement can make
the soup all the more delicious (CY 260).

He displays surprising reservoirs of knowledge about ancient
astronomy, European history, the work of Lactantius, and fiscal
policy. A love of music plays both burlesque and serious roles in
his thinking, as his tribute to an orchestra's flowing tides of divine

sound makes evident. A degree of familiarity with physics leads him to appreciate the value of "nuclei" as a metaphor for his hidden schools and factories, and at the climactic Battle of the Sand Belt, the narrator and Clarence collaborate to make their fortress into a model of atomic structure, with concentric rings of wire carrying a deadly electric charge arranged in a sequence of orbits around a dense core where the narrator and his cadre of skilled boys concentrate the destructive energies of modernity. Merlin's Cave is the final setting where, as Clarence implies, it is time to "unthink" the narrator's dream (CY 418). Until that moment, the sheer delight of thinking had propelled the narrative through an extraordinary procession of interesting things—a fantastic expansion of the keen electrical surprise with which this elaborate inner excursion had begun.

Conclusion

Greatnesses in the Brain

With the last and in some respects most ambitious of Twain's published novels, the *Personal Recollections of Joan of Arc*, he set out to prepare a rejoinder to the disintegration of Hank Morgan's dream. In the process of doing so, he lodges a tentative objection to the stark philosophical convictions that prompt the narrator of "The Tale of the Lost Land" to effectively exterminate the world that he had hoped to perfect. "Ah, what a donkey I was!" he exclaims as he and his fifty-two boy companions wait in Merlin's Cave for their enemies to assault them:

> Toward the end of the week, I began to get this large and disenchanting fact through my head: that the mass of the nation had swung their caps and shouted for the Republic for about one day, and there an end! The Church, the nobles and the gentry then turned one grand all-disapproving frown upon them and shriveled them into sheep! From that moment the sheep had begun to gather to the fold—that is to say, the camps—and offer their valueless lives and valuable wool to the "righteous cause." Why, even the very men who had lately been slaves were in the "righteous cause," and glorifying it, praying for it, sentimentally slobbering over it, just like all the other commoners. Imagine such human muck as this; conceive of this folly! (CY 427)

Training is everything, Twain's narrator had recognized in the depths of Morgan Le Fay's dungeons, as he contemplated the products of the Queen's macabre mental world. The reflexive mindlessness of training both enabled and doomed the utopian fantasy of his sixth-century English republic.

This realization closely resembles the central doctrine of *What Is Man?* Even the most exquisitely gifted human intelligence, Old Man suggests in those pages, is merely a mechanism, an impersonal engine, not an independent ethical or artistic agent. Training and temperament make us what we are. That disquieting assertion is Old Man's deliberately provocative answer to the question that Twain adopted as a title for his 1906 collection of Socratic papers, portions of which he had begun to test on a select cluster of his Hartford neighbors several years before the narrator of "The Tale of the Lost Land" endorses them. However adroit the mental mechanism might be in any individual instance—however comprehensive its ability to assimilate and manipulate the rich streams of thought and feeling in which it was imbedded—it remained only a machine, responsive to a single law: the overriding necessity to secure its own peace of mind, its own spiritual comfort, before all other ends. "Whenever you read of a self-sacrificing act or hear of one," Old Man challenged his young companion, "take it to pieces and look for the *real* motive" (WIM 754; emphasis in the original). Young Man might have been able to frame a more effective reply to Old Man's challenge had his search for literary or personal counterexamples led him to the story of Joan of Arc.

Twain himself had already framed that reply a decade before he published *What Is Man?* Writing in the guise of an eighty-two-year-old veteran of Joan's campaigns, preparing a memoir for "his great-great-grand nephews and nieces," he attached to Joan's character nearly every one of the selfless virtues that Old Man would eventually dismiss as mere tickets: as empty names for things that did not exist.[1] The narrator of Joan's "meteor-flight across the war-firmament of France," Louis de Conte, is one of two surviving brothers out of a family of "small nobility" who had fled the chaos of early-fifteenth-century Paris only to be massacred by a wandering band of mercenaries near the town of Neufchâteau. The boy Louis, "overlooked" by the murderers, is adopted, raised, and educated by the village priest in nearby Domremy, Joan's birthplace, growing up as one of her playmates and eventually serving as her page and secretary, since he and the priest are the only two inhabitants of Domremy who can read and write. This detail initiates the series of elaborately nested translations that are indispensable to the preservation of Joan's story.[2]

Literacy is only the first obstacle that imposes itself between the record of her legendary achievements and a contemporary reader.

CONCLUSION

Joan can offer no direct testimony concerning her inner life, nor correct the transcriptions of others, without the assistance of a trustworthy friend who can read and write on her behalf. Along with his fifteenth-century narrator, Twain invents a contemporary translator, Jean François Alden, to render de Conte's memoir "into Modern English from the Original Unpublished Manuscript in the National Archives of France" (PR ii). The manuscript itself, which de Conte composed in 1492, sixty years after Joan's death, draws in part on trial transcripts written in Church Latin, laced with theological and legal technicalities that only experts can appreciate. On one or two occasions during the relentless succession of trials that Joan endures after the English capture her, she inadvertently stumbles on legal formulations that threaten the standing of the Rouen tribunal, though because her judges suppress any recognition of the potent appeal that Joan has unknowingly invoked, she remains unaware of the technical import of what she has said. Her own words sometimes resist the understanding on figurative grounds. One of Joan's answers to a question from the Court concerning the veneration of her battle standard defies even Jean François Alden's freely deployed linguistic skills. Its "haunting pathos" proves "as subtle as an odor," he confesses in a footnote, eluding "all efforts to convey it into our tongue" (PR 381).

Time itself is both a barrier and a medium of clarification for conveying this remarkable story. In a brief preface to the *Personal Recollections*, Louis de Conte explains that the intervening decades have played an important role in enabling him "to comprehend and recognize" the import of Joan's character. "I was reared in the same village with her," he writes: "I played with her every day when we were little children together, just as you play with your mates" (PR 1). But this early intimacy proves to be a paradoxical form of estrangement. Now that Joan's name "fills the whole world," de Conte confesses, "it is as if a perishable paltry candle should speak of the eternal sun riding in the heavens and say, 'He was gossip and housemate to me when we were candles together.'" How can de Conte hope to explain the stunning turn of events that took place around Joan during two short years in the opening third of the fifteenth century, events that seem to him "ever more strange and wonderful and divine and pathetic" with the passage of time?

In his preface, Jean François Alden emphasizes that Joan was an ethical anomaly of the most profound kind: honest "when honesty was become a lost virtue," given "to great thoughts and great purposes" in a time of petty ambitions, full of pity amid scenes of cruelty, "unfailingly true in an age that was false to the core" (PR vii). She not only embodies most of the ticketed virtues to which Old Man denies any real existence but she does so in a time of transcendent vice.[3] Indeed, de Conte's opening paragraph depicts France, in the years immediately before Joan's birth, to be in a state of postapocalyptic chaos, "where slaughter was a daily pastime and no man's life safe for a moment":

> In Paris, mobs roared through the streets nightly, sacking, burning, killing, unmolested, uninterrupted. The sun rose upon wrecked and smoking buildings, and upon mutilated corpses lying here, there, and yonder about the streets, just as they fell, and stripped naked by thieves, the unholy gleaners after the mob. None had the courage to gather these dead for burial; they were left to rot and create plagues ... Then came, finally, the bitterest winter which had visited France in five hundred years. Famine, pestilence, slaughter, ice, snow—Paris had all these at once. The dead lay in heaps about the streets, and *wolves entered the city in daylight and devoured them.* (PR 5; emphasis in the original)

With the death of the aged and insane French king, Charles VI, a few years later, a youthful de Conte undertakes to convince Joan that the case of the nation is hopeless. One afternoon as they are walking together in the pastures near Domremy, he sets out to provide his friend with unsentimental facts that portray the grim predicament of the country "as plainly as the figures in a merchant's account book." But Joan is unperturbed: "There was a barely perceptible suggestion of wonder in her serious eyes, but that was all; and she said, in her simple and placid way—'The case of France hopeless? Why should you think that? Tell me.'" When de Conte complies in some detail, itemizing the moral and financial bankruptcy of "the French house," Joan remains certain that the nation "will win her freedom and keep it. Do not doubt it" (PR 50). In a final effort to impress upon her the grim future that they face, de Conte sketches a map of France in the dirt, explaining that the "tight grip" of the English on the physical heartland of the nation is already fatal to French hopes. The people had been paralyzed by the disaster at Agincourt twelve years earlier. All opposition is dead.

Joan concedes every feature of de Conte's case, just as Young Man is forced to acknowledge Old Man's "desolating" portrait of the mind, yet she announces "without any doubt in her tone" that the apparently impregnable position of the English will break down and that "before two years are sped" the French heir will receive his crown. "It was inevitable that I should think of madness," de Conte confesses as he reflects on Joan's startling prophecy (PR 52). The first and perhaps the most pervasive battle that Joan must wage, over the course of her story, is with doubt—not her own so much as the incredulity of others who do not have access to her Voices or to the uncanny vision that de Conte describes when he witnesses a *"white* shadow" in the shape of a "robed form" envelop Joan in light and hold a mysterious conversation with her at the edge of the woods above the village.[4] That mystical experience, and Joan's explanation of its significance, brings an end to de Conte's doubts, but Joan's Voices themselves play comparatively little role in the pages that follow.

These supernatural informants had first visited Joan three years before de Conte watched their portentous white shadow drift across a meadow toward his entranced friend (PR 53). Their original messages, however, were vague, as if even these Heavenly agents were compelled to await the fulfillment of some mental process in Joan herself before they could proceed, a process that she appears to be on the point of concluding when de Conte watches her receive her fateful instructions.[5] Much of his story, in fact, is devoted to documenting the development of her thinking. The deciding factor in her success, he comes to recognize, are those "greatnesses in her brain," complemented by "great qualities of the heart," that had been central to Joan's nature long before the Voices singled her out (PR 106). "It took six thousand years to produce her," de Conte observes late in the book, as he meticulously surveys the many injustices of the Rouen tribunal that will sentence her to death: "her like will not be seen in the earth again in fifty thousand" (PR 349). Joan, he implies, is an extraordinary product of evolutionary forces, extending across spans of time that are as vast as an old man writing in 1492 can readily conceive. She is neither a passive instrument of supernatural forces nor a mental mechanism of the kind that Old Man briefly invokes in *What Is Man?* but an intelligence richly equipped to pursue the luxuriant foliage of ideal interests that William James placed at the heart of conscious experience. The complex of mental greatnesses with which nature had supplied her signal their presence very early in de Conte's story.

He begins his memoir with an account of two domestic inquisitions in Joan's life that illustrate her unique intelligence, at the same time that they anticipate the far more bitter trials that destroy her. In the first of these Joan recovers from a childhood fever to learn that the priest at Domremy, Père Fronte, has driven away the woodland fairies that used to befriend the village children as they played around the ancient beech tree that local tradition had named L'Arbre Fée de Bourlemont, the Fairy Tree of Bourlemont. The fairies had apparently broken a centuries-old agreement with Church authorities never, on pain of banishment, to make themselves visible to people. A village matron, however, accidently stumbles upon "the little fantastic atoms" late one night as they are "stealing a dance" in the mistaken belief that they are alone: "tearing around in a great ring half as big as an ordinary bedroom, and leaning away back and spreading their mouths with laughter and song ... in perfect abandon and hilarity—oh, the very maddest and witchingest dance the woman ever saw" (PR 14). When she reports this spectacle to her neighbors, the fairies's doom is sealed. Joan's impassioned protest, when she finally awakens from the delirium of her fever, is too late to save them from exile but not too late to dramatize her instinctive appreciation for legal and psychological distinctions that Père Fronte, in enforcing the Church's penalty, had overlooked.

After her initial storm of anger had abated, she confronted the priest, "made reverence" before him, and systematically exposed his errors. "The fairies were to go if they showed themselves to people again, is it not so?" Joan begins. Père Fronte agrees. Then with a precocious grasp of the sexual energies that the fairies represent, along with an intuitive appreciation for the erotic complexities of priestly life, she makes her case:

> "If a man comes prying into a person's room at midnight when that person is half naked, will you be so unjust as to say that that person is showing himself to that man?"
> "Well—no." The good priest looked a little troubled and uneasy when he said it.
> "Is a sin a sin anyway, even if one did not intend to commit it?"
> Pére Fronte threw up his hands and cried out—

"Oh, my poor little child I see all my fault," and he drew her to his side and put his arm around her and tried to make his peace with her, but her temper was up so high that she could not get it down right away, but buried her head against his breast and broke out crying and said:

"Then the fairies committed no sin, for there was no intention to commit one, they not knowing that any one was by; and because they were little creatures and could not speak for themselves and say the law was against the intention, not against the innocent act, and because they had no friend to think that simple thing for them and say it, they have been sent away from their home forever, and it was wrong, *wrong* to do it!" (PR 16; emphasis in the original)

Pére Fronte quickly tries to deflect Joan's resentment by asking her to help him perform a suitable penance for his mistake: "Find me some way out of this with your wise little head." When he senses an advantage in Joan's struggle to balance her loyalty to the Church with her sense of injustice, he tries to trap her into admitting that the fairies might actually have posed some real danger to the village children since they were (Joan concedes) "kin to the Fiend" (PR 18).

Pére Fronte miscalculates by assuming that Joan's sympathies could not possibly extend to the Devil's children. "The poor fairies *could* have been dangerous company for the children?" she asks: "Yes, but never had been; and *could* is no argument. Kinsmen of the Fiend? What of it? Kinsmen of the Fiend have *rights*, and these had; and children have rights, and these had; and if I had been here I would have spoken—I would have begged for the children and the fiends, and stayed your hand and saved them all" (PR 20; emphases in the original). Joan's wise little head, Old Man might say, is a Gobelin loom reweaving the materials of its time and place into an unexpected emotional and mental fabric: "What can a person's heart be made of," she declares, "that can pity a Christian's child and yet can't pity a devil's child that a thousand times more *needs* it!" But rather than coerce Pére Fronte into an act of repentance that she cannot bear to contemplate, Joan pours ashes on her own head rather than his, while the priest slips seamlessly from a brief realization of error into an attempt to implicate Joan in his sense of moral superiority. Her fierce defense of demons and children is far more potent in its revolutionary urgency than Huck's repeated determinations to go to Hell. She commands the same astute intelligence that Jim displays when she entices Pére Fronte into argumentative traps and erupts with the same impassioned intensity of Mary Jane Wilks or Sally Phelps. All of this remarkable mental abundance precedes by many years the miracle of the Voices with which her legendary exploits begin.[6]

In the second of her childhood trials, Joan's father tries physical rather than mental intimidation when she offers her own bowl of porridge to a hungry wanderer who appears at the family's door on a bitter winter night, as a crowd of neighbors gather around the Arc's roaring fire. Beggars are shiftless rascals, her father declares, in a voice like a "thunder-blast," as he orders Joan to sit down (PR 24). She obeys, but not before asking her father to consider that a hungry stomach is not to blame for the wrongs committed by the head, a point of view that leads the mayor of Domremy to spring to Joan's defense. During the mayor's analysis of culpability and innocence, Joan quietly feeds the beggar, who responds by singing the Song of Roland to his enraptured hosts: "his whole body transfigured, and his rags along with it" as the words of the great poem prompt the kind of emotional excess that Twain associated with the camp meetings of his youth. Joan's family and their guests stand as the beggar sings, tears flowing down their cheeks, swaying "to the swing of the song," panting, moaning, and at last bursting into "sobs and wailing" at the hero's dying prayer (PR 29). The ebbing and flowing tides of divine sound that so moved The Boss, in King Arthur's England, awaken this extravagant outburst of feeling, as they will when August Feldner first hears an organ play in the last of the Mysterious Stranger stories. "Music *is* a good thing," Huck Finn agrees, when a crowd of villagers abruptly breaks out in a spontaneous chorus of the Doxology. It sounds "so honest and bully" in a deceitful world (HF 213; emphasis in the original).

These early episodes in de Conte's book prefigure its entire design. Joan too is a catalyst for the emotional energies of France, just as the unexpected power of Roland's song is a catalyst for the patriotic ecstasy of her neighbors or her impassioned argument awakens the conscience of Pére Fronte. Experience, in turn, reacts upon Joan, as de Conte's story unfolds, drawing out her "faculties" and giving them scope (PR 133). The people of Domremy are, at first, scandalized by her desire to lead a French army against the English, hoping to force her to marry one of her old playmates and remain a village housewife. But Joan successfully defends her liberty in court, before "practiced doctors of the law," turning the fabricated claims of her would-be spouse "rag by rag to ruin under her ingenious hands" (PR 64). The governor of Vaucouleurs, Robert de Baudricourt, ultimately belts his own sword around Joan's waist and sends her to the Dauphin when he, like the judges, succumbs to her influence and to an instance of prophetic knowledge that her Voices provide.

At Chinon, where Joan presents herself to the Dauphin's glittering court, and at Poitiers, where the university faculty examine her character and her religious beliefs, she passes every public test designed to expose her ignorance, while in private she continues to expand her influence through the inner and outer dimensions of her presence. As de Conte consistently does throughout the book, he stresses this developmental feature to her story:

> From the first she was the guest, by invitation, of the dame De Rabateau, wife of a councilor of the Parliament of Poitiers; and to the house the great ladies of the city came nightly to see Joan and talk with her; and not these only, but the old lawyers, councillors and scholars of the Parliament and the University. And these grave men, accustomed to weigh every strange and questionable thing, and cautiously consider it, and turn it about this way and that and still doubt it, came night after night, and night after night, falling ever deeper and deeper under the influence of that mysterious something, that spell, that elusive and unwordable fascination, which was the supremest endowment of Joan of Arc, that winning and persuasive and convincing something which high and low alike recognized and felt, but which neither high nor low could explain or describe; and one by one they all surrendered, saying, "This child is sent of God." (PR 129)

The elements of conviction take hold on this community of prominent doubters without ever conferring a complete understanding of the mysterious "something" that orchestrates the change. Belief penetrates the mind in stages that are half superficial and half profound. A cautious weighing of questionable things ultimately leads to the gradual capitulation of doubt on grounds that no one can explain. Reason, William James would insist, is only one among many of the interior arbiters of consciousness. Together an iridescent consortium of mental aptitudes paves the way for Joan's achievements.

"These were days of development," de Conte remembered much later in the story, as Joan assembled the army that would clear the way to Rheims and the coronation of Charles VII. Some members of her council of war, however, remained impervious to her influence until La Hire, one of her most fervent supporters among the French generals, tries to put Joan's ineffable fascination into words. Her "genius," as La Hire described it, lay in her dual capacity to promote an inward transformation in the French people and then to use that reinvigorated mental resource with complete abandon:

> "The old state of things was defeat, defeat, defeat—and by consequence we had troops with no dash, no heart, no hope. Would you assault stone walls with such? No—there was but one way, with that kind: sit down before a place and wait, wait— starve it out, if you could. The new case is the very opposite; it is this: men all on fire with pluck and dash and vim and fury and energy—a restrained conflagration! What would you do with it? Hold it down and let it smolder and perish and go out? What would Joan of Arc do with it? Turn it *loose*, by the Lord God of heaven and earth, and let it swallow up the foe in the whirlwind of its fires! Nothing shows the splendor and wisdom of her military genius like her instant comprehension of the size of the change which has come about, and her instant perception of the right and only way to take advantage of it." (PR 230; emphasis in the original)

Joan's powers of comprehension and perception, however, must wait on the political deliberations of others who are entangled in the old state of things. "Oh, use me; I beseech you, use me," she begs the pliable but indecisive Dauphin as he hesitates to march toward Rheims for his formal coronation: "I shall last only a year" (PR 216). The words reflect both the ominous hints that Joan has received from her Voices and the sense of interior urgency that is the central feature of her character.[7]

"Truly man is a pitiful animal," Louis de Conte concludes, as he recalls the acts of treachery that ultimately ensnare Joan, just as the human muck of England brought the Yankee's fantasy republic to an end (PR 270). But through the medium of what he terms Joan's "seeing eye"—a metaphor for her unique perceptive gifts as well an emblem of introspective acuity—he captures other dimensions of our mental potential. The pompous braggart known as the Paladin, a childhood companion who reluctantly joins Joan on the dangerous journey to Chinon, becomes her standard bearer and ultimately dies trying to defend her from the Burgundian troops that take her prisoner. His chief characteristic prior to this improbable transfiguration had been a gift for telling lies about his warlike prowess so extravagant and so mutable that they became as real to him as Joan's celestial Voices were to her, an introspective mirror to which Joan's sympathies seem intuitively to respond.

"I watched you on the road," she quietly tells this compulsive buffoon as she prepares to make him the guardian of her banner, "You began badly, but improved. Of old you were a fantastic talker, but there is a man in you, and I will bring it out" (PR 137). These words might have been spoken by The Boss as he sifts through the degraded population of Arthur's Britain in search of promising material for the Man Factories that are the logical outcome of Old Man's conviction that the mind itself is merely a mechanism. But Joan's story is the first of Twain's attempts, in the closing years of his career, to focus on the golden engine in the machine: the hunger for spiritual comfort that is capable at a moment's notice of awakening the tremendous energies of interior life. "Passez outré," Joan wearily and repeatedly replies, as she brushes aside the relentless badgering of her Rouen inquisitors. Though this last phase of her story sometimes reduces her to a vestige of her former self, subsisting on "mere memory, floating in a tired mind," her dismissive response to her persecutors suggests that she is simply waiting for yet another incandescent burst of interest to awaken her inward energies in the restrained conflagration that is the essence of consciousness (PR 446).

NOTES

Preface

1. Albert Bigelow Paine, *Mark Twain: A Biography*, 3 vols (New York and London: Harper Brothers, 1912), 3.1552.
2. From "Experience" in Ralph Waldo Emerson, *Essays: First and Second Series* (New York: The Library of America and Vintage/Random House, 1990), 243.
3. Emerson, *Essays: First and Second Series*, 261.
4. Ernst Mach, who joined the University of Vienna faculty in 1895, included a chapter "On Thought Experiments" in his 1897 study *Knowledge and Error: Sketches on the Psychology of Enquiry*. The Clemens family lived in Vienna from the fall of 1897 through May 1899, where Twain would have heard of Mach's inaugural lecture, "On the Part Played by Accident in Invention and Discovery." Pure experimental inquiry, Mach notes in his lecture, "does not exist": "virtually we always experiment with our thoughts." See Carl Dolmetsch, *"Our Famous Guest": Mark Twain in Vienna* (Athens: University of Georgia Press, 1992).

Introduction

1. Twain tested some of the dialogue's ideas at a meeting of the Hartford Monday Evening Club in 1881. The nature of the club's reactions may have influenced his reluctance to publish. See Kenneth R. Andrews, *Nook Farm: Mark Twain's Hartford Circle* (Cambridge: Harvard University Press, 1950), 103. In April 1899 Twain wrote to Howells that "Mrs. Clemens loathes, & shudders over" Old Man's ideas and would not allow him to print them. See *Mark Twain-Howells Letters: The Correspondence of Samuel L. Clemens and William Dean Howells, 1872–1910*, two vols, eds. Henry Nash Smith and

William M. Gibson (Cambridge: The Belknap Press, 1960), 2.689. An appreciation for the resistance with which the finished dialogue was likely to be met led him to work on its drafts with particular care. Paul Baender notes that "the development of *What Is Man?* was possibly the most intricate, and is surely the most amply documented, in Mark Twain's career." See his commentary to *What Is Man? and Other Philosophical Writings* (Berkeley: University of California Press, 1973), 603f.

2. Sir John Adams first noted this anomaly in *What Is Man?* during his brief discussion of "A Letter from Mark Twain" in *Everyman's Psychology* (Garden City, NY: Doubleday Doran, 1929), 202–206. "Here we have the matter in a nutshell," Adams exclaims: "Spiritual comfort. Spiritual comfort to a machine!"

3. Old Man's refusal to credit mankind with a capacity for self-sacrifice prompts Forrest Robinson to conclude that *What Is Man?* is a "philosophical indictment of human nature." See Forrest Robinson, *The Author-Cat: Clemens's Life in Fiction* (New York: Fordham University Press, 2007), 14, 187–9.

4. William Edward Hartpole Lecky, *History of European Morals from Augustus to Charlemagne*, 3rd edn (1877, rpt. Honolulu: University Press of the Pacific, 2002), 30. Howard Baetzhold treats *What Is Man?* as an elaborate reply to Lecky. See *Mark Twain and John Bull: The British Connection* (Bloomington: Indiana University Press, 1970), 218–24. Sherwood Cummings notes how closely the dialogue follows Lecky's survey of seventeenth-century thought and anticipates elements of contemporary naturalism. See *Mark Twain and Science: Adventures of a Mind* (Baton Rouge: Louisiana State University Press, 1988), 207–10. See too Gregg Camfield's account of Twain's interest in Lecky's work: *Sentimental Twain: Samuel Clemens in the Maze of Moral Philosophy* (Philadelphia: University of Pennsylvania Press, 1994), 113–15.

5. Quoted in Baetzhold, *Mark Twain and John Bull*, 54.

6. Most scholars would dispute this claim on behalf of the dialogue's interest and side with Young Man's dismissive response to Old Man's ideas. See, for instance, Tom Quirk, *Mark Twain and Human Nature* (Columbia: University of Missouri Press, 2007), 242; and Susan Gillman, *Dark Twins: Imposture and Identity in Mark Twain's America* (Chicago: University of Chicago Press, 1989), 10.

7. See "Letters from the Earth" in *Mark Twain: Collected Tales, Sketches, Speeches, & Essays, 1891–1910* (New York: Library of America, 1992), 880.

8. "Letters from the Earth," 881; emphases in the original.
9. Sherwood Cummings writes that "it is nearly impossible to exaggerate the impact of *The Age of Reason* on the mind of Samuel Clemens." See *Mark Twain and Science: Adventures of a Mind*, 20–3. Paine's long discussion of the Old Testament in Part 2 of his book singles out for special scorn Numbers 31, in which the Lord mandates the extermination of the Midianites. Satan cites the same passages at length in "Letters from the Earth."
10. "Letters from the Earth," 882–3; emphasis in the original.
11. Sir John Adams treats the inconsistencies represented by Old Man's "Admonition" as part of a "psychological trap" that ensnares Twain in the opening pages of the dialogue, but Adams does not address Old Man's blunt dismissal of moral admonition as the dialogue ends. See *Everyman's Psychology*, 206. See also Forrest Robinson on the Adams/Twain correspondence in *The Author-Cat*, 13–14.

Chapter 1

1. *Mark Twain—Howells Letters: The Correspondence of Samuel L. Clemens and William Dean Howells, 1872–1910*, 2 vols, eds. Henry Nash Smith and William M. Gibson (Cambridge: The Belknap Press, 1960), 2.778. James Cox cites this letter at length as he introduces the sequence of analogies with which Twain tried to characterize the dictations. See *Mark Twain: The Fate of Humor* (Princeton: Princeton University Press, 1966), 295–303. On the months in Florence leading up to Olivia Clemens's death, see Hamlin Hill, *Mark Twain, God's Fool* (Chicago: University of Chicago Press, 1973), 71–87; and Justin Kaplan, *Mr. Clemens and Mark Twain* (1966, rpt. New York: Touchstone Books, 1983), 368–72.
2. The editors at The Mark Twain Papers reprint the full text of both dedications in the *Autobiography of Mark Twain*, vol. 1, ed. Harriet Elinor Smith (Berkeley: University of California Press, 2010), 535–6. Gregg Camfield treats the incident as a case of "almost perfect plagiarism." See *Sentimental Twain: Samuel Clemens in the Maze of Moral Philosophy* (Philadelphia: University of Pennsylvania Press, 1994), 225–6.
3. In a 1903 letter to Helen Keller, Twain emphatically repeated Holmes's observation: "all human utterance is plagiarism." Shelley Fisher Fiskin cites his remark in *Was Huck Black?: Mark Twain and African-American Voices* (New York: Oxford University Press, 1993),

27. See also Susan Gillman's discussion in *Dark Twins: Imposture and Identity in Mark Twain's America* (Chicago: University of Chicago Press, 1989), 31–52, 136–80.

4. On the composition history of *What Is Man?* see Linda Wagner-Martin's afterword to Mark Twain, *What Is Man?* (New York and Oxford: Oxford University Press, 1996).
5. William James, *The Principles of Psychology* (1890, rpt. Cambridge: Harvard University Press, 1981), 17.
6. James, *Principles*, 519.
7. James, *Principles*, 560.
8. James, *Principles*, 110.
9. James, *Principles*, 521; emphasis in the original.
10. The phrase "inward iridescence" first occurs in James's work in a January 1884 article in the journal *Mind*, much of which he reprints in *The Principles of Psychology*, 219–78. The ongoing, systemic activity of cerebral physiology suggested to James that these outward changes must correspond to inward ones:

    Our earlier chapters have taught us to believe that, whilst we think, our brain changes, and that, like the aurora borealis, its whole internal equilibrium shifts with every pulse of change.... Ever some tracts are waning in tension, some waxing, whilst others actively discharge.... But as the brain-tension shifts from one relative state of equilibrium to another, like the gyrations of a kaleidoscope, now rapid and now slow, is it likely that its faithful psychic concomitant is heavier-footed than itself, and that it cannot match each one of the organ's irradiations by a shifting inward iridescence of its own? But if it can do this, its inward iridescences must be infinite, for the brain-redistributions are in infinite variety. If so coarse a thing as a telephone-plate can be made to thrill for years and never reduplicate its inward condition, how much more must this be the case with the infinitely delicate brain? (*Principles*, 228–9)

    The "stream" of thought is only the first of several metaphors describing subjective experience to which this vivid passage appeals.
11. See *Mark Twain's Own Autobiography: The Chapters from the North American Review*, 2nd edn, ed. Michael J. Kiskis (Madison: University of Wisconsin Press, 2010), xxiv–v.
12. In November 1900 Harvey and Twain had informally agreed that Harper and Brothers, which Harvey owned, would publish Twain's complete autobiography in 2000. Negotiations over the *North American Review* installments didn't begin until almost six years later. See *Autobiography of Mark Twain*, 1.19, 46–57.

13. Twain mentioned to Howells the "wonderful editing" job that Harvey had performed in choosing the contents of the chapters. See *Mark Twain-Howells Letters*, 2.817.
14. Randall Knoper links this focus on the dictates of "interest" to an effort to emulate the transparency of a psychic "medium." See *Acting Naturally: Mark Twain in the Culture of Performance* (Berkeley: University of California Press, 1995), 126–7. Jennifer Zaccara compares the dictation process to talk therapy in "Mark Twain, Isabel Lyon, and the 'Talking Cure': Negotiating Nostalgia and Nihilism in the Autobiography," *Constructing Mark Twain: New Directions in Scholarship*, eds. Laura Sklandera Trombley and Michael J. Kiskis (Columbia: University of Missouri Press, 2001), 101–21. Forrest Robinson sees a pattern of "easy avoidance" in the dictation method. See *The Author-Cat: Clemens's Life in Fiction* (New York: Fordham University Press, 2007), 28–31.
15. See Adams's preface in *The Autobiography of Henry Adams*, ed. Ernest Samuels (1918, rpt. Boston: Houghton Mifflin, 1973).
16. *Autobiography of Mark Twain*, 1.203.
17. *Autobiography of Mark Twain*, 1.220–1; emphases in the original.
18. James, *Principles*, 237.
19. James, *Principles*, 238.
20. Twain first criticized Raymond's acting on the play's opening night in New York City, September 16, 1874. See Ron Powers's account of the stage adaptation of *The Gilded Age* in *Mark Twain: A Life* (New York: Free Press, 2005), 352–60. Randall Knoper notes that New York reviewers largely praised Raymond's performance. See his discussion of Twain's familiarity with contemporary performance practices in *Acting Naturally*, 55–95.
21. The figurative sensibility on display in Twain's account of his meeting with Stevenson is the focus of John Bird's study, *Mark Twain and Metaphor* (Columbia: University of Missouri Press, 2007). Though Bird does not touch on the dictations directly, his close attention to key passages in *Roughing It* and *Life on the Mississippi*, in particular, sheds considerable light on the stylistic intricacies that the dictations exploit.
22. Most critics view the Quarles farm passages, for better or worse, as straightforward exercises in nostalgia. See, for instance, Jennifer Zaccara's comments in "Mark Twain, Isabel Lyon, and the 'Talking Cure,'" 114.
23. In *The Author-Cat*, Forrest Robinson suggests that all the participants in the interchange that Twain describes, including Sandy,

are acting in "bad faith" (20–1). Robinson's reading, while strained, takes seriously the episode's complex psychological undercurrents.

24. Orion's service as secretary of the Nevada Territory was far more distinguished than Twain implies in the dictations. See Philip Ashley Fanning, *Mark Twain and Orion Clemens: Brothers, Partners, Strangers* (Tuscaloosa: The University of Alabama Press, 2003), 60–84.

25. For the two most useful accounts of the Whittier speech and its aftermath, see Henry Nash Smith, *Mark Twain: The Development of a Writer* (Cambridge: The Belknap Press of Harvard University, 1962), 92–112; and Richard S. Lowry, *"Littery Man": Mark Twain and Modern Authorship* (New York: Oxford University Press, 1996), 24–33. Smith calls the speech "an act of aggression" against the eastern literary establishment. Lowry concurs, suggesting that Twain set out to challenge the "rhetoric of reverence" that governed both the dinner and the wider culture it sought to shape.

26. See William M. Gibson's detailed account of this intertwined compositional history in *The Mysterious Stranger*, edited with an introduction by William M. Gibson (Berkeley: University of California Press, 1969), 1–34.

27. Forrest Robinson treats these memorable encounters in "Schoolhouse Hill" as direct attacks on the slave culture of Twain's boyhood, a motive that he considers central to all three of the Mysterious Stranger narratives. See *Author-Cat*, 187–92.

28. Randall Knoper links the intense emotions of the "Mysterious Stranger" stories to Twain's interest in fusing what Knoper calls "seminal 'influence' and passive recipience" in a single imagination. See *Acting Naturally*, 188–91. See also Gregg Camfield, "Transcendental Hedonism? Sex, Song, Food, and Drink in *No. 44, The Mysterious Stranger* and 'My Platonic Sweetheart,'" in *Centenary Reflections on Mark Twain's No. 44, The Mysterious Stranger*, eds. Joseph Csicsila and Chad Rohman (Columbia: University of Missouri Press, 2009), 127–43.

29. Franklin's famous letter "Rattle-Snakes for Felons" from the May 1751 *Pennsylvania Gazette* was familiar to nineteenth-century American readers. See Benjamin Franklin, *Writings*, ed. J. A. Leo Lemay (New York: Library of America, 1987), 359–61.

30. This musical episode, along with many other moments in the "Chronicle," suggests that ecstatic joy is the dominant emotion that Twain depicts in the tale. Susan Gillman is representative of many readers, however, who find the "Chronicle" marked by "bloody and essentially joyless visions of human frailty." See *Dark Twins*, 164.

31. See Twain's 1899 letter to William Dean Howells describing Olivia's reaction to his reading of the "Chronicle," as well as his own sense of drunken delight in the story. *Mark Twain-Howells Letters*, 2.698–9.

32. Tom Quirk's closing assessment of the third of the Mysterious Stranger stories is an astute comment on the series as a whole: "*The Mysterious Stranger* is a drama not of thought but of feeling." Quirk concludes, though, that loneliness is the dominant emotion in the drama. See *Mark Twain and Human Nature* (Columbia: University of Missouri Press, 2007), 274.

33. David S. Sewall explores the castle's allegorical potential as he examines the phenomenon of "linguistic absurdity" in the Mysterious Stranger stories. See his extended discussion of Twain's lifelong interest in mutual incomprehension, "Toward a Chaos of Incomprehensibilities," in *Mark Twain's Languages: Discourse, Dialogue, and Linguistic Variety* (Berkeley: University of California Press, 1987), 126–54.

34. Susan K. Harris sees the list of Stein's workers and family members as a prelude to the final chapter in which Twain appears to treat the whole story as August's dream. See *Mark Twain's Escape from Time: A Study of Patterns and Images* (Columbia: University of Missouri Press, 1982), 29–43.

35. A number of critics link Twain's psychological speculations in these portions of "No. 44, The Mysterious Stranger" to his interest in theories of the conscious and unconscious self. See, for instance, Susan Gillman, *Dark Twins*, 136–80; Jason Gary Horn, *Mark Twain and William James: Crafting a Free Self* (Columbia: University of Missouri Press, 1996), 109–20; and John Bird, *Mark Twain and Metaphor*, 191–204.

36. See Bruce Michelson's perceptive suggestion that "a euphoria related to creative power" plays a central role in the development of "No. 44" in *Printer's Devil: Mark Twain and the American Publishing Revolution* (Berkeley: University of California Press, 2006), 217f.

Chapter 2

1. William James, *Essays in Psychology* (Cambridge and London: Harvard University Press, 1983), 75. This passage originally appeared in "The Spatial Quale," *Journal of Speculative Philosophy* 13 (January 1879), and formed part of James's extensive treatment of spatial perception in *The Principles of Psychology* (1890).

2. The five articles most critical to the development of James's thinking include "Remarks on Spencer's Definition of Mind" (January 1878), "Brute and Human Intellect" (July 1878), "Are We Automata?" (January 1879), "The Spatial Quale" (January 1879), and "The Association of Ideas" (March 1880). A sixth important precursor to *The Principles of Psychology*, "On Some Omissions of Introspective Psychology," appeared in January 1884. All but one of these early pieces are collected in *The Works of William James*, a multivolume series which these notes will cite. "The Association of Ideas" appeared in the March 1880 issue of *The Popular Science Monthly*, a magazine of which Twain was a devoted reader.

3. "Remarks on Spencer's Definition of Mind," in William James, *Essays in Philosophy* (Cambridge and London: Harvard University Press, 1978), 15. Hodgson attributes the experience of mental continuity to the joint action of interest, emotion, effort, and attention. Ideas and sensations, he suggests, are constantly subjected to the antagonistic processes of corrosion and renewal. Interest is "the secret spring" that governs these processes. See *Time and Space: A Metaphysical Essay* (London: Longman, Green, 1865), 219–94. In "The Association of Ideas," James calls Hodgson the "ablest of recent (if not all) English philosophers." See *The Popular Science Monthly* (March 1880), 580.

4. James, *Essays in Psychology*, 46.

5. James, *Essays in Psychology*, 19.

6. On James's early training as a painter, see Gerald E. Myers, *William James: His Life and Thought* (New Haven: Yale University Press, 1986), 18–21; and Ralph Barton Perry, *The Thought and Character of William James*, Briefer Version (1948, rpt. New York: Harper and Row, 1964), 58–62.

7. James, *Essays in Psychology*, 16

8. James, *Essays in Psychology*, 46; emphases in the original.

9. James, *Essays in Psychology*, 35–6.

10. James, *Essays in Psychology*, 51.

11. James, *Essays in Philosophy*, 21.

12. James, *Essays in Philosophy*, 12.

13. James, *Essays in Philosophy*, 12–13.

14. James, *Essays in Philosophy*, 13.

15. "Jim Smiley and His Jumping Frog," in *Mark Twain: Collected Tales, Sketches, Speeches, and Essays, 1852–1890* (New York: The Library of America, 1992), 171.
16. On the complexity of the deadpan consciousness that Simon Wheeler exemplifies, see Randall Knoper's discussion in *Acting Naturally: Mark Twain in the Culture of Performance* (Berkeley: University of California Press, 1995), 56–66.
17. "Jim Smiley," 171.
18. Wheeler's hypnotic appeal is part of the prevailing "queerness" of the experience the story describes. Bruce Michelson treats the tale as "a dadaist monologue," an anachronism that clashes with the gentle simplicity Twain stresses in Wheeler's nature. See *Mark Twain on the Loose: A Comic Writer and the American Self* (Amherst: University of Massachusetts Press, 1995), 26–33.
19. "Jim Smiley," 172.
20. John Bird treats the story's many up/down pairings in *Mark Twain and Metaphor* (Columbia: University of Missouri Press, 2007), 11–17.
21. "Jim Smiley," 176.
22. James Cox stresses that the luxuriance of Wheeler's imagination underscores his role as Twain's artistic surrogate (as well as antagonist) in the story's frame. See *Mark Twain: The Fate of Humor* (Princeton: Princeton University Press, 1966), 26–33. John Bird suggests that the apparent clash of interests between "Twain" and Wheeler points to Twain's "conflicted attitude about his art." See *Mark Twain and Metaphor*, 17.
23. Dewey Ganzel explains that Twain toned down or cut the most inflammatory parts of his newspaper correspondence when he incorporated it into *The Innocents Abroad*, but the sardonic caricature of the other passengers on the *Quaker City* largely remained intact, as did the text of the November 1867 article in the *New York Herald*, which Twain reprinted in the book's final pages. See Dewey Ganzel, *Mark Twain Abroad: The Cruise of the "Quaker City"* (Chicago: University of Chicago Press, 1968), 295–300.
24. See Joe B. Fulton's interesting account of Twain's political journalism between October 1867 and March 1868, when he was living in Washington writing *The Innocents Abroad* and submitting occasional letters to eastern newspapers commenting on the impending impeachment crisis: *The Reconstruction of Mark Twain* (Baton Rouge: Louisiana State University Press, 2010), 120–56.

25. Richard Lowry suggests that *The Innocents Abroad* is, in part, "a sustained exegesis" of the official tour program: a running catalogue of the experiences of a "passionless pilgrim" whose enthusiasms invariably lead to disappointment. See *"Littery Man": Mark Twain and Modern Authorship* (New York: Oxford University Press, 1996), 56–7.

26. These patterns of stagnation are the backdrop for what Bruce Michelson calls the narrator's "guerrilla war against stasis of mood and mind" in *The Innocents Abroad*. See *Mark Twain on the Loose*, 45–63. Forrest G. Robinson, however, stresses the "moral equilibrium" of the book in "Patterns of Consciousness in *The Innocents Abroad*," *American Literature* 58 (1986): 46–63, revisited in *The Author-Cat: Clemens's Life in Fiction* (New York: Fordham University Press, 2007), 84–6. Don Florence emphasizes the volatile "persona" Twain creates as the voyage unfolds. See *Persona and Humor in Mark Twain's Early Writings* (Columbia: University of Missouri Press, 1995).

27. Dewey Ganzel offers a perceptive account of the role that the Horta visit came to play in the evolution of *The Innocents Abroad*. See *Mark Twain Abroad*, 59–74.

28. In *American Palestine: Melville, Twain, and the Holy Land Mania* (Princeton: Princeton University Press, 1999), 161–273, Hilton Obenzinger takes issue with Twain's account of "heart-broken" Palestine, though he recognizes its emotional pertinence to the book. Richard Bridgman and many others note the funereal mood that often seems to seize *The Innocents Abroad*, particularly during the Holy Land portion of the tour. In Bridgman's view, the *Quaker City* excursion led Twain "to misery." See Richard Bridgman, *Traveling in Mark Twain* (Berkeley: University of California Press, 1987), 15–17.

29. Raphael's painting is twice as wide as the four and a half feet that Twain represents it as being in *The Innocents Abroad* and just over thirteen feet high, a striking disparity given the access that he and his readers enjoyed to contemporary guidebooks where such facts could easily be checked. See Luitpold Dussler's description of "The Transfiguration" in *Raphael: A Critical Catalogue of his Pictures, Wall-Paintings, and Tapestries* (London: Phaidon, 1971), 52.

30. Twain's remarks on "The Last Supper" had become standard fare for tourist-authors. See Richard Lowry, *"Littery Man": Mark Twain and Modern Authorship*, 51–5.

31. Twain and his friends had known about the military review for several days before it took place and were eager for a glimpse

of Napoleon III. The caricature of Abdul Aziz was added to the book after Twain had visited Constantinople and developed a caustic view of Turkish rule. See Dewey Ganzel, *Mark Twain Abroad*, 113–16. Twain removed the passage praising the French Emperor from an 1872 English edition of *The Innocents Abroad*, after the Franco-Prussian War and the massacre of the Parisian communards. See Bruce Michelson, "Mark Twain the Tourist: The Form of *The Innocents Abroad*," *American Literature* 49 (November 1977): 395.

32. Five years before the publication of *The Innocents Abroad*, Twain had used the same sententious reference to "the trail of the serpent" to conclude "Lucretia Smith's Soldier," a parody of Civil War sentimental vignettes that appeared in the San Francisco *Californian* for December 1864. At that time the expression clearly struck him as trite, though its tone in *The Innocents Abroad* is more elusive and, for that reason, more interesting. See Bruce Michelson, *Printer's Devil: Mark Twain and the American Publishing Revolution* (Berkeley: University of California Press, 2006), 71–6. Forrest Robinson views the Pallavicini Gardens description as symptomatic of the book's pervasive disenchantment. See "Patterns of Consciousness in *The Innocents Abroad*," 60–1.

33. See Lee Clark Mitchell's stress on *Roughing It* as a "direction of thought" or a verbal construct rather than a documentary narrative: "Verbally *Roughing It*: The West of Words," *Nineteenth-Century Literature* 44 (June 1989): 67–92. Philip Beidler treats both of Twain's first two travel books as efforts to capture the "flux" of consciousness. See "Realistic Style and the Problem of Context in *The Innocents Abroad* and *Roughing It*," *American Literature* 52 (1980): 33–49.

34. See John Bird's discussion of metaphorical repletion in *Roughing It: Mark Twain and Metaphor* (Columbia: University of Missouri Press, 2007), 17–32.

35. Twain's reverie beneath the sage brush is the earliest signal in *Roughing It* of the imaginative appetites that James Cox highlights in Bemis's spectacular buffalo hunt several chapters later. The mind, in effect, is the fire that never needs replenishing. See *Mark Twain: The Fate of Humor*, 100–104.

36. Philip Fanning notes that Brigham Young was not in Salt Lake City when the Clemens brothers passed through on the way to Carson City. See *Mark Twain and Orion Clemens: Brothers, Partners, Strangers* (Tuscaloosa: University of Alabama Press, 2003), 59.

37. Portrayals of drunken befuddlement similar to that of Jim Blaine in this famous episode were staples of the nineteenth-century comic stage. See Randall Knoper, *Acting Naturally*, 68.
38. James Cox suggests that Twain's "What to do next?" in *Roughing It* signals his shift from a hapless (and slightly disreputable) western character to an apprentice professional. See *Mark Twain: The Fate of Humor*, 86–7. Tom Quirk believes that the shift may be aimed at soothing the sensibilities of his Langdon in-laws. See *Mark Twain and Human Nature* (Columbia: University of Missouri Press, 2007), 76–7.
39. In *Mark Twain: The Fate of Humor*, James Cox ties Twain's abrupt departure for San Francisco to the cults of personal invective and dueling that prevailed in Nevada journalism (15–18). Bruce Michelson notes that Twain's familiarity with the kind of violence that contemporary newspaper reporters often invited began long before he left Missouri for the west coast. See *Printer's Devil*, 67–9.
40. Richard Bridgman suggests that Twain rearranges the Kilauea and Haleakala visits in order to make the visit to the dead crater signal a second failed pilgrimage, comparable to the disillusionment Twain experienced at Christian shrines in Jerusalem in *The Innocents Abroad*. See *Traveling in Mark Twain*, 49–59.

Chapter 3

1. Twain visited Haleakala in April 1866. He visited Kilauea in early June. See the explanatory notes to Mark Twain, *Roughing It*, eds. Harriet Elinor Smith and Edgar Marquess Branch (Berkeley: University of California Press, 1996), 735–8.
2. The absence of any reference to this visit to Kilauea's crater floor in Twain's Sacramento *Union* letters suggests that he may have invented the episode, borrowing details from crater walks that other travelers had described. See Mark Twain, *Roughing It* (Berkeley: University of California Press, 1996), 735. The annotation to this edition covers in some detail the full extent of Twain's borrowing for the book (709–39).
3. For the full text of the letter, see *Mark Twain's Letters to Will Bowen*, ed. Theodore Hornberger (Austin: University of Texas Press, 1941), 18–21. On Twain's gradual adaptation to what Jeffrey Steinbrink calls the "sober realities" of his married life, see *Getting to be Mark Twain* (Berkeley: University of California Press, 1991), 176–83.

4. Justin Kaplan describes the turmoil of these months surrounding the composition of *Roughing It*. See *Mr Clemens and Mark Twain* (1966, rpt. New York: Touchstone, 1983), 112–48.
5. Mark Twain and Charles Dudley Warner, *The Gilded Age* (New York: Penguin Books, 2001), 21.
6. Twain's analogy to "reading" the river has long appealed to scholars, but the multiple forms of awareness associated with "knowing" lie at the heart of the *Atlantic* sketches. See, for instance, Richard Lowry, *"Littery Man": Mark Twain and Modern Authorship* (New York: Oxford University Press, 1996), 130–2; and John Bird, *Mark Twain and Metaphor* (Columbia: University of Missouri Press, 2007), 42–55.
7. This depiction of the New Orleans riverfront at the height of the steamboat era introduces the seventh and final installment of the series, a point in the "Old Times" sketches where John Bird suggests that Twain's artistic energy is flagging. His ambivalence about carrying the *Atlantic* articles beyond the May or June issue of the magazine does not seem to have impaired the metaphorical vigor of this passage at least. See *Mark Twain and Metaphor*, 53–4.
8. Twain was rewriting a pirated stage script of *The Gilded Age* in anticipation of its East Coast debut during the spring and summer of 1874. The production premiered in New York City in September 1874, two months before Twain began writing the "Old Times" sketches. See Ron Powers, *Mark Twain: A Life* (New York: Free Press, 2005), 352–60.
9. Richard Bridgman points out that Twain never gets this frantic nightmare of information under firm control in the "Old Times" sketches. Despite the fact that he does succeed in becoming a pilot, he never depicts himself as a master of his profession. See *Traveling in Mark Twain* (Berkeley: University of California Press, 1987), 61–9.
10. Stephen's blend of consummate skill and utter chaos, like the sleepwalking artistry of Mr. X, underscores the inadequacy of the reading metaphor as an account of the pilot's mental accomplishments. Each of these exemplary figures has to blunt the outward forms of awareness that might distract him in order to tap the complex mental reserves on which his skill depends.
11. Lawrence Howe suggests that Mr. B's exemplary skill earns Twain's admiration and, at the same time, arouses his resentment—an ambivalence that may account for Twain's reminder, in this famous episode, that Mr. B is willing to risk the lives of over a hundred

12. innocent passengers in order to display his gifts. Supplanting the commanding figure of the pilot with that of the writer, Howe argues, will play a key role in Twain's artistic growth. See *Mark Twain and the Novel* (Cambridge: Cambridge University Press, 1998), 14–72.

12. William Dean Howells suggested that Twain's key achievement in *The Adventures of Tom Sawyer* was the book's "wonderful study of the boy-mind." Quoted in Tom Quirk, *Mark Twain and Human Nature* (Columbia: University of Missouri Press, 2007), 95. James Cox notes that Twain was writing the "Old Times" sketches and the opening chapters of *Tom Sawyer* concurrently, a fact that makes his reference to "personating" the captain all the more curious. See *Mark Twain: The Fate of Humor* (Princeton: Princeton University Press, 1966), 127.

13. In Randall Knoper's account of the gendered performance conventions to which Twain often responded, keeping mum would be a signal of masculine restraint. Disclosure was a feminine attribute, a loss of mental control triggered by unexpected bursts of emotion. See *Acting Naturally: Mark Twain in the Culture of Performance* (Berkeley: University of California Press, 1995), 112.

14. Forrest Robinson treats the whitewashing episode as an expression of the communal bad faith that pervades St. Petersburg: "Tom Sawyer's plotting serves to emplot *Tom Sawyer*." Though this view results in a sharply reductive account of the mental life on display in Twain's book, Robinson's extensive examination of the novel is important. See *In Bad Faith: The Dynamics of Deception in Mark Twain's America* (Cambridge: Harvard University Press, 1986), 17–108.

15. The conspicuous absence in Tom's makeup of any awareness concerning his past is an early signal of the implicit tie to romance that Twain exploits in the book. The hero's or the heroine's mysterious birth is a familiar element of romance plots, in many instances a precondition for redeeming the corrupt world that is responsible for the concealment of their origins. See Northrup Frye, *The Secular Scripture: A Study of the Structure of Romance* (Cambridge: Harvard University Press, 1976), 65–93.

16. Bill Brown's discussion of Mark Twain in *A Sense of Things* focuses on *The Prince and the Pauper*. These totemic objects in the whitewashing episode, however, are a much richer instance of the mind's capacity to infuse things with an intangible aura. See *A Sense of Things: The Object Matter of American Literature* (Chicago: University of Chicago Press, 2003), 21–50.

17. Cowardice and self-love, James Cox notes, pervade Tom's character, despite the redemptive power of play that Cox finds central to the

plot. See *Mark Twain: The Fate of Humor*, 147. Richard Lowry recognizes the anarchic pleasure principle that motivates much of Tom's behavior, but he considers the story as a whole to be a nostalgic indulgence during which Twain gradually comes of age "as an author of fiction" through the complex vehicle of Injun Joe. See *"Littery Man": Mark Twain and Modern Authorship*, 76–111.

18. John Seelye, among others, dismisses Muff Potter's jail cell speech as a "sentimental set-piece," but Twain clearly gave a great deal of attention to its wording. See "What's in a Name: Sounding the Depths of *Tom Sawyer*," in *Mark Twain: A Collection of Critical Essays*, ed. Eric J. Sundquist (Englewood, NJ: Prentice Hall, 1994), 49–61.

19. This moment in the book introduces what Richard Lowry calls "the sensuous trace of illicit history" in Twain's story: the mysterious incorporation of Murrel's gold into Injun Joe's hoard. See *"Littery Man": Mark Twain and Modern Authorship*, 108–11.

20. See John Seelye's perceptive account of this narrative weave: "What's in a Name: Sounding the Depths of *Tom Sawyer*," 56–61. On the rich generic history behind themes of descent into the "night world," see Northrup Frye, *The Secular Scripture*, 97–126.

21. In a notebook entry dated November 23, 1877, Twain sketches out the book's plot in some detail. He wrote several hundred manuscript pages of *The Prince and the Pauper* the preceding summer, though he wouldn't publish the novel until December 1881. See *Mark Twain's Notebooks and Journals, Vol II (1877–1883)*, eds. Frederick Anderson, Lin Salamo, and Bernard L. Stein (Berkeley: University of California Press, 1975), 49.

22. In Lawrence Howe's dialectical account of Twain's development, *The Prince and the Pauper* is a naïve precursor to the more radical thinking that Twain displays almost a decade later in *A Connecticut Yankee in King Arthur's Court*. Tom Canty's experience, Howe suggests, "discredits reading" in favor of the experiential education that Edward will receive by living a pauper's life and that Hank Morgan exemplifies. Tom Canty's reading in this early portion of the book, however, has real experiential value in Offal Court, as it will prove to have later on in the story. The dialectical oppositions that Howe points out are far from pure. See *Mark Twain and the Novel*, 118–44.

23. Compare this hybrid narrative voice to John Bird's account of the competing sensibilities that he detects in *The Adventures of Tom Sawyer: Mark Twain and Metaphor*, 55–66. In *The Prince and the*

Pauper, Twain's narrator is a much more mysterious entity than the sententious and "drippy" adult intelligence that Bird identifies with several scenes from the earlier book.

24. Bruce Michelson calls Twain's description of London Bridge and its inhabitants the "cadenza" passage of *The Prince and the Pauper*: the moment in the story where Twain's artistic "gusto" seems most in evidence. See *Mark Twain on the Loose: A Comic Writer and the American Self* (Amherst: University of Massachusetts Press, 1995), 148–9. Twain identifies his source for the dialect song that the thieves sing as *The English Rogue* (1665) but doesn't provide a translation. The California editors supply one in their Explanatory Notes:

    Good night then, Drink Woman and Tavern,

    The good man goes away,

    On the gallows to hang near London gallants dining

    For his long sleep at last.

    Go out good women and watch, and watch,

    Go out of London town,

    And watch the man that stole your goods,

    Upon the gallows to hang. (PP 315)

25. See Randall Knoper's discussion of the book's "monarchical theater," and its carnival inversions, in *Acting Naturally* (150–4). Knoper views the pageants as part of a "crisis of representation" in the story to which no form of authority is immune.

26. Mrs. Canty's attempt to elicit this familiar bodily reaction reflects Twain's interest in what Randall Knoper terms "gestural self-betrayal": a "natural language" that undermines disguises. See *Acting Naturally*, 104–5.

27. Compare William James's use of "the gyrations of a kaleidoscope" to illustrate shifts in "brain-tension" in an 1884 article on "The Stream of Thought" that he eventually incorporated into *The Principles of Psychology* (1890, rpt. Cambridge: Harvard University Press, 1981), 228–9. Twain later drew an elaborate analogy between his own creative processes and the outside/inside views of a kaleidoscope, a contrast between external chaos and internal impressions that he revisits several times in his career. Victor Doyno cites the passage in *Writing Huck Finn: Mark Twain's Creative Process* (Philadelphia: University of Pennsylvania Press, 1991), 15–18.

28. Justin Kaplan describes the circumstances behind the Clemens family's 1878–79 European residence. See *Mr. Clemens and Mark Twain* (New York: Simon and Schuster, 1966), 212–23. Twain had

signed a book contract to describe the trip before leaving New York. See also Ron Powers, *Mark Twain: A Life*, 414–26.

29. Richard Bridgman notes the inward turn of Twain's imagination in his discussion of *A Tramp Abroad*, but he remains puzzled by what he considers the book's "numerous pointless and mediocre pages" and by Twain's determination to include in it a number of his own crude drawings. Larzer Ziff concurs in both judgments. See Richard Bridgman, *Traveling in Mark Twain* (Berkeley: University of California Press, 1987), 70–104; and Larzer Ziff, *Return Passages: Great American Travel Writing, 1780–1910* (New Haven: Yale University Press, 2000), 170–206.

30. Sigmund Freud noted the "wild extravagance" of this episode in *A Tramp Abroad* during the course of his 1919 essay on "The Uncanny," though he quickly distinguishes Twain's elaborate record of mental wandering from the psychosexual themes that his essay is exploring. See Nicholas Royle, "Hotel Psychoanalysis: Some Remarks on Mark Twain and Sigmund Freud," in *Angelaki: Journal of the Theoretical Humanities* 9 (April 2004): 3–14.

31. On the largely unremarkable response of the Monday Evening Club to Twain's presentation from "What Is Man?" see Kenneth R. Andrews, *Nook Farm: Mark Twain's Hartford Circle* (Cambridge: Harvard University Press, 1950), 103, 258.

32. William Gibson voices the critical consensus that Jim Baker's yarn is the "high point" of *A Tramp Abroad*. See *The Art of Mark Twain* (New York: Oxford University Press, 1976), 68–71. Twain may have shared that view. He chose to include Jim Baker's tale on its own in his 1888 anthology *Mark Twain's Library of Humor*. Bruce Michelson, however, stresses that a significant measure of the story's impact derives from its unexpected appearance during Twain's description of a walk in the woods outside Heidelberg. See *Printer's Devil: Mark Twain and the American Publishing Revolution* (Berkeley: University of California Press, 2006), 108–109. Compare Twain's portrait of the "Indian crow" in *Following the Equator* (Hartford: The American Publishing Company, 1897), 353–6.

33. Ruskin's comments on the "Slave Ship" emphasize the painting's "indefinite, fantastic forms," followed by an assessment of its significance in Turner's career:

> I believe, if I were reduced to rest Turner's immortality upon any single work, I should choose this. Its daring conception—ideal in the highest sense of the word—is based on the purest truth, and wrought out with the concentrated knowledge of a life; its color is absolutely perfect, not

one false or morbid hue in any part of line, and so modulated that every square inch of canvas is a perfect composition; its drawing as accurate as fearless; the ship buoyant, bending, and full of motion; its tones as true as they are wonderful; and the whole picture dedicated to the most sublime of subjects and impressions—(completing thus the perfect system of all truth, which we have shown to be formed by Turner's works)—the power, majesty and deathfulness of the open, deep, illimitable Sea.

See *Modern Painters*, Section V, "Of Truth of Water," chapter 3. For a more skeptical view of Twain's interest in the nuances of perception, see W. J. T. Mitchell, *Iconology: Image, Text, Ideology* (Chicago: University of Chicago Press, 1986), 40–2.

34. For a detailed account of Twain's extensive involvement in illustrating *A Tramp Abroad*, see Bruce Michelson's chapter in *Printer's Devil*, 77–118. The results of that involvement, in Michelson's view, are both exhilarating and disappointing: a form of technological intoxication, on Twain's part, combined with a great deal of "imaginative cruising on the labor of others" (102).

Chapter 4

1. On the closely interwoven writing projects that Twain pursued between 1874 and 1883, see Ron Powers, *Mark Twain: A Life* (New York: Simon and Schuster, 2005), 348–413. Lawrence Howe views "the Mississippi quartet" that begins with the "Old Times" sketches and ends with the *Adventures of Huckleberry Finn* as a single narrative ensemble. See *Mark Twain and the Novel* (Cambridge: Cambridge University Press, 1998), 73–86.

2. Twain's own introspective goals for the book inevitably differ from the psychological purposes that critics have detected in its pages. Lawrence Howe, for example, sees *Life on the Mississippi* as an "oedipal" turning point in Twain's ambivalent relationship to authority: an attempt to substitute the narrative mastery of the writer for the romantic independence of the pilot. See *Mark Twain and the Novel*, 14–72. Forrest Robinson considers *Life on the Mississippi* a "tormented book," shaped in large part by Twain's sense of personal responsibility for Henry Clemens's death. See *The Author-Cat: Clemens's Life in Fiction* (New York: Fordham University Press, 2007), 44–59, 102–106.

3. Horst H. Kruse notes that the *Harper*'s epigraph was a very late addition to the manuscript. See *Mark Twain and Life on the Mississippi* (Amherst: University of Massachusetts Press, 1981), 123.

4. By contrast, Forrest Robinson sees the book's pervasive discontinuities as "unconscious eruptions and fretful evasions," qualities that he contrasts with the "relative moral serenity of *A Tramp Abroad*" and the warm "nostalgia" of the "Old Times" sketches. See *The Author-Cat*, 101–3.

5. James Cox is among the first to stress the implications of Twain's contrasting portraits of Mr. Brown. See *Mark Twain and the Fate of Humor* (Princeton: Princeton University Press, 1966), 162.

6. Ron Powers, in *Dangerous Water* (New York: Basic Books, 1999), 265–89, gives a detailed account of the *Pennsylvania* disaster and the death of Henry Clemens. See too Forrest Robinson's discussion in *The Author-Cat*, 44–9.

7. Despite Twain's fondness for the character of Uncle Mumford, he too abruptly disappears from the narrative when the *Gold Dust* blows up later in the summer of 1882. Twain makes no mention of his informant's fate among the seventeen dead and forty-seven wounded passengers and crew that newspapers reported after the *Gold Dust* disaster (LM 240).

8. Karl Ritter's story may have originally been part of the manuscript of *A Tramp Abroad*. See Horst H. Kruse, *Mark Twain and Life on the Mississippi*, 24. Bruce Michelson discusses the Ritter episode at some length in *Mark Twain on the Loose: A Comic Writer and the American Self* (Amherst: University of Massachusetts Press, 1995), 80–93.

9. See Gregg Camfield on Twain's ambivalence about the cathartic outbreaks of feeling associated with nineteenth-century sentimental fiction: *Sentimental Twain: Samuel Clemens in the Maze of Moral Philosophy* (Philadelphia: University of Pennsylvania Press, 1994).

10. A brief footnote in *A Tramp Abroad* describes Twain's genuine enthusiasm for Turner's work: "Months after this was written, I happened into the National Gallery in London, and soon became so fascinated with the Turner pictures that I could hardly get away from the place. I went there often, afterward, meaning to see the rest of the gallery, but the Turner spell was too strong; it could not be shaken off" (TA 158). On the impact of the late oils and watercolors in the Turner Bequest, see *J. M. W. Turner: Painting Set Free*, eds. David Blayney Brown, Amy Concannon, and Sam Smiles (Los Angeles: John Paul Getty Museum, 2014).

11. Richard Bridgman considers the visit to Hannibal part of the pervasive pattern of disillusion in *Life on the Mississippi*: a

"cumulatively morbid" collection of episodes, in Bridgman's view. See *Traveling in Mark Twain* (Berkeley: University of California Press, 1987), 105–6.

12. The most perceptive account of Twain's use of dialect in the book is that of David R. Sewell, *Mark Twain's Languages: Discourse, Dialogue, and Linguistic Variety* (Berkeley: University of California Press, 1987), 85–109. See also John Bird, *Mark Twain and Metaphor* (Columbia: University of Missouri Press, 2007), 66–86.

13. See the Explanatory Notes provided by the editors of The Mark Twain Papers on their reasons for restoring this extracted passage to the text of chapter XVI in *Adventures of Huckleberry Finn* (HF 408–9).

14. John Bird notes Jim's metaphorical gifts in these passages, though he sees them as instances of self-deception. See *Mark Twain and Metaphor*, 84–6. See too Forrest Robinson's discussion of what he considers the "proleptic guilt" that pervades Huck's relations with Jim: "The Silences in *Huckleberry Finn*," *Nineteenth-Century Fiction* 37 (June 1982): 50–74.

15. This visit to the lumber raft is the longest of several instances of "overhearing" that shape Huck's book as dramatically as his own speech does. In effect, Huck is the meticulous student of dialect that Twain purports to be in the book's prefatory explanation; he is an acutely receptive listener.

16. Richard Lowry views this encounter with pap as a sign of Twain's interest in replicating elements of Benjamin Franklin's acquisition of literacy in Huck's self-education. See *"Littery Man": Mark Twain and Modern Authorship* (New York: Oxford University Press, 1996), 135–47.

17. On Twain's earliest notes describing the plot of *A Connecticut Yankee*, dating from the fall of 1884, see *Mark Twain's Notebooks and Journals*, vol. 3 (1883–91), eds. Robert Browning, Michael Frank, and Lin Salamo (Berkeley: University of California Press, 1979), 78–9.

18. Compare Twain's remarks on his reading practices late in *Following the Equator*, as he grapples with his inner and outer images of the Taj Mahal: "I am a careless reader, I suppose—an *impressionist* reader ... a reader who overlooks the informing details or masses their sum improperly, and gets only a large splashy, general effect ... built of tinted mists upon jeweled arches of rainbows supported by colonnades of moonlight." See Mark Twain, *Following the Equator* (Hartford: The American Publishing Company, 1897), 577–8; emphasis in the original.

19. The pertinence of "overlap" to the form of *A Connecticut Yankee* is usually confined to the overlap between dreams and reality that introduces the story. Its influence is more pervasive and more varied than that initial duality suggests. See, for example, James L. Johnson, *Mark Twain and the Limits of Power: Emerson's God in Ruins* (Knoxville: University of Tennessee Press, 1982), 130.
20. Randall Knoper compares the frame episodes of the book to manifestations of "mediumship" in Twain: a form of imaginative immersion that secures the sincerity of a theatrical representation and that Knoper's book on performance practices explores at length. See *Acting Naturally: Mark Twain in the Culture of Performance* (Berkeley: University of California Press, 1995), 136–8.
21. Bruce Michelson among others notes the narrator's growing "respect and love" for Camelot's "white Indians." See *Mark Twain on the Loose*, 163. Jackson Lears links the narrator's delight at Camelot's "stir and noise" to the patterns of "anti-modern vitalism" that he traces through the end of the nineteenth century in *No Place of Grace: Antimodernism and the Transformation of American Culture, 1880–1920* (New York: Pantheon, 1981), 165–6.
22. Henry Nash Smith complains about the melodramatic flavor of the narrator's visit to Morgan Le Fay's castle, singling out "the fragrance of greasepaint" in the dungeon scene (145). While Smith seems inattentive to competing sources of interest in these episodes, his lengthy discussion of *A Connecticut Yankee* is a probing treatment of the book. See *Mark Twain: The Development of a Writer* (Cambridge: The Belknap Press, 1962), 138–70.
23. In contrast to this account of the narrator's mental agility and variety, compare Bruce Michelson's focus on the "iron suit" of armor as Twain's emblem for the varieties of mental confinement that fill the book. *Mark Twain on the Loose*, 162.
24. Compare Query XVII of *Notes on the State of Virginia*, where Thomas Jefferson declares that uniformity of opinion among people is no more desirable than uniformity of "face or stature." Torture, Jefferson insists, can succeed only in creating hypocrites, an observation that will influence Twain's account of Joan's "recantation" in *Personal Recollections of Joan of Arc*.
25. The critical consensus of the past fifty years is sharply dismissive of the narrator's spectacular "effects" in *A Connecticut Yankee*, but in focusing on their fraudulent or invidious nature, readers tend to overlook the rich array of inner "effects" in which Twain embeds them. See, for instance, Henry Nash Smith, *Mark*

Twain: The Development of a Writer, 163–6; Randall Knoper, *Acting Naturally*, 155–69; and William Spanos, *Shock and Awe: American Exceptionalism and the Imperatives of the Spectacle in Mark Twain's Connecticut Yankee* (Hanover: Dartmouth College Press, 2013).

26. See Bruce Michelson's appreciative remarks on Sandy's "special moral orientation to romance" in *Mark Twain on the Loose*, 162.

Conclusion

1. Though Tom Quirk has a very low opinion of the *Personal Recollections*, he recognizes its role for Twain as a counterweight to the apparent determinism that lay behind *What Is Man?* See *Mark Twain and Human Nature* (Columbia: University of Missouri Press, 2007), 197–8.
2. On the proliferation of sources and mediators involved in compiling the *Personal Recollections*, see Christina Zwarg, "Woman as Force in Twain's *Joan of Arc*: The Unwordable Fascination," *Criticism* 27 (1985): 57–72; and Jason Gary Horn, *Mark Twain and William James: Crafting a Free Self* (Columbia: University of Missouri Press, 1996), 69–105.
3. Tom Quirk notes that Alden's assessment is largely Twain's as well, a view that Twain made clear in a 1904 essay in which he referred to Joan as a "mental and moral miracle." See *Mark Twain and Human Nature*, 198.
4. The mystical communion that de Conte witnesses in this scene signals Joan's status as a supernatural "medium," a form of translation in itself that Randall Knoper treats as evidence of her essential passivity or transparency in the story. See *Acting Naturally: Mark Twain in the Culture of Performance* (Berkeley: University of California Press, 1995), 171–80.
5. One of the French sources that Twain consulted, J. Fabre's study of Joan's original trial and condemnation, stresses that her Voices needed to wait for Joan "to make up her mind" rather than simply assert their divine authority over her. Cited in Jason Gary Horn, *Mark Twain and William James*, 99. See too Gregg Camfield's discussion of Joan's performance in *Sentimental Twain: Samuel Clemens in the Maze of Moral Philosophy* (Philadelphia: University of Pennsylvania Press, 1994), 199–204.

6. On the importance of the Fairy Tree episodes throughout de Conte's narrative, see Susan Harris's thoughtful afterword to the *Personal Recollections* in the Oxford University Press facsimile. Harris reviews, as well, the contemporary objections to Twain's use of Joan as a means of weaving late-nineteenth-century political and social issues into the fabric of her story.
7. See Forrest Robinson on the resemblances that Twain perceived between the achievements of U. S. Grant and those of Joan: *The Author-Cat: Clemens's Life in Fiction* (New York: Fordham University Press, 2007), 73–9. La Hire's praise for Joan's aggressive tactics in *Personal Recollections* highlights those resemblances. In Robinson's view, the link is part of Twain's lifelong attempt to assuage his feelings of guilt at having avoided serving in the Civil War.

INDEX

Abdul Aziz I (Ottoman sultan) 95
Abelard, Peter. *See* Père La Chaise (Twain's visit to)
Acropolis (Twain's visit to) 99, 101–3
Adams, Henry (*The Education*) 24
Adams, Sir John 250 n.2, 251 n.1
Adventures of Huckleberry Finn 166, 181, 198–217, 219, 221–2, 235
   figurative palette of 213–14
   introspection in 15, 199–200, 210–12, 216
   listening in 199, 201, 244
   noticing as motif 198–9
   raftsmen episode 205–9, 217
   textual evolution of 14, 129
Adventures of Tom Sawyer, The 90, 141–57, 164, 166, 176, 199–200, 203, 205
   consciousness depicted in 142–3, 148
   evocative objects in 144–7, 154
   publication context of 1, 14, 129
   silence in 143–4, 146, 148, 151–2, 155
   tongue motif in 148, 152–5, 161
   underworld motif in x, 143, 146, 154–6
Affre, Denis-Auguste (Archbishop of Paris) 97–8, 101
Agrate, Marco d' (Renaissance sculptor) 99–100
Aldrich, Thomas Bailey 28–31

Alta California (San Francisco newspaper) 105
Asnières sur Seine 97
association (mental process of) 11, 21, 25, 31, 75, 77
Atlantic Monthly 130, 133–4, 141, 160, 182–3, 187
attention (mental faculty) 14, 21, 33, 75–6, 130, 137, 141–2, 199
aurora borealis (as metaphor for brain function) 37
automata (mental analogy to) 76–8, 95, 132, 142, 227
Azores (*Quaker City* visit to) 85–7, 95

Basilica of St. Denis 92, 97
Bates, George Washington (*Sandwich Island Notes*) 126
Bemis, George (*Roughing It*) 108
Bernard of Clairvaux 93
Bixby, Horace ("Mr. B------") 138–41, 147, 183, 185–6, 190
Black Forest (*A Tramp Abroad*) 166, 168–70, 173
Blue Grotto (Capri) 125
Book of Mormon 112
Borroméo, Charles, Bishop of Milan 100–2, 104, 156
Boston Evening Transcript 44–5
Bowen, Will (Twain's 1870 letter to) 128

Cable, George Washington 182, 184, 217
Cairo, Illinois 139, 205–7, 209–10
Capuchin Convent (in *The Innocents Abroad*) 156
Carlyle, Thomas 24
Carson City, Nevada 107, 113–14, 116
Castle d'If (Marseille harbor) 87–8, 91, 95, 108
Chambery, France (in *A Tramp Abroad*) 216–17
"Chapters From My Autobiography" 14, 22–4, 26–46, 65–6. See also *North American Review*
Charles I (1600–1649) 26
cholera (1867 pandemic) 101, 125
"Chronicle of Young Satan, The" 46, 49–51, 53–60, 64, 66, 89
Cincinnati Commercial (newspaper) 190
Civitta Vecchia 96
Clemens, Clara 38
Clemens, Henry 187
Clemens, Jane Lampton 27, 34–5
Clemens, Jean ix, 30
Clemens, John Marshall 27
Clemens, Langdon 128
Clemens, Olivia Langdon ix, 17, 32, 38–9, 46, 55–6, 128
Clemens, Olivia Susan (Susy) 45–6, 49–50, 66
  death of ix, 38–40, 42, 62
  family memoir by 1, 23, 37–8, 43
Clemens, Orion 40–2, 45–6, 50, 57, 61, 106–7, 111–12, 116
Cleveland, Grover 32
Coleridge, Samuel T. 119
Comstock Lode 41, 114, 156–7
Connecticut Yankee in King Arthur's Court, A 14–15, 217–37, 246–7
  consciousness in 217, 221–4, 226, 230
  illustrations 217
  interest motif in 226, 228
  introspective process in 223, 234–5
  partnership motif 218–19, 221, 227
  underworld settings of 223–4, 226
conscience 7, 148, 209–10. See also *What Is Man?*
consciousness (Twain's account of) 2, 6–8, 10–13, 15. See also *What Is Man?*
Constantintople 96
Cooper, James Fenimore (*The Pioneers*) 143

Dagobert I (Frankish king) 92
Damascus 96–7
Darwin, Charles (*The Descent of Man*) 11–12
Da Vinci, Leonardo ("The Last Supper") 91
Dean, Henry Clay 219
deism. See "Letters from the Earth"
De Soto, Hernando 183–5
dictation (autobiographical method of) 17, 24, 31, 37
discrimination (mental process of) 74–5, 82
dreams 10–11, 27, 134–5, 153, 203–5, 218, 221
Dream selves. See "No. 44, The Mysterious Stranger"
Dublin, New Hampshire (Twain's residence in) 22–3, 46

Ecclesiastes 189
Emerson, Ralph Waldo ("Experience") ix–x, 43
emotion (receptivity to) 42–6, 66–8, 92, 130, 230. See also "No. 44, The Mysterious Stranger"

INDEX

Esdralon, plain of (Megiddo) 89, 104
Evening Post (Hartford, Connecticut newspaper) 41

Fayal (Azores). *See* Horta (*Quaker City* visit to)
Florentine Dictations (1904) 17, 22, 28
Flores (Azores) 85–6, 89–90, 94, 104, 124
Florida, Missouri 27, 33
Following the Equator (and impressionist reading) 268 n.18
Franklin, Benjamin 24, 51

Galilee, Sea of 88, 96
Genesis (Book of) 8, 56
Gibraltar 84, 90, 95–6
Gilded Age, The 27, 128–9, 134
Goodman, Joseph 17–18, 20–1, 28, 45, 76, 118
Grant, Ulysses (Joan of Arc compared to) 271 n.7
Great Pyramid of Giza 95

Haleakala (Sandwich Islands volcano) 123–4, 126–7, 130
Hall, Basil 194
Hannibal, Missouri 34, 197–8
Harper's Magazine 183–4
Harte, Bret 28
Hartford, Connecticut 32, 37, 39, 42, 169, 238
Harvey, George 22–3, 37
Heidelberg (*A Tramp Abroad*) 173
dueling clubs 175–6, 178, 195–6
Heilbronn (in *A Tramp Abroad*) 167–9, 171, 200, 216
Héloïse d' Argenteuil. *See* Père La Chaise (Twain's visit to)
Herald (New York City newspaper) 83

Herculaneum 128
Hobbes, Thomas 21
Hodgson, Shadworth Hollway 75, 256 n.3
Holmes, Oliver Wendell 17–22, 43–4, 70, 77, 93, 126, 156, 176
Horta (*Quaker City* visit to) 86–7
Howells, William Dean 17, 23, 55

Innocents Abroad, The 82–105, 125–6, 156, 166
dedication of 17–18, 28, 43–5, 76, 93
fraudulent feeling in 92, 95, 99
interest motif 83–5
introspective goals of 82–3
textual evolution of 83
transfiguration motif 14, 86, 88–9, 91, 94
interest (mental faculty of) 14, 73–8, 91, 133
Interior Master (Twain's trope of) 8, 22, 25, 38, 62, 74. See also *What Is Man?*
artistic gifts of 10, 13–14
introspective nature of 12
spiritual adaptability of 6
volatility of 11, 20, 169

James, William 14, 20–2, 25, 31, 62, 91, 217, 245
"Are We Automata" 76
"Brute and Human Intellect" 76, 81
"On Some Omissions of Introspective Psychology" 22, 33, 252 n.10
Principles of Psychology, The 20–2, 75, 131
"Remarks on Spencer's Definition of Mind" 77–8, 87, 139
"Spatial Quale, The" 74–5, 82

Jamestown, Tennessee 27
Jefferson, Thomas 294 n.24
Jerusalem 96, 99
"Jim Smiley and His Jumping Frog" 14, 79–82, 86
Joan of Arc. See *Personal Recollections of Joan of Arc*
Johnson, Andrew (impeachment of) 83
Joliet, Louis 184

kaleidoscope (as mental analogy) 20, 166, 177–8, 182, 264 n.27
Keokuk, Iowa 42
Kilauea (Sandwich Islands volcano) 105, 122–23, 126–30
Kipling, Rudyard 43

Lake Tahoe 105
Lampton, James 27, 33
La Salle, Rene-Robert Cavelier, Sieur de 185
Lecky, William Edward Hartpole 5
"Letters from the Earth" 8–10, 13
Life on the Mississippi 1, 14–15, 181, 183–200, 213, 216
discontinuity in 185, 188
Longfellow, Henry Wadsworth 43–4
Louis xiv, 185
Loyola, Ignatius 7, 183
Lyon, Isabel 17

Mach, Ernst (on thought experiments) 249 n.4
machine (the mind compared to) 1–4, 8, 78, 238. See also *What Is Man?*
Malory, Thomas (*Morte d'Arthur*) 218–21, 234
Marquette, Jacques 184–5
Marryat, Captain Frederick 194
Master Passion. See *What Is Man?*
Mehemet Ali (Ottoman pasha of Egypt) 95

memory 18–20, 31–2, 34–7, 77, 128, 147, 165–6, 197. See also dictation
"Old Times on the Mississippi" 130–2, 186
mental streaming 3, 20, 22, 24, 33, 37, 62
Milan Cathedral (Twain's visits to) 91, 99–101, 181–2
Monday Evening Club (Hartford men's group) 169, 238
moral sense (Twain's critique of) 12, 60
mosaics (Florentine inlay) 87–8, 90, 104
Mosque of St. Sophia (Constantinople) 96
Mount Tabor (Twain's ascent of) 88–9, 95, 103–4
music (mental receptivity to) 54, 60, 67, 178–9, 230, 232, 244
"Mysterious Stranger" tales 14, 46, 133. See also "Chronicle of Young Satan" "Schoolhouse Hill" and "No 44, The Mysterious Stranger"

Naples (Twain's visit to) 96–7, 125
Napoleon III (French Emperor) 95
National Gallery (London) 267 n.10
Nevada Territory 41
New Orleans 132–3, 138, 159, 182, 184, 195
"No. 44, The Mysterious Stranger" 47–8, 50, 60–2, 64–71, 77, 83, 130, 163
Dream selves in 60–2, 65, 68–9, 83, 85–6, 134
erotic theme in 48, 61
emotional variety in 66–7
interest motif in 66, 73–5

North American Review 14, 22–4, 26–9, 31, 33, 37, 40, 42–4, 50
Notre Dame de Paris 97–9, 101
"Old Times on the Mississippi" 1, 15, 129–41, 159–60, 185–6
Overland Stage Company 109–10
Oxford University (Twain's honorary doctorate from) 43, 45

Paige typesetter, ix
Paine, Albert Bigelow, ix
Paine, Thomas (*Age of Reason*) 9
Palastine (Twain's attitude toward) 88
Pallavicini Gardens 103–4. See also Mount Tabor (Twain's ascent of)
Paris Exposition of 1867 (Twain's visit to) 94–5, 99
Paris morgue (Twain's visit to) 98–9
Parkman, Francis (*La Salle and the Discovery of the Great West*) 184–6
Parthenon 102–3
Pennsylvania (wreck of) 186–8
Père La Chaise (Twain's visit to) 92–3
Personal Recollections of Joan of Arc 237–47
Phelps, William Walter 26–7, 29, 31
Pilot's Benevolent Association 136
plagiarism 19–20, 70, 77
Pompeii 128
Prince and the Pauper, The 1, 157–66, 178, 181
  Henry VIII depicted in 160–2
  madness in 158, 162–3
  mental trials in 161–4
  narrative voice of 158–9
  tongues in 159, 161–2

Principles of Psychology, The. See James, William

Quaker City 82–8, 90–1, 94–6, 101, 166, 181. See also *Innocents Abroad, The*
Quarles, John (family farm) 33–7

Raphael (Raffaello Sanzio da Urbino's "The Transfiguration") 89–90, 103
Raymond, John T. 27
Reconstruction (post-Civil-War policy) 86
relics (Catholic veneration of) 86, 98
Roughing It 14, 105–29, 156, 171
  inundation motif 106, 120, 123–4, 128
  Irish Brigade (Gov. Nye's entourage) 116
  madness in 121
  mental variety in 108, 115–19
  repletion motif 15, 105, 107, 111, 116–17, 123
  Slades's portrait 107–11, 121
  story of the Old Ram 114–15
Rousseau, Jean Jacques 24
Ruskin, John (*Modern Painters*) 173–4, 265 n.33

Salt Lake City 111–13
Sandwich Islands 18, 121–5
Satan (as a character in fiction) 8–9, 46–7, 49, 55–60, 63–4
"Schoolhouse Hill" 46, 48–9, 51–3, 61, 64, 69
self 7–8
self-contentment 4. See also *What Is Man?*
self-sacrifice 2, 4–5. See also *What Is Man?*
Sellers, Colonel Beriah 27. See also *Gilded Age, The*
Shakespeare, William 4, 188

Sherman, William Tecumseh 86
Simonetti (Italian palazzo) 90–1. See also *Innocents Abroad*
slavery (in Twain's childhood) 33–5
"Slave Ship." *See* Turner, J. M. W.
Smith, Joseph 112
Smyrna 96, 105
soul 8, 68–9
Spencer, Herbert (William James's critique of) 77–8, 139
"St. Bartholomew Flayed" (Marco d'Agrate) 99–100
Stevenson, Robert Louis 28–31, 33, 38
Stowe, Harriet Beecher 32
streams of thought. *See* mental streaming

Tangier 95–7
temperament 7–8, 13, 22. See also *What Is Man?*
Territorial Enterprise (Virginia City newspaper) 114, 118–19, 121
thought experiments 3–4, 10, 13, 20, 23–4, 131–2, 229
Titian (Tiziano Vecelli) 91
Tonty, Henri de 185
training 8, 19, 237–8
Tramp Abroad, A 1, 14–15, 166–82, 216
  "Blue Jay yarn" 171–3, 177
  illustrations in 174–5
  introspective mirrors in 177–8
  subjective instrumentation 167–9, 181
  vacancy motif in 168, 171–2
transitive mentality 25–6, 62, 217, 231

Trollope, Frances Milton 194
Turner, J. M. W. 173–5, 177, 196–7, 267 n.10
Twichell, Joseph 166, 169

Vatican Museum (as an index of mental life) 76, 82
  Twain's visit to 89
Vesuvius (Twain's ascent of) 105, 125–6
Vicksburg (testimony of 1863 seige survivors) 191–3, 197
Vienna (Clemens family residence in) 42, 46, 55
Virginia City (Nevada Territory) 18, 105–6, 118–19, 156

Ward, Artemus 80
Warner, Charles Dudley 193
Weekly Occidental (Virginia City magazine) 119
What Is Man? 1–15, 37–8, 229, 238, 241, 243
  consciousness depicted in 2–4, 6, 10–11, 15
  Interior Master in 6, 8, 10–14, 22, 38, 60, 62, 74
  Master Passion 2
  O. W. Holmes and 18–20
  temperament in 7–8, 13
  textual evolution of 1–2, 14, 169
  thought experiments in, x–xi 3–4, 10–11, 13, 78
Whittier, John Greenleaf (70th Birthday Dinner) 43, 166
Winter, Willie 44

Young, Brigham 111–12, 116

2.1 Raphael, "The Transfiguration" (1520), oil on wood. Courtesy of Scala/Art Resource, New York

A WONDERFUL ECHO.

and finally went off into a rollicking convulsion of the jolliest laughter that could be imagined. It was so joyful—so long continued—so perfectly cordial and hearty, that every body was forced to join in. There was no resisting it.

Then the girl took a gun and fired it. We stood ready to count the astonishing clatter of reverberations. We could not say one, two, three, fast enough, but we could dot our notebooks with our pencil points almost rapidly enough to take down a sort of short-hand report of the result. My page revealed the following account. I could not keep up, but I did as well as I could:

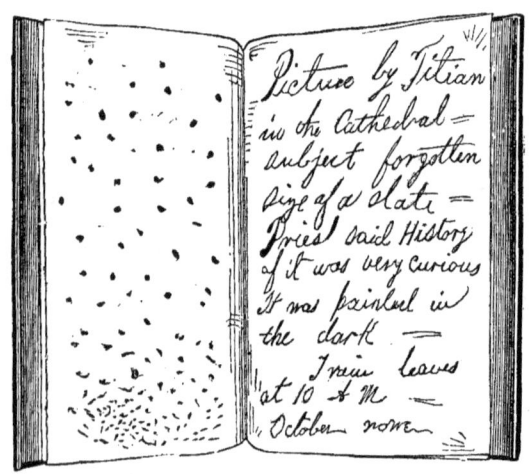

FIFTY-TWO DISTINCT REPETITIONS.

I set down fifty-two distinct repetitions, and then the echo got the advantage of me. The doctor set down sixty-four, and thenceforth the echo moved too fast for him, also. After the separate concussions could no longer be noted, the reverberations dwindled to a wild, long-sustained clatter of sounds such as a watchman's rattle produces. It is likely that this is the most remarkable echo in the world.

2.2 From *The Innocents Abroad* (Hartford: American Publishing Company, 1869), "Fifty-Two Distinct Repetitions" (p. 197)

THE ADVENTURES OF TOM SAWYER

CHAPTER I.

"TOM!"

No answer.

"TOM!"

No answer.

"What's gone with that boy, I wonder? You TOM!"

No answer.

The old lady pulled her spectacles down and looked over them about the room; then she put them up and looked out under them. She seldom or never looked *through* them for so small a thing as a boy; they were her state pair, the pride of her heart, and were built for "style," not service—she could have seen through a pair of stove lids just as well. She looked perplexed for a moment, and then said, not fiercely, but still loud enough for the furniture to hear:

3.1 From *The Adventures of Tom Sawyer* (Hartford: The American Publishing Company, 1876), "Tom at Home" (p. 1)

3.2 J. M. W. Turner, "The Slave Ship" (1840), oil on canvas. Photograph © 2017 Museum of Fine Arts, Boston

Old Blue China.

I also set apart my exquisite specimen of Old Blue China. This is considered to be the finest example of Chinese art now in existence; I do not refer to the bastard Chinese art of modern times but that noble & pure & genuine art which flourished under the fostering & appreciative care of the Emperors of the Chung-a-Lung-Fung dynasty. —

3.3 From *A Tramp Abroad* (Hartford: American Publishing Company, 1880), "Old Blue China" (p. 186) blue; they will bring in some with white hilts presently, and those you can handle freely." When a sword was broken in the first duel, I wanted a piece of it; but its hilt was the wrong color, so it was considered best and politest to await a properer season. It was brought to me after the room was cleared, and I will now make a "life-size" sketch of it by tracing a line around it with my pen, to show the width of the weapon. The length of these swords is about three feet, and they are quite heavy. One's disposition to cheer, during the course of the duels or at their close, was naturally strong, but corps etiquette forbade any demonstrations of this sort. However brilliant a contest or a victory might be, no sign or sound betrayed that any one was moved. A dignified gravity and repression were maintained at all times.

When the dueling was finished and we were ready to go, the gentlemen of the Prussian Corps to whom we had been introduced took off their caps in the courteous German way, and also shook hands; their brethren of the same order took off their caps and bowed, but without shaking hands; the gentlemen of the other corps treated us just as they would have treated white caps,—they fell apart, apparently unconsciously, and left us an unobstructed pathway, but did not seem to see us or know we were there. If we had gone thither the following week as guests of another corps, the white caps, without meaning any offense would have observed the etiquette of their order and ignored our presence.

PIECE OF SWORD.

[How strangely are comedy and tragedy blended in this life! I had not been home a full half hour, after witnessing those playful sham-duels, when circumstances made it necessary for me to get ready immediately to assist personally at a real one—a duel with no effeminate limitations in the matter of results, but a battle to the death. An account of it, in the next chapter, will show the reader that duels between boys, for fun and duels between men in earnest, are very different affairs.]

3.4 From *A Tramp Abroad* (Hartford: American Publishing Company, 1880), "Piece of Sword" (p. 68).

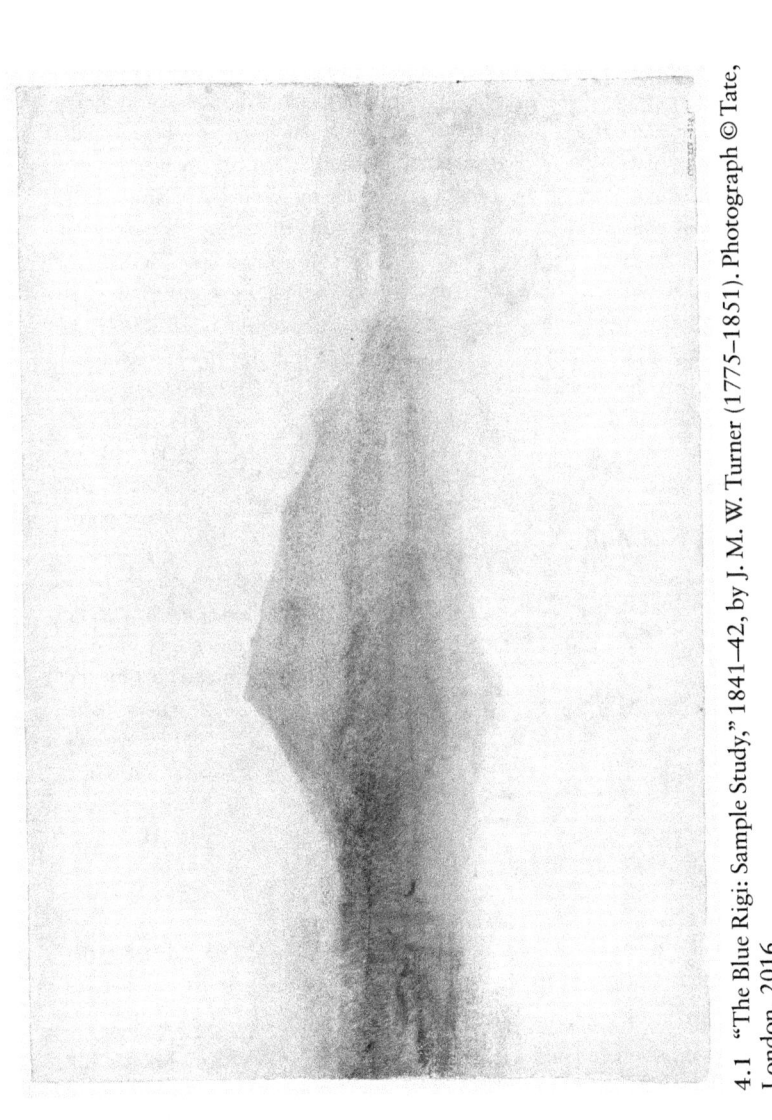

4.1 "The Blue Rigi: Sample Study," 1841–42, by J. M. W. Turner (1775–1851). Photograph © Tate, London, 2016

ed to make a speech—of course a humorous speech. I think
I never heard so many old played-out jokes strung together
in my life. He was worse than the minstrels, worse than the
clown in the circus. It seemed peculiarly sad to sit here,
thirteen hun- dred years before I was born and listen again
to poor, flat, worm-eaten jokes that had given me the dry
gripes when I was a boy thirteen hundred years afterwards.
It about con- vinced me that there isn't any such
thing as a new joke possible. Everybody
laughed at these antiquities—but then they
always do; I had no- ticed that, centuries later. However, of course the scoffer didn't laugh—I mean the
boy. No, he scoffed; there wasn't anything he wouldn't scoff at. He said the
most of Sir Dinadan's
jokes were rotten and
the rest were petri-
fied. I said "petrified"
was good; as I believed, myself, that the
only right way to classify the majestic
ages of some of those jokes was by geo-
logic periods. But that neat idea hit the
boy in a blank
place, for geol-
ogy hadn't
been invented
yet. However,

THE PRACTICAL JOKER'S JOKE.

I made a note of the remark, and calculated to educate the
commonwealth up to it if I pulled through. It is no use to

www.ingramcontent.com/pod-product-compliance
Lightning Source LLC
Chambersburg PA
CBHW052154300426
44115CB00011B/1662